EVERYMAN'S CASTLE

EVERYMAN'S CASTLE

PHILIPPA LEWIS

The story of our cottages, country houses, terraces, flats, semis and bungalows

F

FRANCES LINCOLN LIMITED
PUBLISHERS

Frances Lincoln Limited
74–77 White Lion Street
London N1 9PF
www.franceslincoln.com

ISBN 978-0-7112-3338-6

Designed by Anne Wilson
Printed and bound in China

9 8 7 6 5 4 3 2 1

TITLE PAGES *The Englishman's Home,* by
John Piper, mural painted for the Festival of
Britain, 1951

CONTENTS

INTRODUCTION

T HE 2011 CENSUS categorized British housing types and asked people to specify whether they lived in a house or bungalow (detached or semi-detached); a terrace (including end of terrace); a flat or maisonette (purpose-built block or tenement); or in part of a converted or shared house (including bedsits). All these places are thought of as home by their inhabitants, but the experience of living in each type of dwelling is and has been quite different. Each has also had distinct (but continuously changing) associations for the outside world. British society, perhaps more than that of other nations, has a perennial obsession with its living space and the minute calibrations of class to be inferred from a person's home.

Few people would contradict the maxim that 'An Englishman's home is his castle', which also holds good for the Scots, Welsh and Irish. The concept became enshrined in the public consciousness in 1604, when a law case established the principle that no one could break into a house without stating his business and asking to be let in. The Attorney General summed up with the words: 'The house of everyone is to him as his castle and fortress, as well for his defence against injury and violence, as for his repose.' The first part of his pronouncement is about feeling safe and the second part is about feeling at ease. Behind the front door and beyond the threshold is our defensible space. Is this why the British have historically treated flats with communal entrances and staircases with such suspicion?

There are fictional and actual castles that exemplify both safety and repose. In *Great Expectations* Dickens introduced Mr Wemmick, a south London clerk who transformed a little wooden cottage into a tiny castle. He erected a painted battlement along the roofline, and sham Gothic windows ornamented the façade. Each night at 9 o'clock he fired a cannon and on Sundays he ran a flag up his flagstaff. In order to enter his home he crossed a plank bridge which he drew up behind him. As Wemmick explained to Pip, his home was entirely private: 'When I go into the office, I leave the Castle behind me, and when I come into the Castle, I leave the office behind me.' In the real world, the grocer Julius Drewe had, by the age of thirty-three, accrued enough money from his chain of Home and Colonial stores never to go to his office again. Instead he too turned his energy and fortune to building a

THE COUNTRY HOUSE.
(*What Our Architect has to put up with.*)

Fair Client. "I WANT IT TO BE NICE AND BARONIAL, QUEEN ANNE AND ELIZABETHAN, AND ALL THAT; KIND OF QUAINT AND NUREM-BERGY, YOU KNOW—REGULAR OLD ENGLISH, WITH FRENCH WINDOWS OPENING TO THE LAWN, AND VENETIAN BLINDS, AND SORT OF SWISS BALCONIES, AND A LOGGIA. BUT I'M SURE *YOU* KNOW WHAT I MEAN!"

castle. Drewe's fanciful association with a putative Norman ancestor called Drogo led him to a remote and rocky promontory on the edge of Dartmoor. With Lutyens, the grandest architect of the age, to translate his dreams into reality, he built a granite medieval fortress (albeit one with heating, telephones, a central vacuum-cleaning system and plenty of electricity). Arrow loops pierced the battlements, a working portcullis dropped over the front door, a basement area was designated the dungeon. Here, in the early twentieth century, Drewe and his family lived, played tennis, shot and fished.

There is no shortage of voices recording the delights of home, a place where the inhabitant might be entirely himself. They make comprehensible the unease felt by generations of lodgers living under someone else's roof. Samuel Johnson in 1750 described being at home as 'those soft intervals of unbended amusement, in which a man shrinks to his natural dimensions, and throws aside the ornaments or disguises, which he feels in privacy to be useless incumbrances . . . To be happy at home is the ultimate result of all ambition, the end to which every enterprise and labour tends, and of which every desire prompts the prosecution.' This he wrote from a city merchant's house in Gough Square off Fleet Street, which he rented for £30 and where he compiled his dictionary.

John Clare wrote of precisely the same emotion in 'Home Happiness' (1835), shortly after moving with his wife and seven children to a cottage in Northborough, near his birthplace in Northamptonshire.

"Did I really understand you, Miss Wilson, to use the expression 'A cosy nook' in connection with the house you wish me to design for you?"

Like a thing of the desert, alone in its glee,
I make a small home seem an empire to me;
Like a bird in the forest, whose world is its nest,
My home is my all, and the centre of rest.
Let Ambition stretch over the world at a stride,
Let the restless go rolling away with the tide,
I look on life's pleasures as follies at best,
And, like sunset, feel calm when I'm going to rest.

The words 'comfort' and 'home' were often entwined. Robert Southey thought these two words specifically English, and untranslatable: 'Home is the one, by which an Englishman means his house . . . The other word is comfort; it means all the enjoyments and privileges of home . . .' This was the ideal of the middling classes. The struggle for swathes of the population to achieve any form of comfort or security was slow and laborious.

At the other end of the social scale, the Duke in Benjamin Disraeli's novel *Lothair* (1870) perhaps expressed a truth: 'His Grace was accustomed to say that he had only one misfortune, and it was a great one; he had no home. His family had married so many heiresses, and he, consequently, possessed so many halls and castles, at all of which, periodically, he wishes, from a right feeling, to reside, that there was no sacred spot identified with his life in which his heart, in the bustle and tumult of existence, could take refuge.'

Hermann Muthesius, the German commentator on and enthusiast for British architecture, noted at the turn of the twentieth century, with some astonishment, that the British would always choose to be at home rather than out at the opera or a café. (As our houses and flats get smaller maybe this is no longer true.) Muthesius also thought the weather – another national obsession – shaped our housing: bay windows, he asserted, were 'a substitute for seating in the open air . . . for centuries English architects have shown a special fondness for them.' Robert Kerr in *The Gentleman's House, from the Parsonage to the Palace* (1865) also considered that the climate, along with family reserve, contributed to making a comfortable home 'the most cherished possession of an Englishman'.

This is a book about how different sorts of home made and make for different sorts of domestic life.

"But, Michael, the highly literate, cultivated, superior kind of person who will buy these just wouldn't stare."

COTTAGES

T HE COTTAGE IS JANUS-FACED: one side a miserable and leaking hovel for the agricultural labourer, the other a sunny retreat, the setting for a rural idyll. The medieval peasant built a primitive shelter with the most basic of tools and whatever materials were immediately to hand. It is the qualities of these materials that have come to define the quintessential cottage. The very word conjures up thatch, timber, daub and stone; and thatch becomes mossy, stone grows lichen, timber beams silver with age, walls sag and bulge.

No other kind of housing has such a specific set of words clinging to its foundations: 'dream', 'perfect', 'love in a . . .' John Ruskin's vision was archetypal: 'a cottage all of our own, with its little garden, its pleasant view, its surrounding fields, its neighbouring stream, its healthy air, and clean kitchen, parlours and bedrooms. Less than this, no man should be content with for his nest; more than this few should seek.' The cottage in the mind's eye has been remarkably consistent and Ruskin's description fits precisely. He was looking back – in *Fors Clavigera: Letters to the Workmen and Labourers of Great Britain* – to the Kent of his childhood seen from the inside of a carriage as it bowled down the road from Addington to Shirley in the 1820s – 'one saw no dwellings above the size of cottages or small farmsteads; these, wood-built usually, and thatched, their porches embroidered

with honeysuckle, and the gardens with daisies, their doors mostly ajar, or with one half shut to keep in the children, and a bricked or tiled footway from it to the wicket gate – all neatly kept, and vivid with a sense of quiet energies of their contented tenants.' (This he wrote in the 1870s from his large country house, to which he had recently added a turret, overlooking Coniston Water.)

PRIMITIVE HOVELS

'CONTENTED TENANTS' is something of an oxymoron. It is difficult to imagine from the softness of the early twenty-first century how profound the levels of discomfort were for the majority of cottage dwellers over the years. At the time of the Domesday Book almost a third of the population were peasants; and many of them were cottars, cottage dwellers. Generally the roof over their heads was courtesy of their lord, the landowner to whom they owed labour, goods and arbitrary taxes. The lord or lady of the manor was responsible for providing the main timber beams and maintaining a cottage's overall structure, while maintenance of the fabric – the thatch, lathe and infilling –

LEFT The archetypal thatched cottage, image of sweetness, used since the late nineteenth century on chocolate boxes, and here on a toffee tin manufactured for Harry Vincent Ltd of Birmingham, with the motto 'Take the Home Sweet Home'.
BELOW Woodcut of a rural landscape, dated 1502. Habitations were constructed from whatever material was to hand.

was generally the responsibility of the tenants. Failure in this duty to maintain could lead to the punishment of demolition; and absconding from the area with the building materials was not unknown. Records of the manor court in 1497 for Shepreth in Cambridgeshire name seven whose 'customary tenements' – cottages – were in a state of decay: John Awstyn, Will Lawrence, Will Newman, Robert Felde, Will Beton, Joan Hawsby and Alice Freeman. Defects in woodwork, carpentry, daubing and roofing were ordered to be repaired by Michaelmas on pain of a heavy fine. Repeated notices like this suggest that it was an impracticable procedure. Landlords found it easier to switch to a system by which rent was paid for a lease of a given length.

Freemen paid rent: the fourteenth-century poet William Langland, who knew poverty in the cottage he shared with his wife in Cornhill, described the struggle to find the money in words that stand good for what was a perennial problem.

> . . . the poor in the cottage,
> Charged with a crew of children and with a landlord's rent
> What they win by their spinning to make their porridge with,
> Milk and meal, to satisfy the babes,
> The babes that continually cry for food –
> This they must spend on the rent of their houses . . .

Most housing for the poor in the Middle Ages – and later – was what would now be categorized as hovel, shelter or shed: a single room with an earth floor, a fire in the centre with the smoke finding its way out of a hole in the roof. This was commonly shared with a few animals. A description written at the end of the sixteenth century by Joseph Hall, a moralist and bishop, gave a grim view. 'A starved tenement' one bay wide with the roof beams 'furr'd with sluttish soote a whole inch thick, shining like a black-moors'. At the foot of his bed 'feeden his stalled teme [team of oxen]; his swine beneath, his pullen [chickens] ore the beame.'

GROWING STABILITY

However, for many cottagers life became increasingly comfortable as the sixteenth and seventeenth centuries rolled out, and the authority of the feudal system lapsed. Smallholders emerged as a class, paying rent for a cottage and land. The population increased and farming prospered. The Dissolution of the Monasteries caused a

The house of rest

A woodcut illustration from Wynkyn de Worde's edition of the *Castell of Laboure*, 1506, shows an interior with hearth, chimney and basic furniture.

shake-up of land holdings, releasing land that had belonged to the Church. As men specialized in particular skills such as thatching, joinery and masonry cottage construction improved. Once the technique of timber frame building developed from the basic A-shaped cruck structure to post and truss, a cottage could have more height and the upper part could be 'chambered over', providing the luxury of a place for sleeping or storage, and even dormer windows. The core cottage was spawning brew houses, milk houses, salting rooms and – for weavers, leather and metal workers and the like – space to work. Most revolutionary of all was the invention of the chimney, which sucked the smoke out of the interior and kept the fire, and therefore cooking, far more controllable. Contemporary wills list metal implements, jointed furniture and proper beds.

One of the most informative sources of the history of this period is William Harrison's *Description of Britain and England*, published in 1577 as part of Holinshed's *Chronicles*. Harrison related that Britons no longer had houses made of 'sticks and dirt' – as described by a Spaniard in the reign of Queen Mary – nor were 'slightly set up with a few posts and many raddles [wattles] with stable and all offices under one roof' but that now 'every man almost is a builder, and he that hath bought any small parcel of ground, be it ever so little, will not be quiet till he have pulled down the old house (if any were there standing) and set up a new after his own device.' These builders were likely to have been what he described as 'the third sort of people' – yeomen – 'free men born English . . . these sort of people have a certain pre-eminence, and more estimation than labourers and the common sort of artificers.' It is their houses that survived to be subsequently designated as cottages. Harrison's fourth and last sort, 'day-labourers and poor husbandmen', were likely still to be struggling in hovels; these were the men who Francis Bacon reckoned were totally unsuited to be infantrymen – 'mere cottagers, which are but housed beggars'.

A row of cottages clinging on to the marginal land along the roadside: an unsentimental Victorian depiction.

Beggars were a source of alarm and fear in Tudor England: a disruptive nuisance and a potential burden on the parish. An Act was passed in 1589 with the intention of preventing those perceived as indigent from building themselves a cottage. Permission to build had to be granted by a Justice of the Peace and the dwelling had to stand on four acres: enough to be self-sufficient. Thus, on 28 March 1598 Thomas Rodger, 'an honest true labouring man in his trade of plowright', petitioned Sir Thomas Kitson 'to give him license to build himself up a cottage or poor dwelling-place upon a piece of the common next the east end of your pasture called the Mare Close . . . But because many have interest of common in that plot of ground, as well as in the rest adjoining, and amongst those many, the poor man fears he shall not get all their consent before your worship's good liking thereof may be had.' Rodger got his building permission, plus the gift of a load of timber and two of bricks. The cottage was his for the life of him and his present wife, at a rent of 2 shillings per annum and with responsibility to repair the fence.

The laborious application process was often bypassed by those in urgent need of a home – who included those turned off common land, swathes of which were being enclosed by Tudor landowners turning to profitable sheep farming. The homeless looked for land to build on wherever they could find it: patches of common or thin strips alongside roadways. Although in theory these early squatters could be evicted and their dwellings demolished they were so numerous that the authorities couldn't really keep up with them. The 1571 manor roll of the village of Foxton notes that William Yewle recently and unlawfully erected and built part of a house upon the highway, 30 feet in length and 6 feet in width: a good deal less than four acres. Building a makeshift cottage in this way remained the only way of gaining a home for many rural families into the nineteenth century. There existed the custom, in Wales known as *ty unno*, that a person was entitled to the freehold of whatever shelter they could build over the course of one night, and of the land within a stone's throw.

THE IMPACT OF ENCLOSURE

ENCLOSURE GATHERED PACE in the eighteenth and nineteenth centuries as improvements in agriculture made land increasingly profitable. The face of the landscape changed as landowners fenced and hedged their fields from previously common land (wastes), felled timber and diverted streams. Inconveniently sited cottages were demolished. As Oliver Goldsmith put it in *The Deserted Village*, written in 1770, 'only one master grasps the whole domain', while '. . . poor exiles, every pleasure past,/Hung round their bowers and fondly looked their last'. Lines written by the poet Cowper a few years later, 'God made the country, and man made the town', expressed a generally held view that the transition to an urban life was not for the better.

The fact that empty cottages were rapidly pulled down in order to prevent incomers moving in and becoming dependent on the parish for relief exacerbated the shortage. Extreme hardship among cottagers was observed by the Hon. John Byng, who noted at the end of the eighteenth century in the journal of his travels in East Anglia: 'Here is little fuel to be bought, little to be pick'd up, but that is punish'd as theft, no land allott'd them for potatoes, or ground for a cow; . . . nothing can be more wretch'd; surround'd by heather they dare not collect, and by a profusion of turnips they dare not pluck.'

William Cobbett, who had worked as a farm labourer, noted much the same in his *Rural Rides*, made in the 1820s. In Cricklade in Wiltshire: 'The labourers seem miserably poor. Their dwellings little better than pig beds, and their looks indicate that their food is not nearly equal to a pig. Their wretched hovels are stuck on little bits of ground on the road side, where the space has been wider than the road demanded.' He recalled the productivity of Horton Heath in Dorset before it was swept away by enclosure: a common of about 150 acres on which there had been 30 cottages and gardens, over 100 beehives, 60 pigs, 15 cows and heifers and at least 500 head of poultry.

The Swineherd, by James Ward, 1810. There is an ambiguity about whether the hovel in the background is intended as shelter for beast or human – or, as was often the case, for both.

In his *Cottage Economy* – first published in parts in 1821 and in its seventeenth edition by 1850 – he pronounced: 'I lay it down as a maxim, that for a family to be happy, they must be well supplied with food and raiment.' He offered the usual solution: give the cottagers a small piece of land and they could grow their own fruit and vegetables, keep poultry and a pig or cow and be self-sufficiently happy. He prefaced the section on the economies made by baking bread and brewing beer with 'If the family consists of twelve or fourteen persons . . .'

Cottages, along with a church and maybe a pub, school and shop, constitute a village. Historically they had fallen into two distinct types. In a 'closed' village one landowner, abetted by the laws of enclosure, set the agenda and owned most cottages. A greater number were 'open' villages, the land and cottages owned by an assortment of farmers, rural craftsmen, labourers and independent freeholders. Here the cottages were more varied, ranging from the substantial to the self-built squat on common land. One such was Selborne in Hampshire, described by Gilbert White in 1822: 'We abound with poor, many of whom are sober and industrious and live comfortably in good stone or brick cottages, which are glazed and have chambers above stairs, mud buildings we have none . . . the inhabitants enjoy a good share of health and longevity and the parish swarms with children.'

Life was more brutal elsewhere – in the Highlands of Scotland landowners were even known to set fire to cottages in order to 'clear' the land. In 1807 the Duchess of Sutherland toured her inheritance and was seized 'with the rage of improvements'.

In that year her land agent evicted ninety families, their crops unharvested, to land twenty miles away where they had to live in the open until they could build anew.

IMPROVING CONDITIONS

SOME LANDOWNERS grasped the connection between a healthy and efficient labour force and improved housing. Nathaniel Kent wrote *Hints to Gentlemen of Landed Property*, 1775, a sensible volume aimed at making the most of your land – 'especially useful maybe to those newly come to it'. This was the period when acquiring a large country house and estate was the usual way to consolidate a fortune and position in society. Alongside 'manures considered' Kent reflected on the importance of cottages. He railed against the inadequate hovels of the agricultural labourer, 'without whom even the finest land was worthless'. 'Cottagers are indisputably the most beneficial race of people we have; they are bred up in greater simplicity, live more primitive lives, more free from vice and debauchery than any other men of the lower class; and are best formed and enabled to sustain the hardships of war, and other laborious services' (a definite advance on Francis Bacon's earlier view of cottagers as worthless soldiers). Kent made practical suggestions. The smallest cottage (main room 12 x 12 feet) should be built of brick with a tiled roof, at a cost of £56. Cottages should be near to the farm and built in pairs. He considered it unnecessary to provide separate bedrooms for girls and boys, as boys left home young to become labourers, when they went to live in their employer's farmhouse. He recommended half an acre for growing fruit, vegetables and for keeping a pig; this was the same year that the Tudor act stating that cottages should be built on four acres was repealed.

John Wood the younger, architect star of Bath, was an exception among his peers in making a genuine attempt to design a better cottage for the labourer. This he was inspired to do, he wrote, after a conversation with a landowner on their generally ruinous condition. He went to look for himself, believing that an architect must place 'himself in the situation of the person for whom he designs. I say it was necessary for me to feel as the cottager himself.' He was horrified by 'shattered, dirty, inconvenient, miserable hovels' hardly suitable for animals, let alone 'a proper habitation for the human species . . . It is melancholy to see a man and his wife, and sometimes half a dozen children crowded together in the same room, nay often in the same bed; the horror is still heightened, and increased at the time when the woman is in child-bed, or in case of illness, or of death.' He listed their defects: wet and damp; built against banks; sunken floors; cold and cheerless due to thin walls and lack of porch; steep, inconvenient staircases; lack of ceilings making the cottage either boiling hot or freezing cold; leaky dormers adding to dampness, unhealthiness and decay. In *A Series of Plans for Cottages or Habitations of the Labourer* (1781), he specified brick or stone foundations and rooms facing south or east and at least 8 feet high. He suggested building in pairs, to enable neighbours to help each other out, and specified that there should be a porch, a shed, wide stairs and walls the thickness of one and a half bricks.

By the 1790s anxiety about the state of the rural poor and the shortage of cottages was being aired in books such as David Davies's *The Case of Labourers in Husbandry Stated and Considered* (1795) and *The State of the Poor* by Frederick Morton Eden (1797). The lack of land was one reason given: 'hardly enough ground for a cabbage garden', as small parcels of land had been swallowed up through enclosure and the merging of land holdings. Davies also pointed out that poverty was exacerbated by landowners' absences: instead of staying put to 'exercise hospitality, employ the industrious, and relieve the sick and needy', they were squandering their income on 'amusements and accomplishments in vogue in the capital' or at 'bathing and drinking water places'. Morton gave a good description of the difficulty of finding a place to live – permission to build, even if the labourer had enough money to do it, was still dependent on finding a scrap of land to squat on, so couples stayed with their parents and cottages became more and more crowded. Fuel was scarce and expensive and cooking on an open fire was hopelessly inefficient; he had seen horse dung, sawdust, dried intestines of dead animals and kennel dirt all being used as fuel *in extremis*. The Society for Bettering the Condition and Increasing the Comforts of the Poor published its first report the same year as Morton. Their aim was 'to carry domestic comfort into the recesses of every cottage, and to add to the virtue of the morality of the nation, by increasing its happiness' by means of improvements in cooking hearths, sanitation and sleeping arrangements and by the provision of a privy, a garden and tool space.

THE ROMANTIC VISION

MEANWHILE the middle and upper classes were becoming entranced with the idea of the cottage. An appreciation of the unaffected and simple had become fashionable. Nature was valued for its innocence and, by extension, cottagers, who lived so very close to nature, were idealized (they would doubtless have been astonished to know it). From the 1770s Thomas Gainsborough repeatedly chose to paint scenes of 'peasants'

The Woodcutter's Return, by Thomas Gainsborough, a painting which has hung at Belvoir Castle in Leicestershire since it was bought by the Duke of Rutland in the early 1770s.

outside cottages. Typical was *The Cottage Door*: in front of a windowless cottage under a heavy thatch stands a stately rosy-cheeked woman holding a baby, while around her cluster five boisterous children, artfully *déshabillé* in rags, but reassuringly drinking milk from a bowl and eating hunks of bread. It was, the *Morning Chronicle* stated when the painting was shown at the Royal Academy in 1780, a 'beautiful scene where serenity and pleasure dwell in every spot . . . a scene of happiness that may truly be called Adam's paradise'.

Other painters, including George Morland, Francis Wheatley and Thomas Rowlandson, also worked in this genre of 'fancy pictures' and any number of prints entitled *The Happy Cottager* or *The Sportsman's Return* must have hung on urban walls. Their owners may well have gone to the Theatre Royal Covent Garden in 1783 to see Mrs Frances Brooks's comic opera *Rosina or Love in a Cottage* in which Rosina, it turns out, is too beautiful to be a cottage girl: she is the daughter of a colonel and 'not born to labour'. However, she gleans and spins until the truth is discovered and the squire takes her off to the manor house where she rightly belongs.

As late as 1815 Francis Stevens published *Views of cottages and farm-houses in England and Wales*, a geographically comprehensive collection of etchings intended for the amateur painter. Stevens particularly recommends Gainsborough's style of sketching the effect of light and shadow. He delineated the picturesque dereliction that made cottages so appealing to the artist: 'the component parts of this building

Two Welsh cottages by Francis Stevens, from his *Views of Cottages*, 1815. On the left, a 'sheltered cot' in Carmarthenshire; on the right, an 'ill-constructed hut' on the Isle of Anglesey.

are brick, tile and plaster; materials, which, in a state of decay, usually afford subject for the pencil.' In Carmarthenshire, he notes, 'Surrounded by wood, this sheltered cot, with its window deeply seated in the wall, and chimney peeping through the thatch, excites notions of retirement peace and comfort being possessed by its humble inhabitants.' It is only with the final plate that Stevens's enthusiasm wavers. On the Isle of Anglesey he shows an 'ill-constructed hut [that] affords shelter to the miserable family of one whose occupation is digging poisonous ore in the darksome bowels of the earth. Here no rural charms delight the eye . . . nor are any reflections excited in the mind but those that are associated with the boundless desire of wealth; all is chilling, unsocial, sordid, and remote from that which enlarges the soul, and renders man innocent and happy.' As the plates show little difference between the two cottages, presumably it is the connection to mining and commerce that has taken the paradise out of the picture.

On no account were cottages to be painted white; this theory seems to have originated with Uvedale Price, who was the final arbiter on picturesque taste. 'A cottage of quiet colour, half concealed among the trees, with its bit of garden, its pales and orchard, is one of the most tranquil and soothing of all rural objects; . . . but if cleared up and whitened, its modest retired character is gone, and succeeded by a perpetual glare.' There was a degree of kick-back: in 1798 James Malton pointed out in *An Essay of British Cottage Architecture* that cottages needed to be protected: otherwise, they will 'be found to exist nowhere but on the canvas of the painter.'

Another impatient with the picturesque was George Crabbe, poet and clergyman, who grew up in rural Suffolk and who wrote in *The Village* (1783), addressing the 'gentle souls who dream of rural ease':

> . . . I paint the Cot,
> As Truth will paint it, and as Bards will not:
> . . . Can poets soothe you, when you pine for bread,
> By winding myrtles round a ruin'd shed?

Crabbe describes the cottage interior, where the enthusiasts for the picturesque probably never ventured, and which seems little improved since Langland's description written four centuries before.

Where the vile bands that bind the thatch are seen,
And lath and mud are all that lie between;
Save one dull pane, that, coarsely patch'd, gives way
To the rude tempest, yet excludes the day.

Unsurprisingly, lines that he wrote twenty years later in *The Parish Register* are far more frequently quoted.

Behold the cot! Where thrives the industrious swain,
Source of his pride, his pleasure, and his gain;
Screen'd from the winter's wind, the sun's last ray
Smiles on the window, and prolongs the day;
Projecting thatch the woodbine's branches stop,
And turn their blossoms to the casement's top . . .

By this time Crabbe was chaplain to the Duke of Rutland, and had perhaps partially forgotten the harsh reality of Suffolk as he gazed at his employer's cottage painting by Gainsborough, *The Woodcutter's Return*, on the walls of Belvoir Castle.

COTTAGES ORNÉES

EXPERIMENTS IN SIMPLE COTTAGE LIFE were also played out by a few for whom reality was much grander. It is easy to imagine a longing for small intimate spaces being induced by a life led among the stifling constrictions of court or large aristocratic households. The odd 'cottage' appeared among the temples and grottoes of Georgian landscape gardens, such as Lady's Cottage in the wood at Blickling Hall in Norfolk, built for Mary Anne Drury soon after her marriage in 1761 – a minute edifice intended for the taking of a dish of tea rather than a night's sleep. Queen Charlotte built a thatched cottage in the grounds of Kew Palace. The *London Magazine* reported in 1774: 'The Queen's cottage in the shade of the garden is a pretty retreat . . . the design is said to be Her Majesty's' and it was 'her favourite place with the King'.

The Queen escaped to her garden, but Lady Elizabeth Butler and Miss Sarah Ponsonby, passionately attached and determined to live independently of their aristocratic Irish families, moved to remote Llangollen. Sarah Ponsonby's journal, 'An Account of a Journey in Wales, perform'd in May 1778 by Two Fugitive Ladies', tells how they found the five-roomed cottage with a backdrop of the Welsh mountains. They planned a simple life removed from society and resolved never to spend a night away from home. Their favourite reading was Rousseau's *La Nouvelle Héloïse*, with its chapters on rules for study and simple living. Despite precarious finances they gothicized the cottage, added oriel windows and a library and ornamented the garden with a model dairy, fowl house, gothic arches, cascade and grotto; they employed a housekeeper, kitchen maid, gardener and footman. Their retreat became so famous that the illustrious and curious, including Wellington, Wilberforce, Walter Scott and Southey, all included a visit to the unorthodox household of the Ladies of Llangollen on their Welsh itineraries. Queen Charlotte wrote, as one cottage dweller to another, enquiring as to their progress. They replied enclosing a plan of the cottage and garden and copies of the Italian mottoes that were painted on boards and attached to their trees.

Cottage Industry, an aquatint of 1791. A plate dedicated to the Earl of Moira of County Downe, representing the ideal of productive tenants in their cottage, boiling, spinning and reeling yarn.

They had created what had become known in the late eighteenth century as a *cottage ornée*. An elaboration on a labourer's cottage, the name indicated the cottage's altered status. It had to look markedly different from classical Georgian architecture and include as many rustically inspired accretions as possible, with verandas, gables, polygonal walls, fancy leaded glazing and thatch.

Life in such a cottage could offer social freedom. In 1777 Lord Craven gave his wife a lottery ticket: she won £2,000. The Countess promptly gave him a diamond and with the remainder of the money built herself a Thames-side establishment near Kew, Craven Cottage, where she led a notoriously scandalous life. In her journal she wrote that Lord Cholmondeley had jokingly suggested swapping the cottage for Houghton, his Palladian palace in Norfolk. Later, Craven Cottage was later bought by Pierce Walsh Porter, a friend of the Prince Regent, who was described by *The Gentleman's Magazine* as 'distinguished by the conviviality of his manners and the elegance of his taste'. Walsh Porter's lavish theatrical remodelling (he also composed comic operas) and additions included an Egyptian saloon supported by palm trees, a Gothic dining room, a chapel painted like the Henry VII Chapel in Westminster Abbey, and a semicircular library which opened out on to a large oval balcony. In the 1840s Craven Cottage was bought by Sir Edward Bulwer-Lytton, who retreated there after a scandalous separation from his wife, and so maintained its louche reputation.

Equally extraordinary was the cottage 'A La Ronde' built by two spinster cousins, Mary and Jane Parminter. On their return from the Grand Tour in the late eighteenth century they settled into this sixteen-sided cottage outside Exmouth, and dedicated their lives to tweaking its interior decoration, gloriously ornamented with shells, paper, paint, mirror, quartz and feathers.

Extreme *cottages ornées* were always eye-catchers and few more so than Blaise Hamlet outside Bristol, built by the Quaker banker John Scandrett Harford in the early 1800s to house his old retainers. Architects John Nash and George Repton created for him the ultimate in picturesque cottages in true cottage scale. Encircling a green with a sundial, they were arranged higgledy-piggledy, each different and individually named: Vine, Dial, Sweetbriar, Oak, Diamond, Circular, Dutch, Double and Rose Cottages. Harford asked no rent, but the tenants must have enough money to maintain their cottage. With careful elderly tenants Blaise Hamlet remained pristine, and it became a favourite excursion from Bristol and Clifton. Prince Hermann von Pückler-Muskau, travelling by in the late 1820s, described it as the

Blaise Hamlet, which quickly became a popular destination for an excursion, especially for the amateur artist – such as the one shown here drawing Diamond Cottage.

beau idéal of a village: of 'perfect seclusion and snugness . . . no more delightful or well-chosen spot could be found as a refuge for misfortune.' An 1835 *Bristol Guide* picked out its picturesque features – 'the play of light and shadow produced by their projections and recesses, which afford shelter to a variety of beautiful creepers; the highly ornament and varied character of the chimneys; and the beauty of the surrounding little gardens, glittering throughout the summer with flowers of the brightest hues, and guarded from the intruding hand by hedges of sweetbriar'. The interiors, it noted, were comfortable and well arranged and each cottage had an oven and boiler: some compensation, it is to be hoped, for being continuously on view. It was unsurprising, therefore, that Mrs Dashwood in *Sense and Sensibility* (1811) considered Barton Cottage sadly lacking in picturesque architectural features: 'the building was regular, the roof was tiled, the window shutters not painted green, nor were the walls covered with honeysuckle.'

A classic *cottage ornée*, Knowle Cottage, Sidmouth, built for Lord Despenser in 1810 and including eleven acres of gardens plus conservatories. Painted by Isaac Fidlor in 1818.

The *cottage ornée* became popular in newly fashionable seaside spots such as the Isle of Wight or Sidmouth, and could expand to a ridiculous size. Nash was commissioned by the Prince Regent in 1814 to build a 'cottage' in Windsor Great Park. Its thatched roof was probably the only similarity it bore to the genuine article, since the bill for building it – complete with a cast-iron conservatory and marble fireplaces – was reputedly £200,000. Similarly vast was the seaside cottage of Endsleigh in Devon, built for the 6th Duke of Bedford as a retreat from Woburn for his wife and eight children. Humphry Repton described how the Duke came to think that a cottage style was appropriate: 'Here the good taste of the noble proprietor of Endsleigh was directed by what he saw. An irregular farm-house, little better than a cottage, back by a hill and beautiful group of trees, presented an object so picturesque, that it was impossible to wish it removed and replaced by any other style of building that architecture has hitherto invented, viz. a castle, or an abbey, or a palace, not one of which could have been so convenient and so applicable to the scenery as this cottage.' Built with canted angles to make it appear smaller than it actually was, Endsleigh had bargeboards, a rustic veranda and a floor laid with a mosaic of sheep bones.

ESTATE COTTAGES

GEORGIAN LANDOWNERS saw their country estates as places for 'improvements', which centred on the great country house within its parkland. 'Emparking' frequently involved clearing scruffy old villages and cottages that intruded on the mini Arcadia of lakes, clumps of trees and garden temples. In order to rehouse the labour force – out of sight beyond the park boundaries – designs were needed for cottages, and in some cases entire villages. Goldsmith's *Deserted Village* is said to have been inspired by Nuncham Courtenay where, in 1761, Lord Harcourt, having built a new Palladian mansion, demolished the old village to create his landscape garden. On either side of the turnpike road he built neat brick cottages with dormer windows, an improvement for his re-housed estate workers. On tour in 1788 the Revd Stebbing Shaw noted that 'forty families here, by the liberal assistance of his lordship, enjoy the comforts of industry under a wholesome roof who otherwise might have been doomed to linger out their days in the filthy hut of poverty.'

Harcourt's cottages were neat and utilitarian. The coming vogue was for the picturesque cottage and village and for the first time cottages – or at least their exteriors – were of interest to architects. Pattern books rolled off the presses with plans from which the landowner could pick a design for a labourer's cottage, or choose something 'suitable for persons of moderate fortune and for convenient retirement'. Certainly it should be an ornament in their landscape. Whether for labourer or gentleman, plates were accompanied by much explanatory description. Among W.F. Pocock's *Architectural Designs for Rustic Cottages, Picturesque Dwellings, Villas Etc.*, published in 1807, was a plan for a Woodman's Double Cottage, containing two separate dwellings, each with a living room, closet and two small sleeping rooms which would 'form an interesting object in the scenery . . . If erected near a drive in the wood, and from its elevated situation commanding a prospect, it might be made to bear the appearance of an Hermitage, and have part of the interior fitted up accordingly, still leaving room for

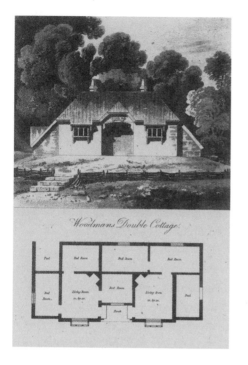

Woodmans Double Cottage.

LEFT Elevation and ground plan for a Woodman's Double Cottage, from W.F.Pocock's *Architectura Designs*, 1807. The carved motto over the door would identify the landowner and estate. Living room 12 x 10 feet.

RIGHT Design no. 19 from P.F. Robinson's *Designs for Ornamental Cottages*, 1826. This was 'a Gentleman's residence upon a scale sufficiently large to acquire the ordinary conveniences, without allowing the building to assume too much importance.' It was vital that the idea of the cottage not 'be lost in the magnitude of the building'. The drawing room measured 18 x 15 feet.

the residence of a Peasant and family.' In the same volume he illustrated a *cabane ornée* in 'the taste of the present day, and though humble in its appearance affords the necessary conveniences for persons of refined manners and habits . . . for the enjoyment of the true pleasures of domestic life, unencumbered with the forms of state and troublesome appendages.' In other words, retirement in a country cottage.

Jane Austen's novels reveal the different social strata living in cottages. In *Pride and Prejudice* Lady Catherine de Bourgh sallies forth into her village 'whenever any of the cottagers were disposed to be quarrelsome, discontented or too poor . . . silencing their complaints and scolding them into harmony and plenty'.

Those who wished to live in a cottage but didn't want to build one could alter their existing house. In *Persuasion* the village of Uppercross contained only two houses superior in appearance to those of the yeomen and labourers: the mansion of the squire and the parsonage which, to house the young squire on his marriage, had been 'elevated' into an eye-catching cottage, 'with its veranda, French windows, and other prettiness'.

Austen also shows how by 1817 it had become commonplace to live in a cottage. In *Sanditon*, Mr and Mrs Parker are searching for a surgeon after a carriage accident, and assume they have found him when they spot 'the neat-looking end of a cottage, which was seen romantically situated among wood on a high eminence at some distance'.

They are mistaken; the surgeon points out that 'it is in fact – in spite of its spruce air at this distance – as indifferent a double tenement as any in the parish . . . my shepherd lives at one end, and three old women in the other.'

Richard Elsam's *Hints for Improving the Condition of the Peasantry in all parts of the United Kingdom by promoting comfort in their Habitations*, 1816, took picturesque theory to extremes. A building should convey its purpose to the onlooker, so for the home of a humble peasant 'the character of the habitation should mingle with such an association of ideas as are most likely to approximate with the occupier's humble station. The lower these buildings are therefore kept the better – even build them half underground so the window sill is level with the ground.'

Such plans generally ignored the large size of working families. Edmund Bartell in *Hints for Picturesque Improvement in Ornamented Cottages and their scenery including some observations on the Labourer and his cottage*, did include labourers' cottages with four rooms. He wondered how a landowner with 'all the luxury and ease and that a splendid habitation and well-furnished table can afford, can calmly pass the squallid [*sic*] dwelling of his lowly tenant, and not feel himself inclined to repair a monument that reflects such indelible disgrace upon his philanthropy.' The landlord's answer, he suggested, would be that his tenants were ungrateful and 'there is a natural tendency to filth and sloth which prevails upon the lower classes of people who are prepared to huddle eight to a dozen in one room.' Overcrowded conditions were a fact of life. William Howitt described entering a Scottish cottage: 'through the eternal cloud of smoke, you most probably find yourself in a crowd. The pigs are running about the floor; hens are roosting over your head, the cows are lowing in, what we should call, the parlour; nine or ten children . . . and the father and mother, are fixing their eyes on the stranger.'

ECONOMICAL RETREATS

FOR THE NON-LABOURING CLASSES the country cottage has frequently been a cheap option. As early as 1782 William Cowper spoke in his poem 'Retirement' of how:

> . . . anticipated rents, and bills unpaid,
> Force many a shining youth into the shade . . .
> There hid in loath'd obscurity, remov'd
> From pleasure left, but never more belov'd.

Is this why friends of Fanny Burney's went off to Teignmouth in the summer of 1773? She wrote in her journal: 'Mr and Mrs Rishton are turned into absolute hermits for this summer, they have left Bath, and to Tingmouth [*sic*] in Devonshire where they have taken a *cottage* rather than a house.' We know that going to live in Barton Cottage was an economy for the Dashwoods in *Sense and Sensibility*, despite Willoughby's clichéd assertion that a cottage is 'the only form of building in which happiness is attainable'.

Living cheaply in a cottage – away from the distractions and expense of town and with nature on hand for inspiration – has frequently been the refuge of artists, poets and writers. The romantic poets were, unsurprisingly, early enthusiasts. William Blake wrote to his friend John Flaxman from Felpham, in Sussex, in September 1800: 'Dear Sculptor of Eternity, We are safe arrived at our cottage, which is more beautiful that I thought it and more convenient. It is a perfect model for cottages, and I think for palaces of magnificence, only enlarging, not altering its proportions, and adding

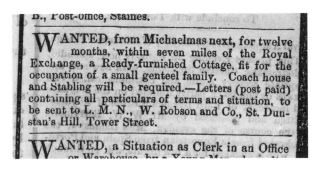

D., Post-office, Staines.

WANTED, from Michaelmas next, for twelve months, within seven miles of the Royal Exchange, a Ready-furnished Cottage, fit for the occupation of a small genteel family. Coach house and Stabling will be required.—Letters (post paid) containing all particulars of terms and situation, to be sent to L. M. N., W. Robson and Co., St. Dunstan's Hill, Tower Street.

WANTED, a Situation as Clerk in an Office or Warehouse by a Young Man

Advertisement in *The Times*, 15 August 1821.

ornaments and not principles. Nothing can be more grand than its simplicity and usefulness. Simple without intricacy, it seems to me to be the spontaneous expression of humanity, congenial to the wants of man. . . Remember me and my wife in love and friendship to our dear Mrs. Flaxman, whom we ardently desire to entertain beneath our thatched roof of rusted gold.'

Dorothy and William Wordsworth had returned to their native Lake District in 1799, not to the handsome Georgian house they had been bought up in, but to Dove Cottage in Grasmere. By the standards of the time it was spacious, with two downstairs rooms and a back kitchen and four small rooms above. They turned the downstairs parlour into a lodging room, covering the stone flags with matting and putting in a camp bed large enough for two people to sleep in. Upstairs they had a sitting room, two bedrooms – one of which Dorothy papered with newspaper – and a lumber room. Outside they grew roses and honeysuckle intertwined with heavy-cropping red-flowering runner beans. They employed Molly Fisher from next door to wash dishes and light fires for a couple of hours a day. Despite the compensations of glorious scenery and a life that inspired poetry, reality impinged. Dorothy wrote: 'We find ourselves sadly crowded in this small cottage . . . The children are now in bed. The evening is very still, and there are no indoor sounds, but the ticking of our Family watch which hangs over the chimney piece under the drawing of the Applethwaite Cottage, and a breathing or a beating of one single irregular Flame in my fire. No one who had not been an Inmate with Children in a *Cottage* can have a notion of the quietness that takes possession of it when they are gone to sleep.' In 1813 William Wordsworth moved his family out of

Dove Cottage to Rydal Mount, a substantial house (with a Turkey carpet in the dining room, reported Dorothy in wonderment).

SENTIMENTALITY VERSUS REALITY

As THE NINETEENTH CENTURY PROGRESSED the recorders of realism and the purveyors of saccharine romanticism continued their divergent paths.

> The cottage homes of England!
> By thousands on her plains,
> They are smiling o'er the silvery brooks,
> And round the hamlet lanes.
>
> Through glowing orchards forth they peep
> Each from its nook of leaves;
> And fearless there the lowly sleep
> As a bird beneath the eaves.

These lines by Felicia Dorothea Hemans were first published in 1827 and continually quoted for the next hundred years. The popular Victorian writer William Howitt was

another creator of pastoral schmaltz. He travelled with his wife Mary to write *The Rural Life of Britain*. At Strath Conan in Scotland they spent the night in a primitive smoky Scottish cottage and dined on oatcakes. Undeterred by the discomfort, he exclaims, 'Ah! Cottage Life! There is much more hidden under that name than ever inspired the wish to build cottages ornées, or to inhabit them. No more beautiful sight than the "primitive simplicity". There are thousands of them inhabited by woodmen, labourers, or keepers, that are fit dwellings for the truest poet that ever lived . . .'

Such sentimental views were dismissed sharply by the topographical writer John Britton in 1850. Rural life was not as metropolitan poets and visionary enthusiasts imagined it, 'replete with sylvan joys, arcadian scenes, primeval innocence, and unsophisticated pleasures', but something far more problematic. George Eliot wrote: 'The notion that peasants are joyous, that the typical moment to represent a man in a smock-frock is when he is cracking a joke and showing a row of sound teeth, that cottage matrons are usually buxom, and village children necessarily rosy and merry, are prejudices difficult to dislodge from the artistic mind, which looks for its subject into literature instead of life.'

In her *Middlemarch*, set in the late 1820s, the character of the devoutly Christian Dorothea Brooke has a passion to build improved cottages: 'I think we deserve to be

OPPOSITE *Loading the Cart for Market*, watercolour by Myles Birket Foster. A late Victorian cottage scene conveying comfort and plenty. Birket Foster was one of the artists used by Cadbury to decorate their chocolate boxes.
LEFT In a *Punch* cartoon, 1861, a squalid cottage is contrasted with an immaculate stable and captioned: 'The Peasant's Petition' to the British Landlord: '*that you will be graciously pleased to treat him like a horse.*'

beaten out of our beautiful houses with a scourge of small cords – all of us who let tenants live in such sties as we see round us.'

Nonetheless, the increasingly urban middle class continued to favour nostalgic images of a world from which they may only recently have moved. Victorian painters churned out cottage scenes. The painter and illustrator Helen Allingham and her husband William moved out of London to Witley in Surrey in the early 1880s, a fashionable rural area for those of an artistic disposition. She and her neighbour and fellow artist Myles Birket Foster had great success with their watercolours of local Surrey cottages; they didn't flinch from recording their decay – some were on the point of demolition – but the sun was always shining and rosy-cheeked children playing in gardens wore spotless white bonnets and pinnies. The overall effect is one of charm and prettiness, which is no doubt what appealed to the eager buyers at Allingham's yearly exhibitions in Bond Street, who had no wish to peer inside the cottages, or see them portrayed on a dark wet November afternoon.

COTTAGE ECONOMICS

Eliot's Dorothea represents a new philanthropic attitude towards both urban and rural housing. Edwin Chadwick's 1842 government report into the Sanitary Condition of the Labouring Population presented chilling facts gathered from all over the country. Conditions were worst in the north, where the cottages were often built of rubble stone and hardly weatherproof. A description from the vicar of Norham was quoted: 'The chimneys have lost half their original height, and lean on the roof with fearful gravitation. The rafters are evidently rotten and displaced; and the thatch, yawning to admit the wind and wet in some parts, and in all parts utterly unfit for its original purpose of giving protection from the weather, looks more like the top of a dunghill than of a cottage.' On the inside rain made a puddle on the earth floor and it was covered with 'the aggregate filth of years, from the time of its first being used. The refuse and droppings of meals, decayed animal and vegetable matter of all kinds, which has been cast upon it from the mouth and stomach, these all mix together and exude from it. Window-frame there is none. There is neither oven, nor copper, nor grate, nor shelf, nor fixture of any kind.' The average size of a cottage was 24 x 16 feet 'and into them crowded 8, 10, or even 12 persons'. In Dorset a medical officer wrote of springs bursting up through the mud floors, one cottage with a single small pane of glass for a window and cottagers living almost wholly on bread and potatoes.

The *Illustrated London News* of September 1846 sent a correspondent to Dorset to investigate the truth of a series of letters in *The Times* on rural poverty. This illustration of the interior of a labourer's cottage in Stourpaine, Dorset, shows the 'privation and suffering of the inmates': 'the atmosphere, especially of the sleeping apartments, to an unpractised nose is almost insupportable.'

The clergy had every opportunity to observe the standard of living in their parishes. The Revd S. Godolphin Osborne, Rector of Bryanston in Dorset, wrote to *The Times* in 1846 that labourers were 'fed like fowls, sheltered like beasts, they are expected to hallow the Sabbath, reverence the game laws, and hold their tongues.' He also expressed horror at what was becoming a burning issue: the need to provide separate bedrooms for boys and girls. 'I do not choose to put on paper the disgusting scenes that I have known to occur from this promiscuous crowding of the sexes together. Seeing, however, to what the mind of the young female is exposed from her very childhood, I have long ceased to wonder at the otherwise seeming precocious licentiousness of conversation which may be heard in every field where many of the young are at work together.' Many cottages in the mid-nineteenth century still had only two rooms, one for living and one for sleeping, plus a scullery. *The Primitive Methodist Magazine* made much the same point in 1864, stating that on some of the largest and richest estates in the land, 'there are labourers' cottages which are a disgrace to this age of civilisation . . . conditions as bad as those witnessed in the cabin of a negro in the swamps of a slave plantation in the southern states of America.' An enquiry into rural housing at this date found that less than 5 per cent of cottages had more than two bedrooms, and the rooms were far smaller than the legal minimum allowed in urban lodging houses.

In the light of this information Cottage Improvement Societies sprang up over the country, among them Northumberland (1841), Hastings (1857), Wimbledon (1858), Nottingham (1861) and Winchester (1869). Some circulated information on good practice; some, like Wimbledon, built groups of model cottages. The 1845 Annual Report of the Cottage Improvement Society for Northumberland reiterated its aim of providing 'at least two habitable rooms in the new cottages' but demonstrated how

Plan for a primitive pair of cottages built on the estate of the Duke of Northumberland, published by the Northumberland Cottage Improvement Society, 1845. Each cottage has a single living room with a bed alcove, plus dairy, cow byre, coal store, privy and ashpit.

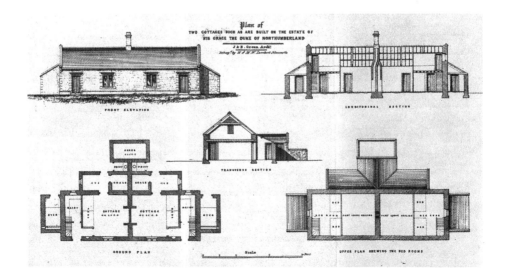

low the county's standard was by holding up as a good example cottages built by the Duke of Northumberland. These had only one room with a small space in the roof for sleeping (saving the expense of two storeys), and the dimensions were 16 feet x15 feet 6 inches and 9 feet high. The Duke's cottages designed for 'public situations' could be built for £77; those for 'obscure and unfrequented positions' and so 'without finishing' could be managed for £72. 0s. 10d.

Progress over a third bedroom was slow. When Scottish architect John Starforth published designs in 1853 for *Farm-houses and Farm-steadings, Factors' Houses and Labourers' Cottages* in 1853, the cheapest cottage, costing £112, had one bedroom 'with space for 2 beds'. This, Starforth admitted, was not ideal, but, he claimed, many cottagers enjoyed the 'time-honoured custom' of sleeping in one room and were prejudiced against innovation – an economy which suited the landlord fine.

The Board of Agriculture had run competitions for model cottages from 1800 onwards, as did various Agricultural Societies. Seventy-six sets of plans arrived from all over the British Isles for the Yorkshire Agriculture Society's 1859 competition – first prize £20. The single cottage must cost no more than £110, to include the cost of a pigsty but not of the land. It must have three bedrooms, a porch, a scullery with a sink, and fireplaces in at least two bedrooms. However, the housing reformer John Birch, who produced *Examples of Labourers Cottages* in print from 1862 onwards, was firm that no family cottage should have less than three bedrooms, living room, scullery, outhouses for coal or wood, privy, piggery, ovens, washing copper, drainage, tank, well, pantry, linen closet, shelving and cupboards. How satisfying to tour the estate and feel pleased with the 'peasant's humble home' he urged the landowner. And some did.

Philanthropists and reformers thought that life in a new clean cottage would also benefit the destitute. 'Villages' of cottage homes, instead of a monolithic Gothic Revival institution, provided something resembling a family unit at the Home for Little Boys that opened in Farningham, Kent, in 1864 or at Dr Barnardo's Village Home for Girls in Ilford. At the home for alcoholic women that she founded near Reigate Lady Henry Somerset felt convinced that the women's self-respect could be better restored 'in cottage life than any institution'.

The boys, girls and alcoholic ladies had little choice in the matter of where they lived, but a number of people fell in with Irishman Feargus O'Connor's scheme – the Chartist Co-operative Land Company, founded in 1845. O'Connor bought six parcels of land which were divided up into plots each with a cottage and fruit trees. One, at Minster

Lovell in Oxfordshire, was called Connorville. The settlers' aims were to become self-sufficient farmers, pay back the company's loan and thereby become landowners, which – most importantly from the Chartists' point of view – would give them the vote. As countless idealistic smallholders bent on self-sufficiency have subsequently found, this is a tough route, particularly when, as here, the majority of inhabitants had come from towns and cities with no experience of country life. But there was much optimism in the new venture. The Chartist agitator, lawyer and novelist Ernest Jones contributed the following encouraging lines on the project to *The Labourer* magazine:

> And how some have chosen wisely
> And how some have acted right:
> How the taverns grow more empty,
> And the cottages more bright.

However much reformers cried out for improved cottages for labourers, the block to progress was always that the cost of building new was out of proportion to the rent that the agricultural worker could pay from his pitiful wage. Cottages represented

ABOVE A bleak view of Snig's End in Gloucestershire, from the *Illustrated London News* of 23 February 1850, endorses the magazine's scepticism about the project.
RIGHT William Snape's 1891 painting matches Flora Thompson's description of a well-furnished cottage.

loss, not profit. In addition, over much of the countryside there were restrictive by-laws insisting that brick or stone be used, rather than cheaper building materials. The agricultural depression of the 1880s augmented the problem: cottage repair bills were unlikely to be top of a straitened landowner's agenda.

As Flora Thompson relates in her memoir of childhood in an Oxfordshire hamlet during the 1880s, *Lark Rise to Candleford*, cottagers were used to problems, and in many cases cheerfully made do. 'Poverty was an inconvenience'; however, 'The inhabitants lived an open-air life; the cottages were kept clean by much scrubbing with soap and water, and doors and windows stood wide open when the weather permitted . . . In nearly all the cottages there was but one room downstairs, and many of these were poor and bare, with only a table and few chairs and stools for furniture and a superannuated potato sack thrown down by way of a hearthrug. Other rooms were bright and cosy, with dressers of crockery, cushioned chairs, pictures on the

LEFT *A Wiltshire Cottage*, watercolour by Helen Allingham reproduced in Stewart Dick's *The Cottage Homes of England*, 1909.
RIGHT A souvenir postcard of the Exhibition Road of Cheap Cottages at Letchworth, 1905.

walls and brightly coloured hand-made rag rugs on the floor. In these there would be pots of geraniums, fuchsias, and old-fashioned, sweet-smelling musk on the window-sills. In the older cottages there were grandfathers' clocks, gate-legged tables, and rows of pewter, relics of a time when life was easier for country folk.' She records that only three of the cottages in the hamlet had their own water supply other than a water butt; drawing water from the various wells and carting it home in buckets suspended on a yoke was hard graft for women.

The parlous condition of old cottages was of national concern, and vernacular architecture was gathering enthusiasts – it represented British craftsmanship and truth to materials. The Arts and Crafts architect M.H. Baillie Scott wrote in 1906: 'You get nearest to heaven' in Tudor cottages. When Alfred Tennyson walked out from his country house in Haslemere, he spotted derelict cottages that he suggested as subjects to his friend Helen Allingham, urging her to paint and record them before they disappeared. Sixty-four of Allingham's watercolours were used in 1909 to illustrate Stewart Dick's *The Cottage Homes of England* (the title taken from Mrs Hemans's poem). The book was a celebration of the cottage and its essential Englishness, regarded even as a reflection of the national character – straightforward but untidy.

TWENTIETH-CENTURY REDESIGN

THE CHEAP COTTAGE EXHIBITION held at Letchworth, Hertfordshire, in 1905 was another attempt to stimulate interest in the rural housing crisis. It was the brainchild of J. St Loe Strachey, editor of *The Spectator* and owner of *The Country Gentleman's*

Land and Water Magazine. Strachey was keen to promote cottages that could be quickly built in modern materials. In Letchworth, the first Garden City, the land was privately owned and not subject to by-laws insisting on traditional building materials. He held a competition for cottages that could be built for under £150 and let for £8 a year. The resulting exhibition was an extraordinary success and attracted nearly eighty thousand visitors, so many that a temporary railway station was needed to deal with the crowds. Cottages incorporating prefabricated concrete, Uralite (asbestos cladding) and Mackolith ('fire-, sound- and vermin-proof') were built. The Bournville Cottage Trust impressed visitors with a large tool shed and an upstairs lavatory. One architect claimed to have lived with a labourer to discover his real needs and designed a large bedroom (since this is where he spent most of his time at home) and a porch with a seat, designed to keep the labourer out of the pub when he came 'home from work weary, and often, unfortunately, to find an untidy, stuffy and sometimes dirty kitchen. His wife may have been at work herself, and not had time to tidy up. Then the children get troublesome. He gets through his evening meal and if there is nowhere for him to sit down with his pipe in peace, you will generally find he goes off to the village public house . . . ' All but Baillie Scott kept to

the price limit. His cottages cost £420 a pair: 'The cottage should be the dream come true, the result of infinite pains.'

In all likelihood it was in the search for a dream come true, rather than cheap agricultural housing, that most visitors went to the exhibition. A reporter for the *Manchester Guardian* described being trapped by a flock of gushing ladies crowding narrow stairs and purring 'Oh, how sweetly pretty!' and 'What a darling wee little place!' Tellingly, one of the most popular cottages at the exhibition was Nook Cottage (which under other circumstances would have been described as a bungalow), featuring an inglenook fireplace at its heart. As a visitor wrote, 'I think the best arranged and prettiest of all the buildings was The Nook Cottage, a marvel of cheapness at £150. The rooms are all on the ground floor, and the kitchen, with its recessed inglenook round the big fireplace, and its box seats to economise space, are reminiscent of the rural homes one finds in real old-fashioned garden cities – the villages and hamlets of old England.' As William Howitt had written, 'happiness is a fireside thing' and the inglenook fireplace, furnished with pokers, chimney ornaments, firedogs, firebacks and trivets, became the mark of a desirable country cottage. The revival of the inglenook was intended to convey a sense of cosiness, and cosiness, it was considered, was what cottages were about.

By the end of the nineteenth century many forward-thinkers were convinced that it would be much preferable to house urban working-class families in individual dwellings with small gardens, rather than in blocks of dwellings or cramped terraces. The word cottage was subsequently applied to low-density schemes in the spirit of what could loosely be called the Garden City movement. The houses built by George Cadbury in his village of Bournville and by the Rowntrees at New Earswick in Yorkshire in 1902 were semi-detached or in short terraces, but they were referred to as cottages. The Fabian pamphlet *Cottage Plans and Common Sense* by Raymond Unwin, the architect of New Earswick, threw out all the preconceived ideas of how a cottage should be and started from scratch. It should face the sun; halls, passages and parlours should be eliminated, to make the most of a small space and create one living room that was as large as possible – with an inglenook recess; this he believed would create an 'almost enchanted space where family members might experience a constant lift of spirits'. He advocated an uncarpeted floor and simple furnishings; this would leave money with which to educate children to think.

The London County Council (LCC) developed what came to be called 'cottage estates', the early ones being White Hart Lane, from 1901, in the north and Old Oak, from 1905, in the west. They were basically much like standard narrow-fronted terraces, albeit with a less rigid street plan; but an effect of cottage-ness was created with gables, tall chimneys and green spaces interspersing the housing.

The need for new rural cottages was also pressing, as pointed out by Hugh Aronson in 1913. *Our Village Homes, present conditions and suggested remedies* noted that although the population of rural Somerset had shrunk by 18,744 people in a decade, numerous disgusting cottages still existed. In one unidentified village, out of 79 cottages 47 had no drainage but depended on earth closets 'of the type with foul pits', a number were without a proper water supply and so dependent on rainwater, and in many back gardens nothing could be grown because the soil was so hot with decaying rubbish. Aronson made a plea for councils to build new cottages in rural areas. Agricultural wages, however, were still so low that when the Board of Agriculture proposed in 1913 to build new rural cottages in villages, it was suggested that they should be let to better paid railwaymen, policemen and postmen, leaving their old cottages available for agricultural labourers to live in. The labourers' 'insanitary dwellings' could then be demolished. This scheme would also provide an alternative to living in a tied cottage.

INCOMERS

BY THE TURN OF THE CENTURY the idea of going away to the country or the seaside for the weekend had taken hold among the middle as well as the upper classes; fewer

'A predilection for week-end cottages', one of Pont's cartoons illustrating the British character, done originally for *Punch* and published in book form in 1938.

RIGHT Design for a new thatched country cottage by C.J. Kay, published in *The Studio*, 1912, the projected cost of which was £1200. In 1904 the magazine had run a competition for 'a weekend cottage'.

OPPOSITE The painter Ethel Walker photographed by *Tatler* in 1941 at home in her workman's cottage in Cholesbury, Buckinghamshire, having been bombed out of Chelsea.

people worked on Saturdays and train companies introduced special weekend return rates. Families began to acquire weekend cottages. Some were even building them. *Modern Cottage Architecture*, published by B.T. Batsford in 1904, included designs for a weekend cottage that could be run with one servant, maybe an amenable villager, and while the author, Maurice Adams, felt that 'a certain amount of roughing it has a charm and makes a change calculated to do most people good', discomfort should be kept to a minimum. Adams recommended a family room and a meal room off it (so that the maid-of-all-work would not be too much in evidence), and a veranda for smoking, wet days and summer evenings.

A humorous paperback of the same period by T.W.H. Crosland called *The Country Life* mocked the trend: 'country-cottageitis is a distinctly modern complaint . . . it is difficult to find within a forty miles radius of Charing Cross any really dilapidated farmhouse, lean-to, or rustic dwelling which is not inhabited during the pleasanter months of the year by persons for whom it was assuredly not built.' The dream cottage was cheap and close to the railway station: 'that sweetly pretty rustic retreat, that remote habitation of your dreams, where all is arborescence, fragrance, simplicity, health and peace . . . You will leave these malodorous, tropic alleys, these hansoms and motor buses, these ABC shops, these fly-blown bars, these stuffy restaurants, these screaming, bloated, underground trains, this desert of a suburb – you will adventure forth into the sweet, the innocent, the beautiful, cow-haunted country which God made – the town, as all men know, having been made by man.'

Life in the country was always thought of as healthier and cheaper, but the reality was often tough for those who chose it, rather than being born to it. 'I want lights, music, people,' was the anguished cry of Katherine Mansfield from the brick semi-detached cottage that she shared with John Middleton Murry at Cholesbury in Buckinghamshire. Her day had involved an attempt to pave the muddy path to the outside lavatory and the disaster of blocking the sink with mutton grease after a failed effort to wash up lunch dishes without hot water or washing powder. First-time cottage dwellers tended to group together for support: Mansfield and Middleton Murry had D.H. and Frieda Lawrence, Mark Gertler and Dora Carrington as neighbours to alleviate the difficulties. Robert Graves rented a cottage from John Masefield before moving to one in Islip in 1921 with his wife, Nancy, and their children, hoping for a quiet life of writing and drawing. Graves cooked and they shared the cleaning, which left them little time for anything else. Their standards were high; they polished their brass ornaments and their children wore five times as many clean dresses as their neighbour's.

In an atmosphere of teething, minor accidents, epidemics and the perpetual washing of nappies, they managed to live on £130 a year, half from Graves's writing and half on presents from family. '"Love in a cottage, I'm afraid" had been the prophetic phrase current at our wedding,' wrote Graves, and commented that while they struggled to manage on 50 shillings a week, their farm labourer neighbours, some with larger families than theirs, were living on 30 shillings: 'Thinking how difficult conditions were for the labourers' wives kept Nancy permanently depressed.'

In accumulating brass ornaments the Graveses were subscribing to the middle-

Illustration from a 1922 *Ideal Home* feature on Apple Tree Cottage, Ansty, Sussex, home of Brighton hotelier Sir Harry Preston and decorated in what was considered appropriate cottage style. The caption reads: 'A closer view of the open fireplace which burns "the old yule log". Note the warming pan – used only as an ornament however.'

class cottage aesthetic which eschewed modernity and sought to hark back to the past. As early as 1904 Heals had bought out a range of Country Cottage furniture consisting of simple furniture in the Arts and Crafts style and linen curtains for casement windows. An authentic cottage interior was described by Harry Batsford and Charles Fry in *The English Cottage* (1938): 'On raising the latch and pushing open the door, we find ourselves in a low room, the ceiling crossed by heavy beams, from which hang hams, bunches of herbs and possibly a frame for washing that can be raised or lowered . . . The window is long and low, of leaded panes . . . The broad window shelf is filled with flowering plants dear to the cottager's heart; their gaiety more than compensates for the loss of light. . . . The chief feature is the fireplace, which occupies most of one side of the room; this opening, six foot or more, is spanned by an oak beam, covered by a curtained valance to increase the draught. The shelf above holds a miscellany of objects – tea canisters, a ticking wooden clock, a brass kettle, candlesticks, china Toby jugs, chained dogs, a pair of simpering pottery figures or a miniature doll's house.' The authors expressed some regret that 'cottage wives now prefer the greater convenience of a range to open-fire cooking, and frequently the open fireplace has been bricked up and a kitchener inserted.'

As a result of the Housing Act of 1930 many rural cottages were condemned as unfit to live in and scheduled for demolition. This humane move was of concern to those who lobbied for the preservation of the countryside; they did, however, regretfully acknowledge that the future of some cottages had to be as townees' play-places. Batsford and Fry dreaded the inevitable result: 'Sometimes the work is done with sympathy and taste, but more often the results are so appalling that one feels that it would have been better for the buildings to have met an honourable end than to have bought their respite at the expense of such vulgarity.' They recall the editress of a ladies journal crying: 'I want to find a Tudor cottage in Sussex, just a beautiful shell to be *gutted*.' Vulgarity is characterized as black-beamed interiors, bottle-glass windows (with here and there a 'stained' pane from a cathedral city antique shop), copper warming pans, faked oak furniture, willow-pattern plates and 'old pewter'. Beverley Nichols, columnist for the *Sunday Chronicle*, bought his weekend cottage in Huntingdon, conveniently just off the Great North Road, on a whim in the early 1930s. It was an 'exquisite thatched cottage', three cottages knocked into one, and had room for his manservant and weekend guests.

Work for agricultural labourers was shrinking as farming became mechanized, and traditional village figures, such as the blacksmith, were gradually disappearing. As a result the village became increasingly middle class. As Mollie Panter-Downes wrote in her 1940 short story *It's The Real Thing This Time*: 'Major Marriot lived with his unmarried sister in a charming cottage, one of the hundreds all over England which, built for the British workingman, are ending their days in gentility as homes for the poor but snug gentry. Chintzes fluttered at its doll windows and a pretty card, hand-painted by Miss Marriot, warned "Heads!" above the lopsided front door, which usually stood ajar and treated passers-by to a glimpse of an arsenal of Zulu shields, bows and assegais.' In highly desirable areas (pretty, near railway station, cathedral town or sea) supply did not meet demand, so villages were augmented by conversions – The Old Shop, The Old Forge, The Old Schoolhouse, The Old Chapel, The Old Stables, The Old Barn, The Old Sail Loft.

Posy Simmonds's *Village Christmas*, 1984. The demographic of rural villages altered dramatically as middle-class incomers replaced redundant agricultural labourers. Second-home owners created ghost villages.

'All we wanted was a country cottage, with decent water to drink, reasonable sanitation, and above all a garden, a bit of untouched earth if possible,' wrote H.E. Bates of his search with his newly wed wife in the late 1920s, but 'every cottage in England seemed to be either sordid or arty.' They finally found a granary in Kent and converted it: 'now a baby has been born here and a novel written and Mozart's music sings through the place as often as the wind once did.'

By the 1960s authenticity had largely been thrown out the window, as the 1963 *House and Garden Book of Cottages* charts. 'A famous decorator transforms the lodge of an historic estate into a weekend cottage with two caravans (to be converted for his guests)'; 'a world-wide traveller and photographer mixes old and new in a highly imaginative conversion of an oast-house'; 'an artist and a designer of wallpapers and textiles convert a house with a ghostly legend in an Essex village'; 'an architect converts two cottages into one spacious weekend escape'; 'a husband-and-wife designing team convert a small East Anglian cottage'; 'an accomplished gardener aided by an eminent son transform a small cottage high on the Oxfordshire hills'. 'What once were labourers' cottages are now the dream objects of thousands, opening up for them all the delights of country life.'

Dream objects are generally bathed in eternal sunshine, while reality is often different. Mollie Panter-Downes conjured up an alternative vision in another short story written in 1940: 'It was before lunch on a dark January day in the Ramsays' country cottage in Sussex. Just how dark January could be, Mrs. Ramsay reflected gloomily, no one would ever know who had not spent it in a delightful little Tudor gem with a wealth of old oak and several interesting original features (such as a beam on which you knocked your head outside the bathroom). The log fire was smoking in its interesting original way . . . '

These disadvantages could be avoided, however, by living the cottage dream solely between the pages of a magazine. *Country Living*, a magazine that has championed rurality since the 1980s, states: 'Whether you live in the town or countryside, in *Country Living* you'll find a wealth of ideas for your home and garden, learn about traditional crafts, keep informed of rural issues, enjoy irresistible dishes using seasonal produce

and, above all, escape the stress and strain of modern-day life [in] the appealing world of rural beauty and tranquillity.'

However, that 'real' cottagers still exist is possibly proven by the prospectus for the 2011 Rackham, Sussex, 65th Annual Fete and Garden Show. Division B (onions, beetroot, runners, parsnip): 'Open to Cottagers of Rackham, Parham, Wiggonholt, Greatham, Crossgates, Amberley, Cootham etc. . . . the Cottagers' division is intended for those who receive wages, and also bona-fida [*sic*] occupiers of a Cottage. The said Cottagers will be excluded if they employ hired assistance. No persons employed regularly in a garden, or their wives, shall be allowed to compete in Division B "open".'

COUNTRY HOUSES

ASTLE, MANOR, HALL, ABBEY, GRANGE, PARK, MANSION, STATELY HOME or just 'the big house'; more is written about country houses than any other kind – exactly as the original builders would have expected. Country houses were homes – albeit often part-time – to two entirely separate groups of people, the owners and the servants. Many were built primarily to impress. Awe-inspiring and packed with treasures, being visited and 'looked round' was to be part of their *raison d'être*. A late sixteenth-century traveller would have stopped in wonder at Bess of Hardwick's initials, 'E S', piercing the skyline of Hardwick Hall above a glittering cliff of expensive glass windows, much as one in 1772 would have gaped at the Marquess of Rockingham's extension of Wentworth Woodhouse's façade to 606 feet. Country houses are landed houses, and land has always represented power – power over the people who live on it, and power to do with it whatever whim or practicality dictates.

Land historically provided a population to fight, vote and work for you. Land gave you sole rights to hunt game, to eradicate villages, to experiment with agriculture. In return the landowner had responsibilities for everything in his care.

Whether a small manor or ducal palace, each country house built between the Middle Ages and the Edwardian period represents success: one individual's moment of power and accumulation of wealth expressed in the creation of a house. Each one is unique, the product of taste, money, time and craftsmanship: cynosure of the nation, or at least the locality.

'Of all the great things that the English have invented and made part of the credit of the national character, the most perfect, the most characteristic, the only one they have mastered completely in all its details, so that it becomes a compendious illustration of their social genius and their manners, is the well-appointed, well-administered, well-filled country house.' Henry James wrote this at the turn of the twentieth century. His gentle term 'country house' has connotations of elegance, comfort, tranquillity – a long haul from its antecedents, the castle and medieval manor.

THE FORTIFIED HOUSE

A CASTLE WAS FOR THOSE with money and ambition. Henry II, alarmed by their number, seized and demolished castles – obliterating twenty and confiscating thirteen between 1174 and 1176, so achieving a more stable society. However, most feudal landowners still chose to live behind some degree of fortification, if not a castle then at least a house protected by solid walls and a gatehouse. Height implied power: towers and turrets impressed. Moats effectively separated a house from its neighbours. Castellations were, in a sense, an architectural expression of noble rank, since the right to fortify was licensed by the king. From 3 July 1482, Edmund Bedingfeld could, at the king's 'will and pleasure, build, make and construct with stone, lime, and sand, towers and wall in and about his manour of Oxburgh, in the county of Norfolk.' These towers and walls could be 'embattled [battlemented], kernell'd [crenellated] and machicollated [given openings below the battlements for dropping missiles through]' so that he and his heirs could hold

The east front of Welbeck Abbey painted in a golden Edwardian glow by Ernest Haslehurst, an illustration for *Our Beautiful Homeland*, c.1905. The medieval abbey was converted into a country house by the Cavendish family in the seventeenth century and continuously altered up to the early twentieth century by the same family, by then the Dukes of Portland.

the property 'forever without perturbation, impeachment, molestation, impediment or hindrance from us or our heirs or others whomsoever'. 'Molestation' was a constant fear; possession was often by force. Only fourteen years earlier and seventy miles away across the county, the ownership of Caister Castle had been in dispute. The Paston family had inherited it from Sir John Falstolf, but the Duke of Norfolk felt it was his and besieged it. Margaret Paston wrote to her husband urging him to take action as 'your brother and his felesshep stand in grete joperte at Cayster, and lakke vetayll [are in great jeopardy and short of food]; and Dawbeney and Berney be dedde and diverse other gretly hurt; and they fayll gunpowder and arrows and the place sore broken . . .' After two months of this, the Pastons surrendered and moved out.

Households such as these were numerous: in addition to the family there were pages, gentlemen-in-waiting, ladies-in-waiting, stewards and retainers – followers recruited from surrounding families who wore the badge or livery of their patron and protected his interests. In return for bed and board they had to be prepared to fight. A potentially volatile system was finally curbed by Henry VII, who granted licences that limited the number of retainers in a household.

At the core of the manor house was the great hall, where rents were collected and manorial courts held. From here the lord of the manor dispensed largesse: not only to his own numerous household, but also to neighbours and any passing traveller – clergy, pilgrims, lawyers, households on the move. The poor were fed at the gate. Competitive building, a theme of this chapter, starts here with the magnitude of the hall: John of Gaunt's at Kenilworth was 90 x 45 feet, that of the Bishop of Bath and Wells 115 feet long. The baron presiding over his medieval great hall with roaring fires, fur-wrapped nobles and carcasses of meat served by knee-buckled serfs, became a symbol of bounteous hospitality. Christmas feasting, lasting for twelve days, was the peak.

Gradually nobles withdrew from the great hall, though some visibility remained important. In the thirteenth century the Countess of Lincoln was advised by Bishop Grosseteste that it was politic to appear at the high table in the hall: 'with your visage and cheer be showed to all men . . . So much as you may without peril of sickness and weariness eat you in the hall afore your many, for that shall be to your profit and worship.' The following century when Langland wrote *Piers Plowman* he noted: 'Now have the rich a rule to eat by themselves / In a privy parlour.' Creating small corners of comfort – and warmth – must have been a continuous struggle; it is hardly surprising that women were first to colonize the solar and the parlour.

The Dissolution of the Monasteries in the sixteenth century provided an unparalleled opportunity for the powerful to acquire Church land, which became the foundation of many great estates. Abbeys were demolished and new houses rose in their stead. As society became more law-abiding, large houses ceased to be part barracks: towers and turrets became merely decorative motifs and the moat an ornamental sheet of water reflecting the size of the house, isolating it from its surroundings. Expressions of power were replaced by displays of splendour. The great hall lost its position as a place for all and sundry, and was transformed into an imposing entrance space. A great chamber, often reached via an impressive staircase, became the centre of the house, a more private room with access only for the privileged. William Harrison commented on the increased grandeur: he observed in Holinshed's *Chronicles* in 1577 that 'the ancient manors and houses of our gentlemen . . . as be lately builded are commonly either of brick or hard stone, or both, their rooms large and comely, and houses of office further distant from their lodgings.' In fact, 'so magnificent and stately as the basest house of a baron doth often match in our days with some honours of a prince in old time.' Wool was a prime source of wealth and many large houses were built on its profits on land recently cleared and enclosed.

Many small well-built manors survived the demise of the feudal system and were gradually enlarged, improved and modernized as their owners' fortunes improved over the centuries. Some became buried in farmsteads and disappeared; others were pulled down and rebuilt, the suffix 'Hall' pointing to their origins. Thousands of small country houses, some with pretensions to fashion and some merely functional farmhouses, have over the centuries sprung up in the rural landscape, but the term has generally been attached to the spectacular.

OSTENTATION

BY THE END OF THE SIXTEENTH CENTURY power was firmly centred at court. Building a house sufficiently splendid to entertain a monarch became an element in the slippery manoeuvring to ascend the hierarchy. A new, more symmetrical style of architecture presented an imposing façade. Interiors and exteriors were enriched with carved wood and stone, glass, gilding, panelling, tapestry, plasterwork and a multitude of chimneys. Ornament was exuberant: outlandish grotesque patterns from the Netherlands, mythic animals, masks, glimmerings of classicism via France and Italy, and elaborate heraldic displays. A deer park provided hunting and hawking as the pursuit and killing of animals was always an essential component of country house amusement.

For the Elizabethans a long gallery, usually on the attic floor, was the new competitive space. A form copied from Burgundy, it was particularly appropriate for British country houses as it created an interior equivalent of the terrace for walking. Here too hung a display of portraits, a new genre of painting which could emphasize lineage and, by inclusion of the monarch's picture, signify loyalty. Catholic families tended to tuck their chapels off the long gallery, out of sight of the main mêlée of the house. The gallery's position as a place where discreet conversations could easily be held led American historian Lena Cowen Orlin to include them among 'Spaces of Treason in Tudor England'. Galleries were also places of assignation: the 1573 fiction by George Gascoigne, *Discourse on the Adventures of Master F.J.*, is set in a northern country house. The young protagonist walks in the long gallery with the married Elinor (an early appearance of marital infidelity in the country house), where the 'coles begin to kindle'. A second

evening, under a full moon, and Elinor succumbs, 'tender limbs against the hard floor', and gamely accepts the discomfort: 'suffised that of hir curteose nature she was content to accept bords for a bed of down, mattes for camerike sheets, and the nightgown of F.J. for the counterpoynte to cover them.' Daybreak comes and they both sneak back to their chambers (a precarious exercise for Master F.J., who has to cross a large courtyard).

The 212-foot-long gallery at Worksop Manor in Nottinghamshire was renowned, yet in a letter written in 1607 to its owner, the Earl of Shrewsbury, Sir George Chaworth taunts him with the grandeur of another being built at Berwick by Lord Dunbar. The gallery at Worksop 'was but a garret' compared to Dunbar's, whose house was a large rectangle of 'exceeding height, and yet magnificent turrets above that height, a goodly front, and a brave prospect open to the meanest and most distant room'.

The twenty-three summer progresses made by Queen Elizabeth I during her reign were, for her most ambitious courtiers, an impetus for building and improvement. A visit from the Queen was both desired and feared: desired because of the favour bestowed and the opportunity to gain her ear, but dreaded because of the heavy financial burden of housing her retinue, which could involve up to 250 horse-drawn carts. Many hosts made do with temporary tents and structures, but Robert Dudley, Earl of Leicester, set the bar high by transforming his medieval castle, Kenilworth, into a palace for the Queen's nineteen-day visit in 1575. Lord Burghley's house Theobalds, in Hertfordshire, was usefully large and conveniently just off the main road north – he entertained the Queen eight times between 1572 and 1596 and doubled its size to avoid the inconvenience of her taking over his principal rooms – great chamber, hall and parlour. Her servants took the place of Burghley's, who were relegated to a converted storehouse, while his steward was ousted from his lodging to house the royal plate. Simultaneously Burghley was tinkering with his other house, Burghley in Cambridgeshire, a project that lasted thirty years.

The Queen never visited Burghley, or Holdenby in Northamptonshire built by Sir Christopher Hatton, one of Elizabeth's favourites and ultimately her Lord Chancellor. A palatial house with two courtyards, it had a complete set of grand rooms in perpetual readiness for the Queen. In 1579, a year after the building had started, Hatton wrote asking Lord Burghley to visit the site and let him know of 'such lacks and faults as shall appear to you'; he was in daily attendance on the Queen and had no time to see it for

A watercolour painted by David Cox in 1838 of the Long Gallery at Hardwick Hall (162 feet), densely hung with portraits. For scale he inserted a figure in early seventeenth-century costume.

himself. Hatton died in 1591, a bankrupt bachelor. Holdenby's subsequent history is typical of many irrationally large country houses. Hatton's nephew sold Holdenby to James I, but ironically the first monarch to spend time amidst its splendour was Charles I, who was imprisoned there for five months. After the Civil War it was bought by a Parliamentarian soldier, who demolished all but one domestic wing, selling off the stone for building. Daniel Defoe saw it in the early eighteenth century and noted 'a kind of odium upon the place, forsaken and uninhabited'. It was going 'daily to decay' and he doubted that its new owner, the Duchess of Marlborough, would manage to revive it; but the family did, and still own it today. Despite its diminution it is still a 'grand country house' and, like so many, now 'a perfect setting for wedding or corporate events'.

The precarious jockeying to bask in the approving gaze of the monarch and so gain lucrative patronage continued under James I. He was disinclined to impose upon his subjects unless invited to hunt or race; however, having a queen he required twice as much space, needing two sets of apartments. Power brokers clustering round the monarch spent more time at court in London than in their prodigious country houses. Travel was laborious: lumbering coaches travelled at little more than three miles an hour. Lord Pembroke arrived at Wilton in Wiltshire one day in 1601 to write the much-quoted statement: 'I have not been a day in the country and am as weary of it as if I had been a prisoner there seven year.' Lady Anne Clifford, journeying in 1603, left a description of a deserted house: 'came to Wrest, my Lord of Kent's, where we found the doors shut and none in the house but one servant, who only had keys of the hall, so that we were forced to lie in the hall all night, till towards morning, at which time came a man who let us in the higher rooms where we slept 3 or 4 hours.'

Ostentatious but empty of inhabitants, such houses were mocked by Ben Jonson in his poem 'To Penshurst', which he wrote c.1616. He lauded Penshurst Place, a fourteenth-century country house that in Jonson's time belonged to Robert Sidney, brother of the poet, Philip. It was famed for its medieval great hall, in Jonson's eyes representing a fine and traditional way of life, 'whose liberal board doth flow with all that hospitality doth know'. The house is 'reared with no man's ruin, no man's groan; / There's none that dwell about them wish them down'; unlike 'those proud, ambitious heaps', with polished pillars, marble, stairs, courts.

Houses inevitably often lay empty when one family owned a number. The Earl Marshall, Lord Shrewsbury, owner of Worksop, owned at least eight others in the north. Lady Anne Clifford (Countess Dowager of Dorset, Pembroke and Montgomery,

A mid-seventeenth-century woodcut illustrating 'Mock Beggar Hall', a ballad which bemoans the disappearance of traditional hospitality and almsgiving because the owners have gone to the city and the court: 'And there they spend their time in sport, / While Mock Beggar Hall stands empty.'

Baroness Clifford, Westmoreland and Vesci, Lady of the Honour of Shipton in Craven and High Sheriffess of Westmoreland, as she styled herself) inherited three in 1643 and moved from one to the other in almost perpetual motion, accompanied by up to three hundred people. 'In these three houses of mine inheritance Appleby Castle and Brougham Castle in Westmoreland and Skipton Castle in Craven I do more and more fall in love with the contentments of country life ... for a wise body might to make their own homes the place of self-fruition and the comfortable part of their life.' She enjoyed ordering repairs, setting things to rights and involving herself in law suits and quarrels.

Anne Clifford had been bought up at Knole in Kent in the early years of the seventeenth century, by then extended to its final considerable size. The number of staff needed to keep such a household in working and comfortable order is recorded. 'A Catalogue of the Household and Family of the Right Honourable Richard Earl of Dorset, in the year of our Lord 1613' lists everyone in the house. One hundred and twenty-seven people are named, including: 'Mr. Matthew Caldicott, my Lord's favourite, and Mr. Peter Basket, who sat at the Parlour Table, one down from My Lord's Table; Henry Keble, Yeoman of the Pantry and Robert Elnor, Slaughterman, who sat at the Clerks' Table in the Hall; Griffin Edwards, Groom of My Lady's Horse, Solomon, the Bird-Catcher and Clement Doory, Man to carry wood, on the Long Table in the Hall; Faith Husband and Prudence Butcher at the Laundry-maids' Table' and finally, in the kitchen and scullery, apparently with nowhere formal to sit, Diggory Dyer, Marfidy Snipt and John Morockoe, a Blackamoor. More than a hundred and fifty years later Caroline Lybbe Powys recorded

a visit to Knole where she was shown round by the Groom of the Chambers, who informed them that the house had 'five hundred rooms, tho' he own'd he never had patience to count them, tho' often had the thirty-five staircases. In the old Duke's time, he said, the company used to be innumerable as the apartments, and made us laugh by an instance of this, having desir'd the housekeeper to count the sheets, she gave out, having delivered fourscore pairs, she said, she would count no longer! One is almost sorry the present owner has it not in his power to keep up this ancient hospitality.'

CLASSICISM AND CONTINENTAL INFLUENCES

DURING THE SEVENTEENTH CENTURY comfort and privacy became increasingly important; one consequence of this was the necessity of separating the servants, purveyors of comfort, from those they served. The architect Roger Pratt, a gentleman himself, and maybe alive to the irritation of meeting a servant carrying slops in a corridor, designed houses whereby the servants' routes were different from those of their masters, and so pioneered both 'below stairs' and 'back stairs'. When, in 1658, he built Coleshill for his cousin, it had a servants' staircase so they 'may not foul the great ones'. Pratt also consolidated the country house into a manageable rectangle, a classical 'double-pile' that eliminated courtyards ('stately indeed, but exceeding costly'). He put

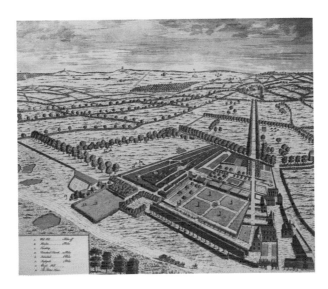

LEFT A painting of *The Tichborne Dole*, by Gillis van Tilborgh, 1671, shows the country house as the fount of charity. A twelfth-century Tichborne landowner had decreed that the villagers should receive in perpetuity the produce from a specific piece of land.
ABOVE An engraving of Copped Hall in Essex, from volume IV of *Vitruvius Britannicus*, 'Views of the Royal Palaces, noblemen and gentlemen's seats in Great Britain', 1739. Bird's-eye views ensured that not only was the house recorded, so was the extent of the land and timber.

service quarters in a rusticated semi-basement 'to keep the servants from encumbering the upper parts of the building by their appearing'. Tenants and estate business could also be confined to the lower, less important parts of the house.

Pratt's architectural vocabulary was classical: pediments and porticoes that expressed status and marked the position of the grand rooms within – elements which stayed good for projecting grandeur for the next two centuries. He also favoured a central rooftop cupola, which, as Celia Fiennes noted, provided a viewpoint for visitors to see clearly the extent (and value) of the property, and 'gives you a great prospect of gardens, grounds, woods that appertaine to the Seate, as well as a sight of the Country at a distance.' Pratt was clear that a house should be built at least a furlong from the road, preferably on a rise in the land and surrounded by green park or pasture. This became the standard position for a country house, frequently remarked upon by foreigners. Nathaniel Hawthorne noted in 1855: 'how comfortable Englishmen know how to make themselves; locating their dwellings far within private grounds, with secure gateways and porters' lodges, and the smoothest roads and the trimmest paths, and shaven lawns, and clumps of trees . . . and all this appropriated to the same family for generations, so that I suppose they come to believe it created exclusively and on purpose for them.'

'Well building hath three conditions: commodity, firmness and delight.' Sir Henry Wotton's translation of the first-century BC Roman Vitruvius was mined for guidance on classical architecture after its publication in 1624. 'Commodity' – or space – in large country houses was lavish. The owner, his wife and their guests all had their own sets of apartments, sequences of rooms spreading out from the central grand saloon. 'Delight' – furnishing this extensive space – was a declaration of the owner's taste and a matter of scrutiny. Continental Europe, particularly France and Italy, was the source of all things cultural and classical as well acquisitions for home. An early Grand Tourist was the 5th Earl of Exeter, who lived at Burghley House in the second half of the seventeenth century, married to the extremely wealthy Anne Cavendish, daughter of the 3rd Earl of Devonshire. They made four journeys to Europe, buying in Paris, Venice, Genoa, Florence, Rome and Naples. In all they returned with over three hundred paintings as well as numerous tapestries, sculptures and *objets de vertu*. Their spending spree left them £8,000 in debt on their deaths and impoverished the estate for at least thirty years, but proved a major draw to Burghley in the late twentieth century.

Travelling abroad also gave British grandees an opportunity to see how their Continental counterparts decorated their *châteaux* and *palazzi*. William Cavendish, later Duke of Devonshire, began rebuilding Chatsworth in 1687, and although this was the wilds of Derbyshire he gilded his external window frames, a notion copied from Versailles. Chatsworth was in effect always open to the public – or at least the well-connected public. Intrepid traveller Celia Fiennes arrived there in 1697 and was astonished by the hot and cold running water: 'There is a fine grotto all stone pavement roofe and sides, this is design'd to supply all the house with water besides severall fancyes to make diversion; within this is a batheing room, the wall with blew and white marble . . . you went down steps into the bath big enough for two people; at the upper end are two Cocks to let in one hott the other cold water to attemper it as persons please.' She noticed that many rooms were still unfinished and that 'they were just painting the ceilings and laying the floores, which are all inlaid.'

The State Drawing Room at Chatsworth, painted by Edward Halliday in 1939, when it was a dormitory for an evacuated girls' school. The girls slept under a ceiling painted by Laguerre in 1690 depicting an adulterous Venus in the arms of her lover, Mars.

Painted ceilings, walls and staircases were the ultimately grand examples of Continental taste, and very effective at covering blank walls to maximum effect. Pratt had warned that British workmen were not up to the task of painting figures on a ceiling and made them look like 'butter prints'. The solution was to import artists, who were also more familiar with classical iconography, gods being appropriately awe-inspiring subjects. Marco Ricci, Antonio Verrio and Louis Laguerre spent years on the vertiginous ceilings and walls of the grandest country houses. After Verrio had painted the Great Staircase at Chatsworth he proceeded to Burghley, where he laboured over a heavily populated Mount Olympus in what became known as the Heaven Room, before moving on in 1697 to spend eleven long and lonely months painting the Mouth of Hell over the staircase. Along the corridor Laguerre was decorating a state dining room with episodes from the life of Antony and Cleopatra, and the Conduct of Scipio towards his Fair Captive. Occasionally an artist removed his wig and sneakily included a self-portrait in a corner, but contemporary figures and scenes rarely appeared – apart from the Duke of Marlborough, who could look up at the ceiling of the Great Hall at Blenheim and catch sight of himself victorious in battle.

Seventy years later such painting seemed faintly ludicrous. Horace Walpole said of Chatsworth: 'The inside is most sumptious but did not please me. The heathen gods, goddesses, Christian virtues, and allegoric gentlefolks are crowded into every room, as if Mrs. Holman had been to heaven and invited everyone she saw.' (Mrs Holman was a pushy social climber of Walpole's acquaintance).

Down the country house scale, manor houses were comfortable, if not elegant. Wye Saltonstall, an impoverished but gentlemanly poet, wrote 'A Gentlemans House in the Countrey' in 1631, describing such a house as 'the prime house of some village, and carryes gentility in front of it'. Here the curate took his Sunday lunch, bread and beer was offered to all comers and even a stranger had 'a napkin and cold meat in the buttery'. Tenants when their leases were about to expire appeared bringing pigs and geese, and maids won sweethearts from among the serving men with promises of cream from the dairy, or free laundry. 'At meals you shall have a scattered troop of dishes led by some black puddings and in the rear some demolished pasties which are not yet fallen to the servingmen . . . All the rooms smell of doggs and haukes.' Mildly indigestible food and rooms smelling of dogs remained elements of country house life for the subsequent three centuries. This was the world of the lord of the manor and his successor, the squire, who in his eighteenth-century heyday epitomized worth and benevolence. The expectation of hospitality that attached to this status, and to temporary posts such as sheriff, was frequently a burden that drove families to the edge of ruin, as they frantically attempted to upgrade their houses.

THE PRICE OF MAGNIFICENCE

THE LANDED GENTRY rose in importance as the role of the monarchy diminished. Power lay with Parliament, and the gentry were its backbone. Sir Robert Walpole (later Earl of Orford) came from that stock but made the leap from Norfolk squire to Prime Minister. Spending the fortune derived from the sinecures that being a Member of Parliament could then bring, he demolished his Jacobean manor house and built Houghton Hall in the 1720s. In this palatial Palladian house, the principal floor was reached by two exterior flights of balustraded stairs. Built in expensive Yorkshire stone rather than brick, it was a very extravagant venture that conveyed permanence. William Kent designed the state rooms, which Walpole filled with superb paintings. But duties rarely allowed him to spend longer than a fortnight there, and when he did it was in an atmosphere of 'a confusion of wine and bawdy and hunting and tobacco', as his son Horace put it. Horace described too a birthday party for his father in 1744, with twenty uncles and cousins 'lowing round me – in short the whole Walpole family are enjoying one another

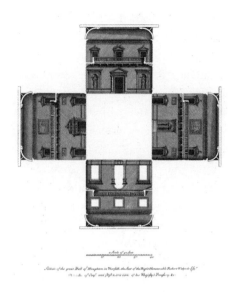

An engraving of the Stone Hall at Houghton, published in *Vitruvius Britannicus*, 1725. The gravitas in this plan was leavened in the actual building by the inclusion of a frieze of riotous putti on the cornice.

and their retirement, and reflecting with infinite satisfaction how little true happiness they ever knew in courts and power.' When he returned to Houghton sixteen years after his father's death he wrote in a letter: 'I have chose to sit in my father's little dressing room and am now by his scrutoire, where, in the height of his fortune, he used to receive the accounts of his farmers, and deceive himself – or us, with thoughts of his economy – how wise a man at once and how weak! For what has he built Houghton? For his grandson to annihilate, or for his son to mourn over!'

The magnificence astonished later visitors. Caroline Lybbe Powys, who went in 1756, commented on how the gilded mouldings and cornices 'makes the whole what I call magnificently glaring' and of the paintings she tells her father, 'I can't even describe one quarter of the pleasure I had in viewing them.' A young Frenchman, François de la Rochefoucauld, visited in the 1770s and found the house inhabited by some of friends of the 3rd Lord Orford. They 'had established themselves in the house, living at their own expense in accordance with a common English custom which seems to me very sensible. Lord Orford does not spend much of each year in the house; its size is so great that he is afraid of living in all the year round in view of the expense in which he would be involved.' It was he who sold the art collection to Catherine the Great. The roller coaster of family fortunes is a constant theme in the history of country houses; how relatively quickly the ambitions and wealth of one generation can be dissipated by a single black sheep, leaving behind a stranded white elephant.

The most spectacular example of a dramatic crash was probably Cannons (modern spelling Canons), built by James Brydges, who was created Duke of Chandos in 1719 for no great achievement. A Member of Parliament from 1698 to 1714, he amassed a vast fortune as Paymaster General to the Queen's Forces Abroad, since he took a cut from all pay made to soldiers fighting the War of Spanish Succession. As the war drew to a close he resigned and converted his wealth into a new country house in Middlesex that was exceptionally lavish in scale and size. Chandos consulted, and then dismissed, a number of leading architects; he commissioned artists and craftsmen to decorate it and employed agents to stuff it with paintings and works of art, many of which he bought sight unseen. 'The whole is built with such a profusion of expense', as Daniel Defoe put it. Chandos kept a private orchestra of about thirty-two players that included members of the Scarlatti and Bach families, and for several years Handel was composer in residence. In 1720 the house and its elaborate gardens were barely complete when Chandos's wealth was severely dented by losses suffered in the South Sea Bubble. Account books reveal panicky attempts at economizing: the Duke compelled one of his valets also to wait at table, copy letters and do accounts; later footmen also had to do the mangling and help in the pantry, and in 1730 the auditors announced that in future 'the breakfasts allowed the family shall be milk porridge or water gruel, and that those that will have tea must have it at their own expense.' Visitors to the house were charged a fee.

A literary spat in 1731 boosted the number of visitors. Alexander Pope had published a poem, 'Epistle IV to Richard Boyle, Earl of Burlington, Of the use of Riches', which attacked the bad architectural taste of aristocrats: 'A description of the False Taste of Magnificence. The first great error of which is to imagine that Greatness consists of size and dimension instead of proportion and Harmony of the whole.' The poem describes with satirical wit 'Timon's Villa', which was generally believed to be Cannons. Pope denied the charge, but Cannons became notorious. Pope's lines include barbs such as: 'Where all cry out, "What sums are thrown away" . . . The whole, a labour'd quarry above ground.' And jibes at the philistinism of the owner, with a library of unread books: 'For all his Lordship knows, but they are wood.' The poem ends, as it happens presciently, with wheat growing where the house once stood: 'Deep harvests bury all his pride has plann'd, / And laughing Ceres reassume the land.'

Cannons was demolished in 1747, just three years after Chandos's death, the estate so encumbered that his heir found it impossible to keep it standing. The contents and architectural material were auctioned off and the house reduced to lots, from 'A painted ceiling by Sgr. Belluci – Represents in the middle the Seven Liberal Arts & Sciences with the Temple of Honour & Mercury offering the genious of youth to Eternity ... £350' to 'A Japan'd close stool ... £1.5 shillings'.

GRAND ASPIRATIONS

WHILE ONE HOUSE WAS BEING DEMOLISHED, many more were being built. A new class of landowner was identified by Daniel Defoe in his *Tour Through the Whole of Great Britain*, in 1724: 'There are several very considerable estates purchased, and now enjoyed by citizens of London, merchants and tradesmen, as Mr. Weston an iron merchant near Kelvedon, Mr. Cresnor, a wholesale grocer, . . . I mention this, to observe how the present increase of wealth in the city of London spreads itself into the country, and plants families and fortunes, who in another age will equal the families of the ancient gentry, who perhaps were bought out.' Not only iron merchants and grocers, but also brewers, bankers, slave traders, nabobs retiring from India, naval officers with prize money to spend and even cabinetmakers – as was William Hallet,

An eighteenth-century print of 'Architecture' showed clients viewing a ground-plan. Peripheral buildings such as stabling, garden pavilions and gate piers also received close attention.

ARCHITECTURE.
London, Printed for Rob.t Sayer . . . 15 Printseller near the Golden Buck near Serjeants Inn Fleet Street.

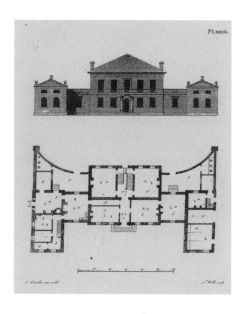

'Design of a House for a Gentleman or Merchant retired from Business, to be placed on some pleasing Eminence in a Healthful Soil', a plate from *Familiar Architecture, Consisting of Original Designs of Houses for Gentlemen and Tradesmen, Parsonages, Summer Retreats, Banqueting Rooms and Churches*, a pattern book by Thomas Rawlins, 1789. In this design the main room is 10 feet high and the kitchen has been placed in the wings so that 'every unpleasing Stench [is] avoided, and the whole render'd commodious as well as wholesome.'

who built a modest country house on the site of Cannons. These were the new gentry, and country houses were the sign of success. Existing landowners rebuilt and extended too, marriage to an heiress, as ever, sometimes footing the bill.

Building a large country house was a public gesture, and critical scrutiny followed. As Lord Shaftesbury realized in the early eighteenth century, 'The ordinary Man may build his Cottage or the plain Gentleman his Country-house according as he fansys; but when a great Man builds he will find little Quarter from the Publick, if instead of a beautiful Pile, he raises, at vast expense, such a false and counterfeit Piece of Magnificence as can be justly arraigned for its Deformity by so many knowing men in Art . . .' 'Deformity' – not getting classical details right – was a pitfall. The detailed engravings of the works of Palladio, as well as books such as *Vitruvius Britannicus*, which from 1715 onwards illustrated the latest British Palladian architecture, were valuable cribs. James Gibbs introduced his folio edition, *A Book of Architecture*, in 1728, as being designed to be 'of use to such Gentlemen as might be concerned in Building, especially in the remote parts of the country where little or no assistance for Designs can be procured'. Isaac Ware (born into a chimney-sweeping family but spotted and mentored by Lord Burlington, so maybe particularly conscious of the need to be correct) contributed *The Complete Body of Architecture* in 1756–7. Any number of small manuals provided guidance for builders, such as Abraham Swan's *One Hundred and Fifty New Designs for Chimney Pieces* (1758), which ran into four editions in ten years.

The economics of building and owning a country house were usually dependent on an estate producing revenue from rents as well as – in good times – agriculture. Large landowners had the resources to experiment with agricultural improvements which increased productivity – and wealth. Landholdings were greatly increased by enclosures of common land, either by agreement or through a petition to Parliament by the principal landowner, quickly granted since landowners dominated Parliament. The new-built country houses – unlike the old manor houses, situated near the church in the heart of the community – were surrounded by a park, a *cordon sanitaire*, separating them from the labourers and village. A luxuriously unproductive and very decorative landscape became the backdrop to country house life.

Many country houses were in a constant state of change and alteration, inside and out. In 1784 François de la Rochefoucauld visited Heveningham in Suffolk and admired how Sir Gerard Vanneck had pulled down all the interior walls of the old house to make a 'splendidly lofty' pillared hall and surrounded it with a 'magnificent modern building'. Vanneck was 'in need of a few statues' and the drawing room was unfinished. Building was a lengthy process, some owners dying before seeing plans completed. John Byng on one of his summer journeys in the1780s characteristically observed that old trees were being felled at Tixal[1] Park, in Staffordshire, and that the owner 'is now demolishing the remains of the grand old mansion, to erect offices upon; adjoining his new mansion house'. At Ingestre Hall the old magnificence is 'ruin'd by a late modern alteration; the grand drawing room is so fritter'd out with French festooning (contraband probably) as to make me sick.' Raby Castle has a carriage drive that has been driven through the medieval great hall and chapel: 'This sounds grand – but must chill the house with winds; and it felt so cold, and so resounding with eccho [*sic*] – that I hastened to the other apartments.' He wrote a satire entitled *Modern Taste*: 'if you should have purchased a good OLD FAMILY HALL, seated low and warm, encircled by woods, and near a running stream, pull it down, and sell all the materials; on no account preserve any of the carving, old wainscoting, painted glass or lofty mantelpieces; because all these things are entirely out of fashion . . . never think of stone or slate, as nothing looks grander, or is seen further, than a RED BRICK HOUSE, with long wings . . . CUT DOWN ALL TREES that are near your house, as they will spoil the prospect, and . . . Grub up all the HEDGES around you, to make your grounds look Parkish . . . Make the APPROACH to your house as meandering as possible . . .'

Approaching Barrington Court in Somerset, Byng wonders if it will look like the print. Engravings of individual country houses were made by the thousand as illustrations for the popular books of views – more than a hundred were published between 1715 and 1870. Usually funded by subscription, they were designed to flatter the owners. The highly prolific J.P. Neale produced eleven volumes in as many years of his *Views of the Seats of Noblemen and Gentlemen in England and Wales, Scotland and Ireland* from 1819 onwards. They revealed the 'number and splendour of the mansions of our nobility and opulent gentry, which while they attest to the wealth of our nation, exhibit also in the most impressive manner, our national taste for whatever is beautiful in nature, or classical in art, presenting that happy union of splendour and comfort.' His choice was based on 'historical celebrity', plus friends, as 'grateful remembrance of past favours, may have induced me to insert the view of a residence possessing no remarkable features either of locality or architectural arrangement.' Subscribers

Wentworth Woodhouse in Yorkshire, an engraving after J.P. Neale, from Jones's *Views of Seats, Mansions, Castles etc of noblemen and gentlemen in England, Wales, Scotland and Ireland*, 6 volumes, 1829–30. 'Accompanied by descriptions of the mansions, list of pictures, statues and genealogical sketches of the families.'

were principally owners or prospective owners of country houses. Neale's list included Jane Austen's brother Edward Knight of Godmersham Park, Sir Richard Bedingfeld of Oxburgh (still crenellated and going strong), as well as John Hodgson, East India Merchant of Hampstead, James Gillespie, an Edinburgh architect, William Ashburner in Bombay and J. Levy of Mount Terrace, Mile End.

As usual, size equalled status: competition in the eighteenth century focused on the length of the façade. Country house gazetteers supplied trainspotterish detail: Stowe, we read in F.O. Morris's *A Series of Picturesque Views of the Seats of Noblemen and Gentlemen etc.,* had a frontage of 916 feet and a drive two miles long, the entrance to the park being marked by a 60-foot Corinthian arch. In an attempt to achieve political prominence in the county, Lord Verney beggared his family by striving to make Claydon even more spectacular than Stowe. Such vast spaces were clearly sometimes alarming. In *Mansfield Park* ten-year-old Fanny Price found 'The grandeur of the house astonished, but could not console her. The rooms were too large for her to move in with ease, whatever she touched she expected to injure, and she crept about in constant terror of something or other.' Even Thomas Creevey, a man of the world, found arriving at Petworth in 1828 daunting: 'How we got into the house, I don't quite recollect, for I think there is no bell, but I know we were some time at the door, and when we *were* let in by a little footman, he disappeared *de suite*, and it was some time before we saw anybody else . . . Every door of every room was wide open from one end to the other, and from the front to behind, whichever way you looked, and not a human being visible.' An Edwardian guest at Wentworth Woodhouse, reputedly with five miles of corridor, was supposed to have crumbled wafers to mark the route from bedroom to dining room, a technique later formalized by presenting guests with crested silver caskets each containing a differently coloured confetti.

COUNTRY HOUSE VISITORS

TRAVEL FOR THE GEORGIANS was quicker and more comfortable, as turnpike trusts improved roads and coach-building advanced. The country became more accessible and impassable roads no longer imprisoned country visitors for months. Summer journeys involving day trips to local houses of note were commonplace and by presenting convincing credentials to servants houses could be toured in the absence of owners. In *Pride and Prejudice*, when Elizabeth travels with the Gardiners to Derbyshire: 'she must own that she was tired of great houses; after going over so many, she really had no pleasure in fine carpets or satin curtains.'

Horace Walpole was a relentless and often splenetic visitor. In May 1736 he wrote to George Montagu enumerating recent visits: 'Stopped at Duke of Kent's at Wrest. On the great staircase is a picture of the Duchess's, I said 'twas very like; "O dear Sir," said Mrs. Housekeeper, "its too handsome for my lady Duchess, her Grace's chin is much longer than that." . . . Coming back we saw Easton Neston, a seat of Lord Pomfret's, where in an old greenhouse is a wonderful statue of Tully, haranguing a numerous assembly of decayed emperors, vestal virgins with new noses, Colossuses, Venuses, headless carcasses, and carcassless heads, pieces of tombs and hieroglyphics . . . I forgot to tell you I was at Blenheim, where I saw nothing but a cross housekeeper, and an impertinent porter; except a few pictures; a quarry of stone, that looked at a distance like a house, and about this quarry, quantities of inscriptions in honour of the Duke of Marlborough; and I think of her Grace too, for she herself is mentioned, as putting 'em up, in almost all of them.' Ninety years later Blenheim is still mouldering, as the German traveller Prince Hermann Pückler-Muskau records: 'The present possessor, with an income of seventy thousand pounds, is so much in debt that his property is administered for the benefit of his creditors, and he receives five thousand a year for life . . . As we entered, there was such a smoke that we thought we had to encounter a second fog in the house. Some very dirty shabby servants – a thing almost unheard-of here – ran past us to fetch the "Chatelaine", who, wrapped in a Scotch plaid, with a staff in her hand and the air of an enchantress, advanced with so majestic an air towards us, that one might have taken her for the Duchess herself. As a preliminary measure, she required that we should inscribe our names in a large book: unhappily, however, there was no ink in the inkstand, so that this important ceremony was necessarily dispensed with. We passed through many chill and faded rooms.' Daniel Defoe, who had looked at it in 1724, with the Duke of Marlborough dead and the palace still unfinished, saw that it represented 'the bounty, the gratitude, or what else posterity pleases to call it, of the English nation', but also that only royalty could ever afford to live there. In fact money arrived, with an injection of Vanderbilt railroad dollars, handed over when Consuelo married the 9th Duke in 1895.

The showpieces did not necessarily engender envy in visitors used to living on an ordinary scale. Nathaniel Hawthorne wrote after a visit in 1854 to Eaton Hall, a massive Gothic Revival pile erected by Earl Grosvenor in the early nineteenth century, that he thought it 'impossible for the owner of this house to imbue it with his personality to such a degree as to feel it to be his home. It must be like being a small lobster in a shell much too large for him.'

Many country houses were inhabited only intermittently by their owners and the space was only properly used when filled with guests. They were crucial gathering grounds for aristocrats and gentry: leisured weeks spent in each other's company consolidated their social class. Here marriages were arranged and political alliances made. Social equals were often thin on the ground in country areas, so when, in *Pride and Prejudice*, nearby Netherfield Park is leased by Bingley, a single young man of large fortune, Mrs Bennet, mother of daughters, is overjoyed at the opportunities this presents.

Country houses could serve a useful political purpose, providing opportunity for discussion and horse-trading away from Westminster. Sir Robert Walpole took fellow politicians to Houghton during recesses. Such politicking is revealed in the

A family, possibly the Rasheighs of Menabilly in Cornwall, posed by the painter Edward Smith in frivolous activity among classical garden features, *c.*1770. Their house is displayed in the background.

correspondence between Earl Grey and Thomas Creevey in 1827: 'I had a letter this morning from good old Fitzwilliam. Brougham had been at Wentworth *uninvited*, and evidently for the purpose either of making recruits, or of holding out the appearance of his being well in that quarter – probably both. Fitzwilliam smoked him, and took care that he should not go away deceived as to his opinions, which are exactly what you would have expected from a good honest Whig . . .' Most country estates, even after the Reform Act, had a seat or two in Parliament under their patronage. Ninety years later, during the First World War, Lady Ottoline Morrell described how she and her husband hoped that their country house, Garsington in Oxfordshire, would 'make a centre for those who were still under control of reason, and who saw the War as it really was, not through false emotional madness, and the intoxication of war fever. We hoped that they would at least meet and think and talk freely, and realise that there were other values in life.' When, in 1917, Lord and Lady Lee decided to hand over their refurbished country house, Chequers, to the nation, it was to give the new class of politician, such as Lloyd George, a country retreat.

Letter writing was a time-filler during a country house stay, particularly for women, idle while men shot or hunted. Caroline Lybbe Powys was prolific. Of a 1788 visit to the James family at their new house, Langley Hall in Berkshire, she wrote describing the 'Large hall, drawing-room, two eating-rooms, library, an inner hall, grand staircase, and some small rooms, many apartments above so spacious and convenient; out of every bed-chamber a large dressing-room, and light closets as powdering rooms to each. The grounds are laying out now. We were particularly happy to see Lady Jane so happily married to a man so pleasing as Mr. James . . . They have a fine fortune, which they spend elegantly, without any form or ceremony, making every friend partake of the happiness and good-humour they so eminently possess themselves.' Less elegant were the later incarnations of Langley Hall: in the early years of the twentieth century it was a boys' prep school; in 1915 it became The Actors' Orphanage and School; during the Second World War it was RAF Bomber Command HQ, after which it became the Road Research Laboratory of East Berkshire College. Recently it was transformed again, into one of the country's earliest free schools.

The Georgians had abandoned private apartments and migrated to communal drawing rooms, dining rooms and libraries, backdrop to days such as Lybbe Powys described in Shropshire with an 'agreeable set' of never less than sixteen or eighteen. 'Monday, the morning as usual divided into parties of riding, walking, shooting, reading, working, drawing. Never met at dinner till after four.' Company was essential in such vast surroundings. Reduced to that of only her family, Lady Louisa Stuart wrote from her father's house, Luton Hoo, in July 1778, of days spent 'trailing to the farm and dawdling in the flower garden'. Her mother was in good spirits, 'considering the ennui that I believe is inseparable from this house, and which I own has at last infected me. For my part, I am sufficiently accustomed to dumb people, for here are Frederick and William [her brothers] who speak about six words a day, and instead of being any company or comfort, only serve to give me the vapours by walking up and down the room without ceasing . . . or now and then flinging themselves on the couch, yawning, and asking me questions as "When do we go to London?"'

Foreign visitors wrote home with precise descriptions. François de la Rochefoucauld stayed at Euston Hall with the Duke of Grafton in the 1780s. 'The morning papers are on the table and those who want to do so, read them during breakfast, so that the conversation is not of a lively nature.' After a day amusing yourself, 'at 4 o'clock precisely you must present yourself in the drawing-room . . . This sudden change of social manners is quite astonishing and I was deeply struck by it. In the morning you come down in riding-boots and a shabby coat, you sit where you like, you behave exactly as if you were by yourself, no one takes any notice of you, and it is all extremely comfortable but in the evening unless you have just arrived you must be well-washed and well-groomed. The standard of politeness is uncomfortably high – strangers go first into the dining room and sit near the hostess and are served with seniority in accordance with a rigid etiquette. In fact for a few days I was tempted to think it was done for a joke. Dinner is one of the most wearisome of English experiences, lasting, as it does, for four or five hours. The first two are spent in eating and you are compelled to exercise your stomach to the full in order to please your host . . .' He was homesick for sauces and noted that 'all the dishes consist of various meats either boiled or roasted and of joints weighing about twenty or thirty pounds . . .' He claimed that when the ladies retire after dinner, 'there is not an Englishman who is not supremely happy. Fresh toasts are ready to hand, politics supply plenty – one drinks to the health of Mr Pitt or Mr Fox, or Lord North.'

Prince Hermann von Pückler-Muskau's letter to his wife in the late 1820s revealed that the library was for ' "rendezvous" . . . Here you have an opportunity of gossiping for hours with the young ladies, who are always very literarily inclined. Many a marriage is thus concocted, or destroyed.' On a typical evening after dinner, 'Our suffering host lay on the sofa, dosing [*sic*] a little; five ladies and gentlemen were very attentively reading in various sorts of books; another had been playing for a quarter of an hour with a long-suffering dog; two old Members of Parliament were disputing vehemently about the "Corn Bill"; and the rest of the company were in a dimly-lighted room adjoining, where a pretty girl was playing on the piano-forte, and another, with the most perforating voice, singing ballads.'

The novelist Maria Edgeworth, evidently a favourite guest, corresponded regularly with her half-sister Honora in the 1820s. She wrote of arriving at Bowood in Wiltshire one December evening: 'at 5 o'clock – dusk – up to our rooms – red breeches footman lighting us up and lighting our 6 wax candles informed us "My lady has just come in from a long walk and *gone to change herself*" – But we found her quite unchanged.' She described one evening there when a fireside discussion with Lord Lansdowne was interrupted by a game of charades: 'Suddenly with a great burst of noise from the breakfast room door, a tribe of gentlemen neighing and kicking like horses. You never saw a man look more surprised than Lord Lansdowne did – putting his glass up to his eye – and afterwards same performers on all fours grunting like pigs and then a company of ladies and gentlemen in dumb shew acting a country visit – ending with asking for a frank – curtseying – bowing and exit.' The word was neighbours: 'Perhaps this will all be very dull in the sober reading but I assure you it produced much laughter in the acting.'

Staying with a family at Easton Grey in Gloucestershire she found it a model country gentleman's house: 'convenient, comfortable, perfectly neat, without the teizing precision of order – the library-drawing-room furnished with good sense – delightful armchairs low sofas, stools, plenty of moveable tables – books on tables and in open bookcases and in short all that speaks the habits and affords the means of agreeable occupation.'

Maria Edgeworth also documented the vacuity of enforced leisure. At Wycombe Abbey she wondered if she would escape without having broken her neck on 'these horribly slippery beautiful floors and stairs'. Here, 'Lady Carrington sits on a sofa all day long or drives or walks out just for health and is always poorly – Very like Lady

Country house life drawn at first hand by Olivia de Ros, aged twenty, in 1827, before her marriage to Henry Wellesley. She contrasts the boredom of the ladies 'Before Tea' with their animation 'After Tea', when they have been joined by the men. From an album at Hatfield House where she was a visitor.

Before Tea

After Tea

Bertram in *Mansfield Park* . . . One of the Miss Smiths is a perfect walking red book – knows all the fashionable marriages – births and deaths and who is to inherit titles and fortunes. I should be extinguished if I lived with them long.' Thomas Creevey was thrown in with equally disagreeable company at Stapleton (Park) in Yorkshire while staying with Robert Edward Petre in 1827. 'What a fool this good-natured Eddard [*sic*] is to be eat and drunk out of house and harbour, and to be treated as he is. The men take his carriages and horses to carry them to their shooting ground, and leave his fat mother to waddle on foot, tho' she can scarcely get ten yards. Then dinner being announced always for seven, the men neither night have been home before 8, and it has been ¼ to 9 that Dow. Julia and her ladies have been permitted to dine. Then those impertinent jades, the Ladies Ashley breakfast upstairs, never shew till dinner, and even then have been sent to and waited for.'

The expense of entertaining visitors was significant: Pückler-Muskau was convinced that 'many families atone for this public extravagance by eating meagrely when alone, a reason for never turning up uninvited.' He also suspected that after a hospitable month the family then had to recoup their losses by visiting others. For the neighbourhood visitors were an economic boon. The diarist Joseph Farington noted in 1801 that the Duke and Duchess of Devonshire had spent the entire winter at Chatsworth: 'The Duke was in a great stile, having sometimes in his house 180 persons including Visitors and their servants. He kills on average 5 bullocks in a fortnight and 15 or 16 sheep a week.'

AN ARMY OF SERVANTS

WILLIAM HOWITT listed in 1838 the paraphernalia needed to sustain a proper country house: 'its offices, out-buildings, gardens, greenhouses, hothouses; its extensive fruit-walls, and the people labouring to furnish the table simply with fruit, vegetables, and flowers; its coach-houses, harness-houses, stables, and all the steeds, draught-horses, and saddle-horses, hunters, and ladies' pads, ponies for the ladies' airing-carriages, and ponies for children; and all the grooms and attendants thereon; to see the waters for fish, the woods for game, the elegant dairy for the supply of milk and cream, curds and butter, and the dairy-maids and managers belonging to them: and then, to enter the house itself, and see all its different suites of apartments, drawing-rooms, boudoirs, sleeping-rooms, dining and breakfast rooms; its steward's, housekeeper's and butler's rooms: its ample kitchens and larders, with their stores of provisions, fresh and dried;

its stores of costly plate, porcelain and crockery apparatus of a hundred kinds; its cellars of wine and strong beer; its stores of linen; its library of books; its collections of paintings, engravings, and statuary; the jewels, musical instruments, and expensive and interminable nick-nackery of the ladies; the guns and dogs; the cross-bows, long-bows, nets and other implements of amusement of the gentlemen; all the rich carpeting and fittings-up of day-rooms, and night-rooms, with every contrivance and luxury which a most ingenious and luxurious age can furnish; and all the troops of servants, male and female, having their own exclusive offices, to wait upon the person of lady or gentleman, upon table, or carriage, or upon some one ministration of pleasure or necessity.' When this was compared to a labourer's cottage, he wrote, 'we might almost be persuaded that they could not be the same class of animals.'

Nearly a century later Nancy Mitford, in her novel *A Christmas Pudding*, described Compton Bobbin, a house encumbered by possessions. Once 'inhabited by persons of taste and culture . . . it must have been, for instance, a person of taste who introduced the Chinese Chippendale mirror now hanging where only housemaids can see it in the back passage, the tails and wings of its fantastic birds sadly cracked and broken, victims of the late Sir Hudson Bobbin's addiction to indoor cricket. . . . Whose Venetian glass chandelier ruined by electric wiring carelessly and locally performed, which hangs, draped in dust sheets, in the disused ballroom? Whose enamelled snuff-boxes, whose Waterford glass jumbled together with so much horrible junk in glass-fronted cupboards on the landing?' It is a characteristic of large country houses that the attics, where servants once slept, and stables, where horses were no longer kept, have gradually silted up with the broken and the outdated. This has provided a valuable seam of domestic archaeology, as the National Trust discovered when it took on Calke Abbey. Periodic attic turnouts have frequently given a welcome fillip to straitened finances.

A large country house was in effect home to two entirely separate communities. The prodigious number of servants needed to make it function changed little between the Knole list of 1613 and Howitt's 1838 description, the servants in both far outnumbering those they served. Job descriptions varied widely: Knole had a log carrier in 1613, Woburn in the 1770s a hairdresser and a confectioner, Longleat in the 1880s a 'steel boy' who burnished the metal parts on harness. The complexity of the housekeeping, and the work involved, could be gauged from the fact that at Harewood House the 1836 inventory listed 600 towels, all marked for different purposes.

A strict hierarchy prevailed in the servants' quarters. The housekeeper was in charge of the female staff, as the butler was in charge of the men. These two acted as filters between the master and mistress and the servants. At the lowest rung servants were unlikely even to see their employers, and all were expected to lower their eyes, or even turn their back, in their presence. The tunnels at Uppark that ran from the main house to the service quarters kept servants dry, but also out of sight. The late Georgian invention of bells that summoned servants up from the servants' hall accentuated the barrier between the two groups, as servants no longer had to wait within earshot for instructions.

Male servants performing services deemed as non-essential, such as butlers, footmen, valets and coachmen, were annually taxed at a guinea per head from 1777, so an array of footmen was a status symbol. They were often selected – like carriage horses – to be of matched heights; fine calves and tall stature were especially highly prized. A footman would stand behind each diner. One visitor of the period noted that in order to keep up numbers grooms and coachmen were sometimes called in, filling the dining room with the smell of stables. The custom of dressing footmen in eighteenth-century knee breeches, silk stockings, braided waistcoats and, on formal occasions, powdered hair survived into the twentieth century, symbolic of an attempt to keep the modern age at bay.

A servant's life was secure in terms of food and clothing but offered little freedom. Although many servants were treated benevolently, they were routinely believed to be irresponsible and untrustworthy. Susanna Whatman lived at Turkey Court in Kent, which her husband, a paper-maker, had substantially enlarged in the 1760s on being made High Sheriff. Her housekeeping book logged her servants' duties: the garret bedrooms, where eighteen servants slept, were to be swept three times a week. 'In every room care must be taken not to open the windows with dirty hands. The locks in every room should be kept bright, the keys kept clean.' She writes to her housekeeper from London in June 1800 with instructions that temptation should not be left in the way of servants and meat should be put away: 'There are two keys to the little wire safe, one for cook and one for housekeep, that there may be no excuse for the leaving roast, or boiled beef, legs of pork etc in the open safe . . . [this] is very necessary, as it would be difficult to detect depredations on a large joint.' Suspicion of malingering and petty wrongdoing in the relationship between servants and employers was perennial, and took on an extra dimension during owners' long absences. In Tobias Smollett's *The Expedition of Humphry Clinker* (1771),

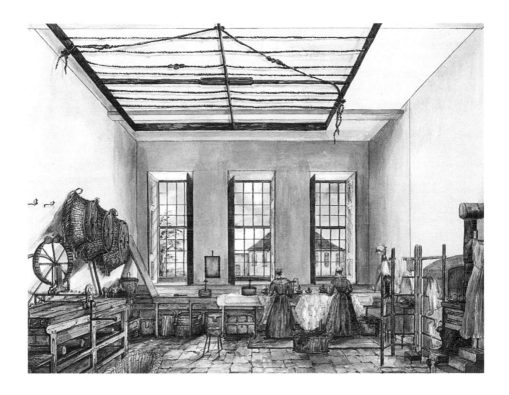

The laundry at Aynhoe Park in Northamptonshire, as recorded by Elizabeth Cartright, Bavarian daughter-in-law of the owner, Tory squire William Cartright. She meticulously recorded the interiors of the house as an antidote to boredom during the winter months. As her journal relates: 'Sunday passed like all Sundays in writing letters in the morning and in being bored in the evening.'

Tabitha Bramble writes from Gloucester to her housekeeper at Brambleton-hall: 'Let none of the men have excess to the strong bear – don't forget to have the gate shit every evening before dark. – The gardnir and the hind may lie below in the landry, to partake the house, with the blunderbuss and the great dog; and I hope you'll have a watchful eye over the maids. I know that hussy, Mary Jones, love to be rumping with the men.'

Servants could, and did, retaliate. By the mid-eighteenth century vails or tips expected by servants had become exorbitant, and despite a group of Scottish aristocrats boycotting

RIGHT The servants ranged on the entrance steps at Ashridge, a country house built to massive proportions by the Bridgewater family on the profits from canals. OPPOSITE Cecil Beaton's imagining of the Christmas Grand Servants' Ball in the dining room at Longleat, where the Marquess of Bath opened the Ball with the housekeeper. An illustration from *Before the Sunset Fades* by the Marchioness of Bath.

the system, it continued. Country house visits were particularly expensive since they involved tipping gamekeepers and ghillies as well as the inside staff. Failing to tip a footman after dinner could result in covertly insolent behaviour during a subsequent visit. Dean Swift consistently refused invitations to Lord Halifax's house, calculating it would cost him a guinea in vails, more than the 12 shilling coach hire to reach it.

Houses could not run without servants and it was sometimes a seller's market. On newly fashionable Windermere an observer commented in 1811: 'Land, half rock, is bought up at any price, merely on account of the beauty of the spot. The complaints about scarcity of servants and labourers, and their consequent high prices are general. It is plain there are too few poor for the rich.' Servants' manuals specifically stated that information on an employer's conduct should not be passed on, but gossip was obviously rife, and as early as the nineteenth century tip-offs to the press could produce the odd cash bonus. A furore was caused in 1911 when it was discovered that an American magazine had been actively seeking gossip from among servants in the great houses.

Employers traditionally showed their appreciation with treats such as summer garden fêtes and Christmas servants' balls. These were markedly different from medieval feasts, as appearances by the upper echelons were brief. Caroline Lybbe Powys recorded the tenants' annual feast at Fawley Court on Twelfth Night in 1789: 'The young people all as usual danced with the tenants six or eight dances; then we came

up to cards and supper . . . droll toasts given after dinner. Among the toasts were: 'May the rich be charitable and the poor happy.' The playwright Richard Brinsley Sheridan bought the estate of Polesden Lacey in 1797 and threw himself with gusto into the role of landowner. The 'grand harvest home on Tuesday, to the labouring people in the neighbourhood of his beautiful seat at Polesden' was reported in 1802. He put up a tent for three hundred, 'who were treated with true English cheer and ancient hospitality, and the industrious and deserving girls of character, were rewarded each by an harvest present from their amiable hostess. A select party dined at the mansion house, which was enlivened by the vivacity and gaiety of Mr. Sheridan, and the peasantry departed, after preserving the utmost regularity, order and decorum . . . all filled with gratitude for hospitable and kind reception.' Gratitude could seem pinched. Jane Carlyle watched Lady Ashburton hand out cheap toys from the Lowther Arcade to forty-eight children at the servants' ball at the Grange in Hampshire in 1851 under a banner proclaiming 'Long Live Lord and Lady Ashburton' and contrasted their cost of £2. 12s. 6d. with the £700 spent on giving a ball. A dress length for each child would have been preferable, she thought. This was the traditional Christmas gift that the Marchioness of Bath gave to each undermaid at Longleat, a ritual followed on Christmas night by the gentry watching the maids dance in the courtyard: 'On the rough paving stones, in their thin dresses, they would bob around in the cold.' The birth or coming of age of an heir was similarly occasion for lavish celebrations and presentations which served to confirm the continuation of the line.

Ownership of a large country house involved *noblesse oblige* (and occasionally the reverse of the coin, *droit de seigneur*). Whereas alms were distributed to all comers in early periods, by the nineteenth century benevolence was focused on estate tenants. Improved cottages, village halls and sports clubs were built, but also small gifts of clothing and food were given to the newly born, the sick and the old. No large kitchen would have been without a recipe for a nutritious beef tea, calf's foot jelly or gruel. The account books at Longleat show that port, gin and whisky were given, as well as joints of meat, to households where the wage-earner was sick. Less thoughtful were the buckets of leftovers that were taken down to the villagers from the dining room at Blenheim. It was the American Duchess of Marlborough, Consuelo Vanderbilt, who insisted that the meat and vegetables should be separated from the desserts, rather than all jumbled together. At Wentworth Woodhouse an early twentieth-century Countess Fitzwilliam toured the local villages in her yellow Rolls distributing gruel, milk, eggs, clothes and live chickens. Since the family's vast wealth came from coal mining and their tenants were mainly miners on minimal wages, this bounty was welcome. During the General Strike of 1926 Earl Fitzwilliam taught miners riding pit ponies how to play polo on the front lawn, and as miners continued their strike he undertook to feed over 2,500 of their children daily.

EXTRAVAGANCE AND DECLINE

NEW VICTORIAN FORTUNES derived from sources such as industry, brewing, commerce or finance; as ever social elevation was consolidated by the acquisition of a country house. Typical was financier Baron Ferdinand de Rothschild, who built Waddesdon Manor, a Loire château dropped on to Buckinghamshire farmland. Finished in 1883, its purpose was to provide a setting for his celebrated Saturday to Monday house parties. The house included a bachelors' wing, intended for well-bred but impecunious younger sons, who tended to lead purposeless lives in the billiard and smoking rooms of country houses. William Gibbs's fortune made from shipping guano from Peru translated into an ecclesiastical Gothic Revival mansion at Tyntesfield, while the engineer and armaments manufacturer Lord Armstrong built Cragside as a vastly expanded medieval manor into which he put an hydraulically powered lift and cooking spit and, in 1880, hydro-powered electric light.

New money combined with old to keep the country house system alive. Some landowners were reaping large rents from encroaching towns. The Duke of Omnium, in Trollope's novel *The Duke's Children* (1880), tells his son Lord Silverbridge: 'As to property. I am so anxious that you should enjoy all the settled independence which can belong to an English gentleman.' His heir, gazing at the distant view, is asked if all the land will be his, and replies: 'Some of it, I suppose. I don't think it is all ours . . . for extent of acres, one ought to go to Barsetshire.' 'Is that larger?' 'Twice as large I believe, and yet none of the family like being there. The rental is very well.'

Extravagant entertaining remained a hallmark of many country houses. The 5th Earl of Lonsdale, a bon viveur and sportsman, reputedly spent £4,000 a week when in residence at Lowther Castle, an estate that had been in the family since the Middle Ages, and which he inherited in 1882 aged twenty-five. He had a penchant for yellow, which coloured the livery of his servants, his fleet of cars, his dogs and the gardenias in his hothouses. Each morning the Lowther coat of arms was pounced in coloured powders on fresh sand in the stable yard. The Prince of Wales, during his long wait to

A country house party photographed at Polesden Lacey in 1909. On the right-hand side of King Edward VII (in the centre) is Mrs Ronnie Greville, the famous hostess; on his left, one away, is his mistress, Alice Keppel, whose husband, George, is at the end of the back row.

become Edward VII, was a prized guest at house parties, often arranged to coincide with race meetings, regattas or shoots. Formal groups photographed around an imposing entrance give no indication that in some houses social rules were quietly bent. In a world where marriages were often made for money and status, a country house party provided cover for extra-marital affairs, with the hostess allotting adjacent bedrooms according to the latest gossip. This world was exposed to the wider public when the Prince of Wales was called as a witness in a case that involved Sir William Gordon-Cumming, who was accused of cheating at after-dinner baccarat in 1890. The incident took place at Tranby Croft, a new house built in the Italianate style by a friend of the Prince, shipowner Arthur Wilson, who arranged an illegal gambling game for the Prince's amusement. The Prince's mistress, Lady Brooke, spread the story. Gordon-Cumming sued for libel.

Toward the end of the nineteenth century cracks began to appear in the fabric of the grand country house. The landed class, who, as Trollope wrote, 'felt the absolute necessity of luxurious living', were feeling the pinch. The agricultural depression of the 1870s and 1880s reduced incomes that, for over a century, had come rolling in from estates. Simultaneously, the landed gentry lost their power over rural administration – held since the manorial system – when county and rural district councils were established. As early as 1886 Henry James saw aristocrats as being on the 'very edge of the ground that was beginning to fail them; yet looking over it, looking on and on always, with confidence and still unalarmed'. Fossilized in the 'gilded bondage' of the country house, they spent their time 'in vain sitting and strolling about'. In 1951 the Marchioness of Bath wrote *Before the Sunset Fades*, a memoir of life at Longleat before the First World War. 'My husband's grandmother had her loose-change coins washed every day. The valets ironed their gentlemen's boot ribbons; and the morning papers were toasted and ironed before appearing on the breakfast table.'

John Galsworthy looks at their fate in his novel *The Country House*, set in 1891. Horace Pendyce lives a delightful life in his country house, Worsted Skeynes, with 'its perfect cleanliness, its busy leisure, its combination of fresh air and scented warmth, its complete intellectual repose, its essential and professional aloofness from suffering of any kind, and its soup – emblematically and above all, its soup – made from the rich remains of pampered beasts . . . He considered it a *duty* to live this life, with its simple, healthy, yet luxurious curriculum, surrounded by creatures bred for his own devouring, surrounded, as it were, by a sea of soup!' But his heir has gambling debts and an imminent divorce, and Pendyce recognizes that 'country houses are not what they were'. His wife longs for life in a cottage with her dog and her flowers.

In 1894 death duty on estates worth over a million pounds rose to 8 per cent. As Lady Bracknell topically comments in *The Importance of Being Earnest*, which Oscar Wilde wrote that year, 'land has ceased to be either a profit or a pleasure. It gives one position and prevents one from keeping it up.' In 1909 a further raid on country house exchequers was made by Lloyd George, who, despite ferocious opposition from the landowning peers in the House of Lords, introduced new taxes on profit from land in order to finance the Liberal government's new social agenda, such as old age pensions. A tax on mineral rights was put at one shilling in the pound, denting the income of families such as the Fitzwilliams at Wentworth Woodhouse, whose fortune came from coal.

1909 was also the year that H.G. Wells published *Tono-Bungay*. Both author and hero were bought up in large country houses, and the mothers of both were housekeepers, in Wells's case at Uppark in Sussex. Wells conveys the imminent change. While 'the great houses stand in the parks still, the cottages cluster respectfully on their borders, touching their eaves with their creepers', the house's supremacy of the neighbourhood has nearly ended and it will no longer represent 'the Gentry, the Quality, by and through and for whom the rest of the world, the farming folk and the labouring folk, the trades-people of Ashborough, and the upper servants and the lower servants and the servants of the estate, breathed and lived and were permitted.'

The founding of *Country Life* magazine in 1897 symbolized this shift. Although aimed at the new, less ambitious middle-class country house owner, it both featured houses of the *ancien régime* – halls encrusted with stags heads and weapons – and also advertised what was being surrendered. The first issue advertised the sale of Stowe: 'a noble seat . . . in the centre of a magnificent deer park of 1100 acres . . . splendid marble vestibule 66 ft x 45 ft . . . several complete suites of rooms . . . large number of best and secondary bedrooms besides accommodation for a large establishment of servants . . . glasshouses and vineries proportionate to the place.' By 1923 it was home to ninety-nine public school boys. Choice stretches of countryside became available as landed families sold off chunks of their estates, and country houses were deprived of the land that often supported them. Between 1911 and 1914 the auctioneers Knight Frank and Rutley disposed of over two hundred estates.

REINING IN: THE SMALLER HOUSE

THE CHARM OF LIVING IN THE COUNTRY grew as the process of doing it became simpler. Many of the well-heeled middle classes chose to live there, instead of in town; they sought out old houses to restore and extend, or conveniently placed plots to build on. They had no historic attachment to a particular piece of land or sense of duty to local life. There was a boom in building country houses on a smaller scale, unpretentious houses in the Arts and Crafts style, designed by architects such as Edwin Lutyens and Robert Lorimer, typically within easy commuting distance of big cities. The countryside was no longer a two-class society and the difference between the small country house and the extended cottage was becoming blurred.

The country house party survived. 'Already everyone feels that they have the right to leave for the country after work on Friday and return on Monday morning,' was an

A country house in Troon, Ayrshire, designed by Arnold Mitchell, 1912. This house, built of local stone and overlooking the sea, was described as 'small'; however, the ground floor still had both a servants' hall and a billiard room.

observation made by architect and diplomat Hermann Muthesius, reporting on the British in 1904. Trains and motor cars transported people speedily: shooting, dances, croquet and tennis games could be fitted into a long weekend. Muthesius observed the peculiarly British attitude to house guests: 'It is amiably taken for granted that no special arrangements will be made for the visitor. He is one of the family and can do or not do as he wishes, like any of the others. His host does not feel obliged to drag him round the sights of the neighbourhood, nor his hostess to put special delicacies before him . . .' The passion for hunting, fishing, walking and cycling that was integral to country house life was, he thought, 'the only antidote' to the depressing climate, and the popularity of billiard rooms was 'probably attributable to the isolation of houses in the country, because of which, on rainy days when the house is full of people, billiards is the only cure for deadly boredom.'

'Happily the weather was fine, the food good, & we flowed about happily enough, & without serious boredom, which is more than one can ask of a week-end' – this was how Virginia Woolf described a July weekend at Garsington with Ottoline Morrell

ABOVE Recording the occasion in photography was part of the country weekend ritual. From Lady Ottoline Morrell's album of Garsington in Oxfordshire, left to right: Aldous Huxley, Dorothy Brett, Ottoline and Philip Morell.
OPPOSITE Egginton Hall, Derbyshire, became a military hospital in 1917. The ground floor was converted into wards and an operating theatre; ambulance trains of wounded were received directly from the Front. After occupation by troops in the Second World War its condition was considered irredeemable and it was demolished in 1955.

in 1918. 'I suppose we spoke some million words between us; listened to a great many more, (chiefly from the mouth of Mrs Hamilton, who strains at her collar like a spaniel dog) . . . There was Gertler; Shearman & Dallas for tea, Brett. Ottoline, 3 children & Philip . . . I think Ott. was a little bored. In fact for some reason I was rather well content. My bed was like layer upon layer of the most perfect springy turf; & the garden is almost melodramatically perfect . . .' After an aimless walk: 'We trailed back through the village, where all the peasants were lounging in the road, with their pipes & their dogs & their babies. The most affable, & I'm afraid obsequious greetings were exchanged; the dazzling appearance of Ott. & her pearls seeming to strike the agricultural labourer neither as wrong or ridiculous, but as part of the aristocratic show that he'd paid for. No one laughed.'

During and after the First World War survival in a large country house became deeply problematic: the death toll among both heirs and servants, the continuing agricultural

depression, post-war nervousness about bolshevism and socialism followed by the General Strike and the fall-out from the 1929 crash made the future seem fraught with difficulties. Families owning several country houses, as many still did, retrenched to one. Large houses were almost impossible to sell, despite fat brochures listing historical background, royal connections, ghosts, hunting six days a week and sizeable game bags. Knight Frank and Rutley's copy for Taymouth Castle in Perthshire advertised shooting with an annual bag of 13,435 grouse. In 1931 they even arranged that the Flying Service would take prospective buyers to the nearest landing place. Houses that didn't sell were stripped out, demolished or left to rot, and the land frequently snapped up by developers. Creeping industrialization had left some houses stranded in areas that were no longer rural, and the overblown grandeur that had seemed an entitlement in the eighteenth and nineteenth centuries had often become a millstone. During the war people had become accustomed to country houses being requisitioned as barracks or military hospitals, which may have eased the decision by families to abandon them to prep schools, hotels or golf clubs.

Conflicting views on the rights and wrongs of one family owning such houses were explored by Vita Sackville-West in *The Edwardians*, a novel set in 1904 but written in 1930, shortly after her discovery that as a woman she was barred from inheriting Knole. It centres on young Sebastian, Duke of Chevron, and his great country house, Chevron. 'There was always plenty of money at Chevron, and there still was, even with the income-tax raised from 11d to 1/- in the pound.' The author recognizes the qualities of good landowners: Sebastian was an ideal landlord – ' "wish there were more like him" they said, forgetting there were, in fact, many like him; many who, in their quiet unobtrusive way, elected to share out their fortune, not entirely to their own advantage – quiet English squires, who, less favoured than Sebastian, were yet imbued with the same spirit, and traditionally gave their time and a good proportion of their possessions as a matter of course to those dependent upon them . . . But did it, Sebastian reflected, sitting with his pen poised above his cheque-book, carry with it a disagreeable odour of charity?' The burden of historical possession is expressed by the outsider Leonard Anquetil: 'Not only will you esteem material objects because they are old . . . but, more banefully, you will venerate ideas and institutions because they have remained for a long time in force; for so long a time as to appear to you absolute and unalterable.' Chevron's house and name 'were tied on to him like so many tin cans to the tail of a poor cat.'

The novelist Evelyn Waugh also had first-hand knowledge of country house life in the 1930s. He frequently visited the Lygon family, who for twenty-eight generations had lived at Madresfield Court, a moated manor house in Worcestershire extended in the 1880s to a house of unmanageable proportions with 160 rooms. In his novel *A Handful of Dust* Brenda and Tony Last are at home at Hetton Abbey:

> 'I was thinking how delightful it is, that it's Saturday morning and we haven't got anyone coming for the weekend.'
>
> 'Well, it sometimes seems to me rather pointless keeping up a house this size if we don't now and then ask some other people to stay in it.'
>
> '*Pointless*? I can't think what you mean. I don't keep up this house to be a hostel for a lot of bores to come and gossip in.'

The weekend house party in the 1930s was a pale shadow of an Edwardian one. 'What a bore weekends are, forty-eight hours social crucifixion', the politician Chips Channon wrote in his diary in July 1936. Jottings on his recent invitations only partially endorse his statement: '20 June Sutton Courtenay, roses, the river, and the youth of England splashing in the Thames . . . Russian ballet, food in the courtyard, Chopin, colour, gardening, a riot, but a healthy riot of the senses, and a deep thirst for life . . . 4th July Tredegar: glorious house, but the feel and even smell of decay, of aristocracy in extremis, the sinister and the trivial, crucifixes and crocodiles.'

Many families struggled to keep their houses on with little income for upkeep, tradition and beauty being hard to relinquish. The writer and editor Diana Athill was bought up in a large eighteenth-century country house in Suffolk with gardeners, grooms, a chauffeur, butler, footman, cook, kitchen maid, scullery maid, three housemaids and her grandmother's lady's maid. She recalls 'The tables loaded with cut flowers, the flowery chintzes, the indifferent watercolours of beloved places expressed the life lived from the house . . .' As a child she felt that was what a house should be – 'even cold was a matter of pride'. She observes that life in such a house engenders 'that smug, matter-of-fact assumption of superiority', noting that people such as her family had 'been snug all their lives, and snugness breeds smugness – but smugness is too small a word for what it feels like from *inside*. From inside, it feels like moral and aesthetic *rightness* . . .'

Evelyn Waugh's Brenda Last was exasperated: 'Do you know how much it costs just to live here? We should be quite rich if it wasn't for that. As it is we support fifteen servants indoors, besides gardeners and carpenters and a night-watchman and all the people at the farm and odd little men constantly popping in to wind the clocks and cook the accounts and clean the moat, while Tony and I have to fuss about whether it's cheaper to take a car up to London for the night or buy an excursion ticket.' Brenda's brother Reggie St Cloud contributes the thought: 'There's a lot in what these Labour fellows say, you know. Big houses are a thing of the past in England . . . I daresay you will find it quite easy to sell to a school or something like that . . . schools and convents always go for Gothic.'

The future was bleak. In the 1930s Noel Coward parodied Felicia Hemans. Her 1827 cloudless verse (that introduced the term 'stately home'):

The stately homes of England
How beautiful they stand
Amidst their tall ancestral trees
O'er all the pleasant land

became:

The stately homes of England
How beautiful they stand,
To prove the upper classes
Have still the upper hand . . .

The state apartments keep their
Historical renown.
It's wiser not to sleep there,
In case they tumble down.

But still, if they ever catch on fire,
Which, with any luck, they might,
We'll fight
For the stately homes of England.

And some did burn down or, having no foreseeable future, were demolished, a process that continued up to the 1970s.

SWANSONGS AND SURVIVORS

JUST BEFORE THE SECOND WORLD WAR the realization that many country houses were indeed *in extremis* led the National Trust to draw up a list of imperilled houses of architectural importance. James Lees-Milne made tours of inspection. At Lyme Park, on 25 November 1943: 'A butler met me at the front door and conducted me through the central courtyard, and up some stone steps and into the hall on the *piano nobile*. Lord Newton lives and eats in the great library with a huge fire burning, and two equally huge dogs lying at his feet . . . The world is too much for him, and no wonder. He does not know what he can do, ought to do or wants to do. He just throws his hands up in despair. The only thing he is sure about is that his descendants will never want to live at Lyme after an unbroken residence of 600 years . . . There were forty evacuated children in the house, but they have now gone. The park is cut to pieces by thousands of RAF lorries, for it is at present a lorry depot.' At Temple Sowerby he found the house occupied by the Railway Wagon Repairers and their families. The owners were in one small wing, using a caravan as a bedroom.

During the Second World War country houses were virtually servantless but once again bustled with inhabitants – soldiers, doctors, nurses, wounded, evacuees, schools and displaced families. Their size and remoteness had positive advantages, and for some this was their swansong. Wilton Park, Buckinghamshire, built in 1779 by a returning Governor of Madras, was turned into an interrogation centre for senior

Nazi prisoners; Gopsall Hall, Leicestershire, built by ironmasters in 1750, became an experimental radar base for the Royal Engineers. Both were demolished after the war.

The National Trust could only solve a fraction of the problem. From 1945 through the 1950s supertax was at 90 per cent. Houses were becoming irrevocably dilapidated, and many families could no longer hope to maintain them. They were put up for sale at the same price 'as a small villa in a pleasant part of Surrey', as one MP remarked. Many owners applied to demolish. The guidebook to Bowood opens with an explanation by its owner, Lord Shelburne, as to why most of it is no longer there: 'My father, who inherited as a consequence of his two cousins being killed in action within a few days of each other in 1944, was faced with difficult choices. He decided that it was the Park, Pleasure Grounds and the Estate which should be given hope for the future, and so with the greatest regret he demolished what was called the Big House in 1955.' For a government with a national housing shortage and a country to reconstruct, Sir Ernest Gowers's 1950 report on the state of Historic Houses in Britain was not a priority. The report was finally debated in 1953, and this resulted in the establishment of the Historic Buildings Council and tax relief for owners opening their houses to the public. A contemporary spin on the Victorian hymn 'All Things Bright and Beautiful' went 'A poor man in his castle, brings trippers to his gate, from whom he seeks the florins to salvage his estate . . .'

For many houses, opening to the public for money was salvation: the Marquess of Bath was among the first, opening Longleat in 1949. An elegant little illustrated guidebook sold to early visitors was written by his wife and ended with the words: 'The heart of a house is the human life within its walls . . . [At present] there are no children being measured against the nursery door. But the house is not divorced from life. It is being visited as a thing of beauty in a drab and dreary world.' The family did move back to the house, thanks to their fearless experiments in moneymaking. The Beatles played at Longleat in 1964, but opening a safari park in 1966 was a more radical first – visitors caged in their cars while the animals roamed free. Currently Longleat's attractions include the Postman Pat village, the Jungle Express Railway and King Arthur's Mirror Maze, as well as the present Marquess's murals of his 'wifelets'. At Woburn Abbey the Duke of Bedford also opened a safari park, but only when plans to transform some of the 3,000-acre deer park into a Butlin's holiday camp had failed. Savvy aristocrats added extra attractions to the house tour: Lord Beaulieu first showed his father's historic car collection for 2s. 6d. in 1952, while in 1974 the Lyttons turned

Knebworth into the Stately Home of Rock with a Bucolic Frolic for 60,000 featuring Van Morrison. Large parks proved to be endlessly flexible in accommodating crowds for whatever lucrative events owners could devise. Many schemes evoked disapproval. 'I do not relish the scorn of the peerage,' said the Duke of Bedford, who had offered a secluded corner of his park at Woburn to a nudist society, 'but it is better to be looked down on than overlooked.' He fought to keep Woburn Abbey, stating: 'I do not know of any great family that has survived the loss of its house' and seeing the future in a 'kind of happy Hampstead atmosphere' rather than being perceived as a 'bloated landlord holding on to his property and robbing the poor tenant'. Even with tax breaks and tourists, keeping a house upright remained a struggle. The National Trust perfected the art of presenting country houses as beautiful works of art, but by the end of the twentieth century had realized that many visitors identified more with the life below stairs and were investing the same care in their kitchen quarters.

Populating houses was the key to their survival. Demolition ceased to be an option once public opinion recognised their unique beauty and architectural importance.

Turning country houses into hotels was one way in which they could fulfil their original purpose: to provide a period of idleness being fed and nurtured by people paid to do so – in much the same ratio as in their heyday. Many hotels successfully recreated the atmosphere of the country house party, with fires burning brightly, comfortable sofas, wellingtons in the hall and croquet on the lawn. Despite the difficulties inherent in converting listed buildings with ballrooms, drawing rooms and libraries into flats, it frequently happened – and saved the house. Their fates varied: a timeshare company, Diamond Resort International of Las Vegas, bought Gothic Revival Stouts Hill in Gloucestershire (originally built by a successful local weaver), whereas in 1975 seven young North London couples bought Regency Thedden Grange in Hampshire (originally built with naval prize money) and brought up sixteen children to roam the park, milk the cow, climb the trees and eat their own vegetables. Some houses became corporate headquarters, bringing them into direct contact with commerce in a way that their original builders had meticulously avoided.

While people attempt to realize the dream of a country house on a shoestring, it is, as always, the wealthy who slip easily through the portals. The new country house owners are bankers, musicians, film stars, entrepreneurs, artists and impresarios. Many are not British. Indoor pools, gyms and cinemas replace the long gallery. Retreat from an over-curious world to a house within a park, a scheme devised by the Georgians, is equally valued today.

Do you call this your 'think-tank' colonel, so that it qualifies as a legitimate expense for tax purposes? I find I do my serious long-range thinking here. Which reminds me, I want to consult you about my campaign to get a knighthood. I seem to have missed it this year, in spite of my well-publicised gifts to charity.

OPPOSITE 'Summer Day Out', Osbert Lancaster's view of the public arriving in coaches and caravans at a stately home which closely resembles Longleat.
RIGHT A frame from 'Grace and Favour', a cartoon by Marc (Mark Boxer) published in *The Listener* in 1968. The media mogul angles for a knighthood to match his newly acquired country house.

TERRACES

TERRACE HOUSES have ranged from mean, grimy back-to-backs to gleaming stucco palaces. Between the two extremes lie hundreds of thousands of middling-sized terraces – most British people have probably lived in one at some point in their lives.

Such housing is defined by a uniform exterior behind which lie individual houses. These have proved over time to be extraordinarily flexible at accommodating changing living patterns. To make maximum use of the street the frontage of each house is narrow, so the space within is vertically arranged. The staircase forms a spine from basement to attic, with rarely more than a couple of rooms on each floor. Such apparently impractical vertical living, causing inhabitants to flutter up and down from one floor to another, has led to comparisons between life in a terrace house and that of a caged bird. When George Montagu wrote to Horace Walpole in 1770, he described how he had 'taken a house, indeed, a bird-cage, for a year; I flatter myself you will be glad to hear I am become a

Londoner.' Louis Simond, a French-American visitor to London in 1810, was mystified by this standard British housing form. 'These narrow houses, three or four stories high – one for eating, one for sleeping, a third for company, a fourth underground for the kitchen, a fifth perhaps at the top for the servants – and the agility, the ease, the quickness with which the individuals of the family run up and down, and perch on the different stories, give the idea of a cage with its sticks and birds.' But the British always accepted the inconvenience, embraced it even: as the twentieth-century writer A.P. Herbert, who lived in Hammersmith Terrace, explained: 'I am one of those old-fashioned folk . . . an obsolete fellow, I like to have stairs about a house. I get much exercise prancing upstairs to change a collar. I like to live vertically, like a squirrel, forever popping up and down my tree. If we were birds this vertical method of living would be understandable; but we are like rabbits, and ought to live in a flat.'

AN URBAN FORM

THE GROWTH OF TERRACE HOUSING represents the gradual move from a rural to an urban society. A move to urban life grew increasingly attractive for all classes from the eighteenth century onwards, offering opportunities for work, freedom from a static rural existence, new pleasures and entertainments. By 1851 more than half the population of England lived in towns. The terrace house, providing the maximum number of homes in the minimum amount of space, precisely suited this new mobility.

Initially a group of uniform houses was simply called a row – as in Maids of Honour Row in Richmond, four identical houses built in 1724 by the Prince of Wales to house the women attending the Princess of Wales at nearby Kew Palace. A terrace at this date was a gravel garden path for strolling along. When, in 1772, the Adam brothers named their row of houses fronting the Thames 'Royal Terrace' (it later became Adelphi Terrace), the name was intended to draw attention to its unusual broad riverside walk. Subsequently it was attached to the houses themselves.

In terms of town planning terraces proved flexible, as they could be built in straight lines as streets and squares, or curved into circles and crescents. The grandeur of a square was realized as early as 1661 in the 4th Earl of Southampton's plan for Southampton

A cross-section of a three-storey terrace house, showing foundations, drainage and back extension: frontispiece illustration to *Our Homes* by S.F. Murphy, published in 1883, when terrace building was at its peak.

97

(later Bloomsbury) Square. Dublin's position as the secondary imperial capital was emphasized by an entirely new city plan created by the Wide Streets Commission of 1757, which overlaid the medieval city with squares and streets bounded by uniform terrace housing. John Wood pioneered a dramatic circle at Bath in the Circus (1754) while his son, John the younger, bent terraces into crescents opening out on to dramatic views, first at Bath's Royal Crescent (1767–75). Changes in terrain were no problem: the Georgians swept terraces picturesquely over hillsides, while Victorian builders did not hesitate to plunge them straight up and down precipitous slopes in the coal villages of the Rhondda Valley. Terrace houses can be sliced in a variety of ways: to house families with servants, families without servants, or, subdivided, to spawn apartments, lodgings and bedsits. They can be built in any size, to suit any class of person or scale of rental. The precarious nature of finance and fashion has meant that many terraces have moved up and down the social scale within a few decades.

It was realized very early on that terrace housing is an efficient way of accommodating a specific working population. One of the first examples of terrace housing is to be

found in Vicars' Close in Wells, where there are two opposing rows of houses built for the vicars, who stood in for absentee members of the clergy during cathedral services, so needed to be on the spot. Dating from the mid-fourteenth century, they pre-empt by four hundred years the hundreds of thousands of subsequent terraces built for weavers, miners, railway and factory workers.

SPECULATION

MOST TERRACE HOUSING has originated as a speculative venture. The shape of houses to come appeared in 1630 in the Piazza at Covent Garden. Here stood at least eighteen identical houses linked in blocks on two sides, designed in a classical style pioneered in Britain by Inigo Jones and inspired by Continental models. The impressive stone arcading at ground level did not become a regular feature of terrace houses, but the grand first floor and long thin back gardens did, a pattern that lasted well into the nineteenth century. Round the corner from Covent Garden an early speculator, one William Newton from Bedfordshire, acquired Purse Field in Great Queen Street in 1635 and permission was given to 'build 14 faire dwelling houses or tenements . . . fitt for the habitacon of able men'. Newton marked out the plots, some a single width of 44 feet and some double at 88 feet. Made of brick and stone, each individual house was marked by classical pilasters. They were described as 'stately and magnificent' and creating 'ye first uniform street'. Newton leased some plots to builders such as Francis Thriscrosse; others he built himself and sold. Early inhabitants included aristocrats and courtiers – Lord Arundell, the Earl of St Albans,

LEFT The Royal Crescent, from *Bath illustrated by a Series of Views* by J.C. Nattes, 1804. Finished in 1775, the Crescent faced open fields to the south and west and looked down on to earlier building in the city.
ABOVE A night view of a pithead and miners' terrace housing by Rowland Hilder, *c*.1930.

the Earl of Bristol, Sir William Paston, and the Parliamentary General Lord Fairfax. However, in a way that is characteristic of the form, the area lost its appeal and within fifty years one house was already occupied by two families, the Stonors and the Brownes. Recorded in 1718 were their attempts to rationalize the division by swapping 'the cellar under the foreparlour next Queen Street and the uppermost room or garret over said parlour' for 'the kitchen under a room heretofore called Mr. Stonor's dressing-roome and a larder backwards next the garden.'

The Restoration of Charles II made the prospect of time in London and at court appealing once again, and this, combined with the destruction wrought by the Fire of London, led to a lively demand for houses. An Act of 1667 controlled the rebuilding: the individual ornamented and gabled houses and the desnsely packed courts that had burnt so ferociously were to be replaced by uniform façades and wide roads. A new class of town dweller was emerging with no need of workshops, storage or trading space and no desire to live in the old way, over the shop. New regular brick houses were profitable. 'Building', wrote Nicholas Barbon, was 'the most proper and visible Distinction of Riches and Greatness, because the Expences are too Great for Mean Persons.' Barbon emerged in the 1670s as the prototype property speculator. A contemporary, architect Roger North, described him as 'the inventor of this new method of building by casting of ground into streets and small houses, and to augment their number with as little front as possible, and selling the ground to workmen by so much per foot front, and what he could not sell build himself', leading, as he put it, to 'a super-foetation of houses about London'. Barbon grasped that economies could be made by repetition on a grand scale. Some of his schemes failed – his cheaply built houses in Mincing Lane collapsed – and some of his methods were dubious: he started to build Red Lion Square without permission, demolished houses inconveniently in his way and fell into debt. Roger North considered this new form of city house, 'where divers houses stand contiguously in a range', inelegant. With only two rooms per floor, windows, chimneys, doors and closets were 'cluttered together' and both noise and 'smells that offend, are a nuisance to all the rooms, and there is no retiring from them.'

To build a terrace the landowner divided his land into plots and sold building leases to builders or craftsmen, who were referred to as the 'undertakers'. A ground rent would be due on the land throughout the period of the leases (originally these were for forty-two years but by the late eighteenth century they had generally been extended to ninety-nine years). A peppercorn rent was sometimes charged for the first few years while the house was being built. The house was erected at the expense of the builder, who would then sell the lease as quickly as possible. Until he had done that the builder himself bore all the expenses of paying the craftsmen – the carpenters, masons, bricklayers, glaziers, plumbers, and so on. Frequently purchasers would buy the shell of the house which could then be finished to their own specifications. By putting covenants on the leases the ground landlord could try to control the tenor of the area: no business on the premises, and certainly no cow-keeping, bone-boiling or dog-skinning. Subletting was frequently forbidden. When the lease expired the house became the property of the ground landlord, who usually took the opportunity to rebuild, reface, modernize or even demolish and start again.

In London it was the aristocratic families with large landholdings close to the burgeoning West End of London who had most to gain from this system. During the eighteenth century the Crown, the Bedfords, the Portmans, the Grosvenors, the Welbecks and the Cadogans all followed in the footsteps of the Earl of Southampton. He had developed his Bloomsbury manor in the 1660s with a specific plan. His own imposing house would open on to a large square which was lined with rows of houses. Thus a house with a mere 24-foot frontage became part of a grand piece of townscape. He also added smaller streets with less expensive houses, a church and a market, thus creating a desirable neighbourhood. Innumerable bodies and individuals over the next couple of centuries took to this form of property development, attaching the names of their country houses (Eaton Terrace,

Detail of an engraved view of Southampton (later Bloomsbury) Square in 1746, when the area was the northern limit of fashionable London.

Grosvenor Estate); schoolboys (Oppidans, Eton College Estate); pious fifteenth-century women (Lady Margaret [Beaufort] Road, St John's College Cambridge Estate) to the addresses of ordinary terrace houses in Belgravia, Belsize Park or Kentish Town.

To succeed terraces had to appeal to potential inhabitants and it was vital that this happened quickly; unfinished houses did not inspire confidence in an area's future. Occasionally builders resorted to holding lotteries to get rid of empty houses. Mrs Hunt, wife of a Piccadilly grocer, and her lodger Mrs Braithwaite won a centre house in Grosvenor Square in 1739 supposedly worth £10,000. The Adam brothers too sold tickets in order to finish their ambitious but financially precarious venture the Adelphi, where they had added adjoining streets to Adelphi Terrace. The houses did not sell despite the presence of their celebrated friend David Garrick in No. 5 Adelphi Terrace. His wife, Garrick wrote in 1772, was 'almost killed with fatigue of moving to the Adelphi . . .' He had the drawing room ceiling painted by Zucchi and he spent £300 on a chimneypiece. Fanny Burney saw it a month after the move, 'a sweet situation', and an impressed Dr Johnson was held to have remarked, 'Oh, David, these are the things which make death dreadful.' By 1773, running out of money, the Adams announced the lottery. The eight main prizes included houses on John Street, Adam Street and a coffee house, and they sold 4,370 tickets at £50 a ticket. Despite this they were forced to sell their art collection. Fanny Burney went to the auction and noted, 'the undertaking was I believe too much for them, and they suffered much in their fortunes. I cannot but wonder, that so noble and elegant a plan should fail of encouragement.'

Speculative building could be boom or bust. It was affected by national and local events: confidence could falter at the outbreak of a war, or blossom at news of a peace treaty, the successful completion of a canal, an improved turnpike road or arrival of the railway. Some people made money, and some went bankrupt. Some did both. In Dublin the closure of Parliament after the Act of Union in

BY MR. WHITE,
At the King's Arms Tavern, Palace-yard, Westminster, on Tuesday, the 29th inst., at 2 o'clock, in four lots.

FOUR neat new-built Leasehold Dwelling Houses, erected in a substantial manner, containing eight rooms each, with yards and other conveniences, two whereof are situate in Smith-square, St. John's, near Millbank-street, Westminster, and the other two houses adjoining in St. John's-street. Let to good tenants, at moderate rents, amounting to £75 12s. per annum. Held for a term of 50 years from Midsummer, 1792, subject to a ground rent of 3 guineas each for two of the said houses, and 2 guineas each for the other two houses per annum.

To be viewed till the sale on application to Mr. Minshull, attorney, No. 53, Millbank-street, Westminster, of whom printed particulars may be forthwith had, and of Mr. White, Storey's Gate, Westminster.

Advertisement from *The Times* of 26 January 1793 for newly built houses in Smith Square.

1800 led to the loss of the city's *raison d'être*, and the governing aristocratic elite and all who had served them abandoned it. At the time of the Napoleonic Wars Robert Southey wrote from Bath of the fate of Norfolk Crescent, 'one of the melancholy new ruins which the projectors were unable to complete, and so were ruined themselves, a sudden check having been given to all such speculations when the last war broke out.' Expansion over Notting Hill in London stalled when the builder couldn't absorb the sharp rise in interest rates in 1853 and went bust. With half-finished houses rapidly becoming ruins, the *Building News* reported four years later that 'we regret to observe a very great number of buildings still standing in their deplorable condition, some in carcase with their roofs on, others partly roofed in, and some in rough carcase with some of their walls not yet up to their eaves, presenting a most melancholy instance of the waste of capital.' In 1860 Ladbroke Gardens was still 'a desert of dilapidated structures and decaying carcases' in which few 'would care to dwell . . . [a] dreary desolation, with the wind howling and vagrants prowling . . .'

However, the inexorable expansion of the cities in the eighteenth and nineteenth centuries provided thousands with the opportunity to make money by turning farmland into streets and squares. Thomas Cubitt, son of a Norfolk carpenter, made a fortune building swathes of fine housing in Bloomsbury, Belgravia and Pimlico and by 1828 was directly employing a thousand men. He invested in good working practices and properly organized drains. Small opportunistic profits were also made, as typified by a character in George Gissing's novel *The Odd Women* (1893), who became rich because 'in consequence of some mortgage business he came into possession of a field at Clapham. As late as 1875 this field brought him a rent of forty pounds; it was freehold property, and he refused many offers of purchase – well, in 1885 the year before he died, the ground-rents from the field – now covered with houses – were seven hundred and ninety pounds a year.'

DEVELOPING A TERRACE STYLE

GEORGIAN TERRACE HOUSE ARCHITECTURE was quite plain and unornamented; fear of fire had resulted in successive Acts of Parliament prohibiting individual wooden cornices and eaves, protruding door canopies and wooden window surrounds. Such simplicity was remarked on by James Stuart in his *Critical Observations on the Buildings and Improvements of London* (1771): the new wide straight streets produced 'a grand effect' but the 'street houses', as he called them, conveyed 'neatness, more than magnificence'. He was rattled that the aristocracy, 'whose proud seat in the country is adorned with all the riches of architecture, porticos, and columns', chose in town to live in something that was merely convenient within, and unornamented without, for all the world like the house of 'a packer or a sugar baker'. Social status was not necessarily visible from the exterior: 'Would any foreigner, beholding the insipid length of wall broken into regular rows of windows, in St. James's Square, ever figure from thence the residence of the first Duke in England?' Intricate fanlights, doorknockers and bootscrapers were often the only opportunity to express individuality on the strictly controlled exterior design.

However, as John Wood the elder discovered in 1728 at Queen Square in Bath, it was possible by 'uniting several houses so as to have the outside appearance of one magnificent structure' to create something grand. Instead of a row of houses there appeared instead to be one splendid Palladian house with a central pediment and giant Corinthian columns. Many terraces in prominent places subsequently attempted

Architect's drawing for central pedimented house in terrace. Signed by Michael Searles, 'built 1795', Surrey Square, London. Michael Searles worked over south and south-east London.

to look like 'one magnificent structure'. No architect went to more extreme lengths than John Nash, who crowded the pediment of Cumberland Terrace in Regent's Park with the figure of an enthroned Britannia, crowned by Fame and accompanied by a raft of attendants. On one side stood Literature, Genius, Manufacture, Agriculture, and Prudence, bringing the youth of different nations for instruction; on the other the guardian spirit of the Navy, surmounted by Victory, Navigation, Commerce, and Freedom, extended her blessings to the Africans. And at each end there were figures of Plenty.

Generally, however, terraces followed the standard patterns. Unnecessary ornament was expensive, and often builders saw no point in building houses that would last longer than the lease. Such shoddy workmanship was spotted by Pierre-John Grosley, a Frenchman whose *New Observations on England and its inhabitants* was translated and published in 1772. 'Those which are let for a shorter term have, if I may be allowed the expression, only the soul of a house. It is true, the outside appears to be built of brick; but the wall consists only of a single row of bricks; and those being made of the first earth that comes to hand, and only just warmed at the fire . . . In the new quarters of London, brick is often made on the spot where the buildings themselves are erected; and the workmen make use of the earth which they find in digging the foundations. With this earth they mix, as a phlogiston, the ashes gathered in by the London dustmen. I have even been assured, that the excrements taken out of the necessary-houses entered into the composition of bricks of this sort.' He was shocked too at other miserly practices such as using extremely thin deal beams: 'This makes the rooms wider, and contributes to lessen the expense.' There may have been an element of Gallic *schadenfreude* here, but Louis Simond also observed of the new houses lining the roads out of London: 'Their walls are frightfully thin, a single brick of eight inches, – and, instead of beams, mere planks lying on an edge. I am informed it is made an express condition in the leases of these shades of houses, that there shall be no dances given in them.' Over a century later, fear that 'floors come to pieces under the first waltz' was still current, as Mrs Haweis, a writer on domestic matters, warned buyers of new houses in the Queen Anne style.

In theory a 1774 Building Act was designed to rationalize and set standards for the building of terrace housing, thus avoiding precarious party walls, joists too flimsy to support a quadrille, and bricks fired from dubious substances. It specified a standard of materials and strengthened the anti-fire regulations. Terrace houses were put into

four categories, from the First Rate of over 900 square feet of space down to the Fourth, which occupied less than 350 feet and was one storey above the ground. Work that did not comply could be demolished and the builder fined and 'committed to the house of correction'.

PLANS AND LAYOUT

BEHIND THE FAÇADE there was some variation in layout – builders produced slightly different configurations for different buyers. But generally the bird-cage plan prevailed, servants in basement and attic with eating, receiving and sleeping sandwiched between. Few architects, or publishers of pattern books, bothered with the form. *The Modern Builder's Assistant*, by the William and John Halfpenny, Robert Morris and T. Lightoler (1757), was unusual in illustrating a row of three houses each with a 20-foot frontage. Interestingly, it states that it didn't matter where the kitchens were put, since 'where Families are intermixed, such Places must be rather adapted to the Use and Convenience of them, than if they were designed for private Families, in which

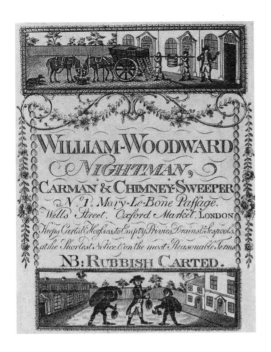

OPPOSITE The flimsy construction of terrace houses was a joke with a long history: 'The Battle of the Pianos', a *Punch* cartoon of 1855, shows two families on either side of the thin dividing wall of a Victorian terrace house, each determined to drown out the sound of the other.
LEFT Late eighteenth-century trade card which demonstrates the inconvenience of the fact that few terrace houses had back entrances: everything, including the contents of the privy, had to come out through the front door.

the Disposal is often at the Caprice and Humour of the Inhabitant, or the Wants and Necessities of his Employment.' The possibility that the house might become lodgings was recognized from the outset.

The architect Isaac Ware, more comfortable with grander projects, in his 1756 edition of *A Complete Body of Architecture*, deplored 'those little commone houses where the extent of the front is limited to a few feet' and where the door was 'thrown' to one side, so creating a passage parallel with the fore parlour instead of a decent hall. For 'a fore parlour is a room of very little use or value in a small house in London; it is too near the street, and too much in the way of disturbance from the entry.' Fifty years later Robert Southey reiterated: 'the inconvenience of living on a level with the street: the din is at your very ear, the window cannot be thrown open for the dust which showers in, and it is half-darkened by blinds that the by-passers may not look in upon your privacy.' Ware had attempted to improve matters with a central door, proper hall and back parlour; when faced with the basement, he despaired: 'Offices in the common way of London building . . . are all placed underground; but this is unwholesome, inelegant and inconvenient.' Especially if there was not enough room in the garrets to sleep all the servants, and it was necessary to lodge a man or two maids in the kitchen: 'But in this case the necessary care of those peoples healths requires that it should be boarded.' It was

The servant in the basement: one of a series of Victorian advertising cards for Crane's black lead, 'the servant's friend', used on kitchen ranges and fireplaces.

best that the basement storey 'is faced with rustick, it gives an air of solidity to the superstructure; *it looks likes a rock upon all the rest is raised.*'

Basements were a necessary feature of terrace houses, because roads were generally constructed above ground level. Thus the front basement window looked on to the base of the raised road. A Frenchman, César de Saussure, writing home in the mid-eighteenth century, was astonished at the very small footprint of the British terrace. He explained the nature of the basement: 'In all the newly-built quarters the houses have one floor made in the earth, containing the kitchens, offices, and servants' rooms . . . In order to accomplish this a sort of moat, five or six feet in width and eight or nine deep, is dug in front of all the houses, and is called the "area". The cellars and vaults where coal is stored are very strongly built beneath the streets, and to reach them you cross the area.'

Basements were generally held to be horrible. William Tayler wrote from the servants' point of view in 1837: 'In London, men servants has to sleep down stairs underground, which is jenerally very damp. Many men lose their lives by it or otherwise eat up with the rhumatics. One mite see fine blooming young men come from the country to take services, but after they have been in London one year, all the bloom is lost and a pale yellow sickley complexion in its stead.'

When houses descended into multiple occupancy, it was the landlord or landlady who lurked in the basement, monitoring the front door traffic. A typical Bloomsbury terrace fallen on hard times in described by S.F. Murphy in *Our Homes* (1883): 'Take an ordinary lodging-house in such a locality as Bloomsbury, for instance. The House itself is, including the basement, five storeys in height. Originally intended for one family, it is now inhabited by three or four. The basement, dark and damp, and stuffy, is occupied by the proprietor and his family. In rooms seldom or never visited by the genial rays of sunlight, reeking oft-times with foul exhalations of defective drains or of decaying refuse under the floor-boards, the accumulations of years, a family of five or six adults pass the greater part of their existence.' After the mid-nineteenth century basements were generally eliminated or the ground floor was raised to create a much lighter half-basement, such as the illustration of The Laurels, Brickfield Terrace Holloway, home of the Pooters in George and Weedon Grossmith's *Diary of a Nobody* (1892). Carrie, Mr Pooter's wife, with only one servant to help her, was not going to suffer long hours below ground.

HOUSING THE PERIPATETIC

THERE WAS A DEARTH OF ACCOMMODATION for the increasing number of people wishing to live in towns and cities, or just to stay for a season – those, as J. Gwynn put it in *London & Westminster Improved* (1766), 'quitting their innocent country retreats for the sake of tasting the pleasures of this great city'. As Edinburgh ran out of space in its existing courts and tenement houses to accommodate the enlightened society flourishing around the law, the university and medicine, the city announced a competition in 1766 for a new town plan. By the 1780s it was well under way. Mrs Piozzi wrote in her journal: 'Within these last 20 Years have grown up in this great City . . . private Dwellings of a uniform & symmetrical Beauty sought for elsewhere in vain; Squares of uncommon Magnitude, and Streets unrivalled . . .' She thought that Edinburgh excelled in 'Symmetrical Singularity and Dignity of Appearance', appropriate for a city that regarded itself as the modern Athens. The crisp grey stone no doubt contributed to what Louis Simond described as its look of 'superior consequence'. Once the accommodation was in place, people came flocking. Robert Burns visiting in 1788 wrote to a friend that 'everything was going on as usual – houses building, bucks strutting, ladies flaring, blackguards skulking, whores leering . . .' The only complaints lay in Edinburgh's disorganization in the matter of sewage: 'With this Town I am delighted and surprised, tho' it is as offensive to the nose as it is delightful to the eye,' wrote Sydney Smith in 1796.

Georgian towns, cities and ports all expanded with lines of terrace housing. Spa towns in particular flourished, as the well-to-do travelled in the pursuit of health, an occupation ameliorated with a good dose of pleasure – dancing, gambling and gossiping.

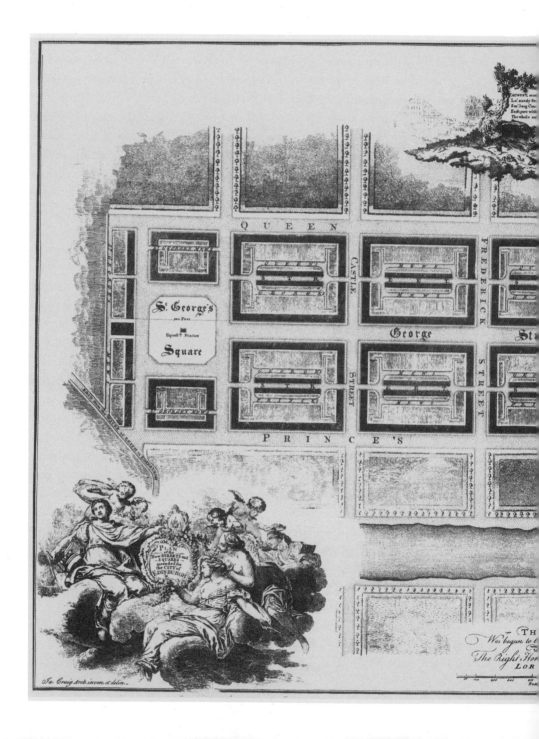

Ja. Craig Arch. inven. et delin.

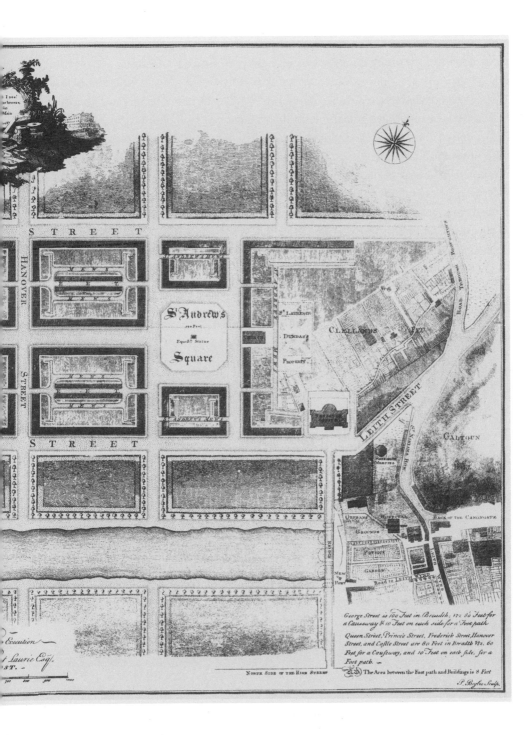

Bath outshone them all. The first step taken by the 5th Duke of Devonshire when he decided to turn the remote Derbyshire hamlet of Buxton into a fashionable spa was to turn to an architect, John Carr of York, to build a crescent near the baths. Duchess Georgiana declared to her mother in 1783, while it was being built, that she had never seen anything so magnificent 'tho' it must half ruin one'. Buxton's crescent incorporated not only lodgings, but also two hotels, an assembly room, a card room, a billiard room and lending library. The unsuitability of terrace housing for the infirm was noted early: Lady Louisa Stuart wrote in a letter of 1806, 'Lady Ailesbury grumbled sadly when she first went to Buxton, being lodged in one of the Crescent houses (which indeed are strangely contrived for invalids).' Bath staircases were often wide enough to allow for a sedan chair.

As the seaside ousted the spa as a fashionable destination, coastal towns also turned to terrace building. In 1817, Jane Austen, in *Sanditon*, portrays a small seaside town trying to attract visitors. There is, on the highest spot of the down, 'one short row of

smart-looking houses, called the Terrace, with a broad walk in front, aspiring to be the Mall of the place'. It is on the brink of success (the sound of a harp is heard coming out of one house), or – is it? Lady Denham, an investor in the Terrace, is worried: 'If people want to be by the sea, why don't they take lodgings? Here are a great many empty houses – 3 on this very Terrace; no fewer than three lodging papers staring me in the face at this very moment, Numbers 3, 4 and 8.' Basking in the approval of the Prince Regent, Brighton became the most popular resort. With seafront terraces, interspersed with squares and crescents that eventually stretched for a mile and a half, it beat off competition from Scarborough, St Leonards, Folkestone, Southsea, Hastings, Torquay, Eastbourne, Llandudno and Weymouth.

Letters and journals dating from this period are peppered with descriptions of searching for satisfactory houses and refer to continuous new building. George Montagu wrote to Horace Walpole, in November 1768, asking about a lodging he was interested in. But he was worried about the house next door which was being built by Mr Beauclerc: 'Now I shall be obliged to you if you would let down your chariot glass when you next pass by, and take a peep at it; for if it lays open and exposed, I know how dilatory London workmen are . . .' Walpole replied that only the ground floor had been built. 'I fear nothing for you but the noise of workmen, and of this street in front and Piccadilly on the other side. If you can bear such a constant hammering and hurricane, it will rejoice me to have you so near me . . .'

A good West End house was essential for those wishing to enter society in London. The leasehold could be purchased or annual rent paid. All that London had to offer was described in Fanny Burney's novel *Cecilia*, published in 1782. The orphaned heroine stayed with her childhood friend Mrs Harrel in 'one of the most elegant houses in Portman Square'. She found Mrs Harrel 'immersed in the fashionable round of company and diversions . . . sucking in air impregnated with luxury and extravagance'. Her husband 'seemed to consider his own house merely as an Hotel, where at any hour of night he might disturb the family to claim admittance, where letters and messages might be left for him, where he dined when no other dinner was

PREVIOUS PAGES *Plan for Edinburgh*, by James Craig, engraved 1768. The plan shows the grid of the terraced streets, each end culminating in a square; this was in radical contrast to the old town.
LEFT *The Crescent*, a lithograph of 1821 by Daniel Egerton. This Regency terrace in Cheltenham typifies the accommodation being erected in expanding spa and seaside towns.

offered him, and where, when he made an appointment, he was to be met with. His lady, too, though more at home, was not therefore more solitary; her acquaintance were numerous, expensive and idle, and every moment not actually spent in company, was scrupulously devoted to making arrangements for that purpose.' Expenditure on their country villa, Violet-Bank, concerts, balls, suppers and masquerades lead them into debt. Desperate economy is why their friends the Belfields, a brother and sister, lodge in only two rooms up two flights of stairs in Portland Street. The brother – who tried to rise above his station as a tradesman's son – is indulged with 'the use of a very good parlour in which [to] see his friends. "And this," added she, "is a luxury for which no body can blame him, because if he has not the appearance of a decent home, no gentleman will employ him."' In a terrace all were outwardly equal, even if you had only a small slice of it. A further social level is revealed when Cecilia helps the wife and five children of an injured carpenter who live in a small room up two flights, 'the three eldest of whom were hard at work with their mother in matting chair-bottoms, and the fourth, though a mere child, was nursing the youngest'. Lodgings at the top of the house were inevitably the cheapest. Garrets were the last resort. It was in Brooke Street, Holborn, in the attic of a house belonging to a sack-maker called Mrs Angel, that the poet Thomas Chatterton died of arsenic poisoning and starvation in August 1770. As fashionable London moved west, older houses in the east, such has this, had lost their lustre.

For short visits, as to Bath to take the waters, it was customary either to rent a suite of rooms from a landlady and order food to be sent up from a communal kitchen in the basement, or to take an entire house. Cook shops in the city provided ready-made dishes and sauces. Fanny Burney described arriving at Bath in her journal for 1780. 'We alighted at York House, and Mrs. Thrale sent immediately to Sir Philip Jennings Clerke ... He came instantly with the usual alacrity to oblige, and told us of lodgings upon the South Parade, whither in the afternoon we all hied, and Mr Thrale immediately hired the house at the left corner. It was deliciously situated; we have meadows, hills, Prior Park, "the soft-flowing Avon".' They moved in the next day. But the experience caused anxiety for Jane Austen, who wrote to her sister, Cassandra, in January 1801. 'The houses in the streets near Laura Place I should expect to be above our price – Gay Street would be too high, except only the lower house on the left hand side as you ascend; towards *that* my mother has no disinclination; – it used to be lower rented than any other house in the row, from some inferiority in

Poverty in a garret, shown in William Hogarth's *The Distrest Poet*, 1741. Bare cupboard, crying baby, wife making do and milkmaid presenting bill surround the poet frantically seeking inspiration.

the apartments. But above all other's, her wishes are at present fixed on the corner house in Chapel row, which opens into Prince's Street. Her knowledge of it however is confined only to the outside, & therefore she is equally uncertain of it's being really desirable.' Choice naturally related to status: Sir Walter Eliot in *Persuasion* considers his house in Camden Place, high above Walcot Street, 'a lofty dignified situation, such as becomes a man of consequence'. One pastime in Bath was to visit building sites and judge the desirability of new housing for future seasons. Tradesmen were adept at meeting demands and one even boasted that he could provide all furnishings needed for a house within three days. To Louis Simond the effect was that the city was 'cast in a mould all at once; so new, so fresh, and regular'. He was less sure about its society: 'a sort of monastery, inhabited by single people, particularly superannuated females. No trade, no manufactures, no occupations of any sort, except that of killing time. Half the inhabitants do nothing, the other half supply them with nothings.'

Criticism of terrace housing's exterior uniformity persisted; perhaps it went against the nation's desire for individuality. Robert Southey complained of 'extended brick walls, about forty feet high, with equally extended ranges of windows and doors, all precisely alike, and without any appearance of being distinct houses. You would rather suppose them to be hospitals, or arsenals, or public granaries, were it not for their great extent.' This was in 1807, just before the passion for facing brick with stucco – a smooth, light-coloured render – really took hold. After some failed attempts a stable compound was manufactured that reliably produced the effect of finely dressed stone for roughly one-quarter of the cost. With the help of this transforming material, John Nash in Regent's Park for the Crown Estate, Thomas Cubitt in Belgravia and Pimlico for the Grosvenor Estate and Thomas Kemp in Brighton built startlingly impressive terrace houses ornamented with rustication, columns, pilasters, capitals and pediments, aimed at attracting the most prosperous residents. Success or failure, as usual, was dependent on whether or not this was achieved. Thomas Kemp, his funds boosted by marriage to a banker's daughter, managed to draw fashionable Brighton eastwards to his Kemp Town Estate, but his most spectacular development, Sussex Square, a crescent 200 feet longer than Bath's Royal Crescent, was a struggle, still unfinished in 1844, eighteen years after the first tenants moved in. The arrival of the Duke of Devonshire in 1828 raised the social stakes, despite the fact that he was, he said, 'surrounded by the shells and carcases of the houses that compose Kemp Town'.

Belgravia was secure in its central and fashionable location and Thomas Cubitt built stucco terraces to suit all households. Belgrave Square had the largest houses and rapidly acquired rich and aristocratic residents. Unlike many developers, Cubitt took responsibility for road building, street lighting and sewerage. And although an inhabitant of Chesham Place complained in 1834 that the street was too dark to distinguish door numbers, and one from Lower Belgrave Place groused in 1835 that 'after every shower of rain we are over our shoes in mud when we step out at our front doors', it remained consistently desirable. Extraordinarily, life in Belgravia was put into verse – seventy-nine pages of it – by Mrs C.L. Gascoigne, who also happened to be the niece of Lord Carrington, who ran the bank of Smith Payne Smith, which invested in Cubitt's properties. She gave him due credit for his achievement: 'Thine the praise, O Cubitt! Thine the hand / That being gave to what thy mind had planned' and continues her public relations exercise with 'Of this stupendous town – this "mighty heart" / Of England's frame – the *Fashionable* part!' Of a titled mother 'with her train of well-dressed daughters', she writes, 'No wish have they on earth – no higher aim / Than to attain *position*, and a *name*! / An elder son! A house in Belgrave Square, / A country seat . . .' With characteristic Victorian sentiment she points out that death comes to the rich and poor alike in Cubitt's development : 'But not alone in proud Belgravian homes / Does death appear! – Lo, *everywhere* it comes! / The darkened window in the noisy mews . . .'

THE MEWS

SUBSTANTIAL TERRACE HOUSES in Belgravia, and elsewhere, had access to nearby mews, small narrow streets lined with buildings that combined stabling, coach houses and living quarters for grooms and coachmen. Having a carriage in town put you on a particular social standing. In the 1880s the Marchioness of Bath recalled that eleven horses and five stablemen were sent to the mews behind the family house in Grosvenor Square, but generally by this date many families had abandoned carriages and hired broughams when necessary. As their true purpose ceased, mews were colonized by small traders such as cobblers, flower girls, knife-grinders and chimney sweeps or used as garages. In the early twentieth century, when pressure of space began to be felt in 'good' areas, their transformation began. The Grosvenor Estate in 1915 successfully converted a mews property in Mayfair into what the estate surveyor Edmund Wimperis described as 'the best bijou house in London' (since when the words 'bijou' and 'mews' have rarely been parted). A character in a 1933 novel by Cecil Roberts, *Pilgrim Cottage*, wonders how Kitty has come to be living in such an expensive area as Bruton Street: 'Perhaps she had one of those mews flats in which people, with the aid of a bright door and a little interior decoration, persuaded themselves they were living like gentlefolk instead of like stablemen. Strange how the decay of the horse and groom had conveniently coincided with the growth of Income Tax! Squeezed out of their front mansions, reduced gentility had taken refuge in horse-boxes – horse-boxes, however much bright paint, pseudo panelling and chintz curtaining had been incorporated with a geyser, bathroom-kitchen, electric light and a telephone.'

Michael Flanders and Donald Swann's 1950s song 'Design for Living' conjures up mews chic twenty years later.

> When I started making money, when I started making friends
> We found a home as soon as we were able to.
> We bought this freehold for about a thousand more than
> The house, our little house, was once the stable to.
> With charm, colour values, wit and structural alteration
> Now designed for graceful living, it has quite a reputation . . .
> With little screens and bottle-lamps and motifs here and there
> Mobiles in the air
> Ivy everywhere
> You mustn't be surprised to find a cactus in the chair
> But we call it home sweet home.

HOUSING FOR THE INDUSTRIAL NORTH

WHILE THE INHABITANTS of salubrious Bath, Brighton or Belgravia could probably not have imagined a cellar basement to have any other purpose than to house servants, a radically different type of terrace house was common in the north. In Lancashire cellars under terraced rows had been excavated for cotton weavers to work in, as they provided the damp atmosphere needed for cotton. When weaving was centralized in mills, these and other cellars became living quarters for the poorest and most destitute inhabitants of the country. Friedrich Engels's *The Condition of the Working Class in England in 1844* (published 1892) described an area of Manchester known as Little Ireland. 'The creatures who inhabit these dwellings and even their dark, wet cellars, and who live confined amidst all this filth and foul air – which cannot be dissipated because of the surrounding lofty buildings – must surely have sunk to the lowest level of humanity.' Further description was provided by a journalist, Angus Reach, in 1849, of a cellar in Angel Meadow. 'The place was dark, except for the glare of a small fire. You could not stand without stooping in the room which might be about twelve feet by eight. There were at least a dozen men, women and children on stools, or squatted

Cope Place, Kensington, painted by Charles Ginner in 1924: a small service street with large terrace houses looming behind.

RIGHT A wood engraving in the *Punch Almanack* for 1850, after a drawing by John Leech, of a family in a rat-infested cellar resisting the rent collector.
OPPOSITE Illustration from Gustave Doré's *London*, 1872. View of house backs from the train on the railway line between Vauxhall and Charing Cross.

on the stone floor, round the fire and the heat and smells were oppressive . . . the inmates slept huddled on the stones, or on masses of rags, shavings and straw which were littered about.' Statistics suggest that in 1851 nearly 12 per cent of Manchester's population lived in cellars.

Silk weavers worked at attic level, where the light was best. The French Huguenot silk weavers, expelled from France in 1685, settled in Macclesfield and the Spitalfields area of London, where they adapted their early Georgian terrace houses with large top storeys and wide windows to accommodate looms for their sought-after lustrings, brocades and paduasoys. By the time Charles Dickens visited Spitalfields in 1851 machine competition had reduced the once-wealthy community to penury, and he found some weaving families reduced to living in the attics alone. A partitioned-off corner contained 'bedstead, fireplace, a chair or two, a tub of water, a little crockery. The looms claim all superior space and have it. Like grim enchanters who provide the family with their scant food, they must be propitiated with the best accommodation. They bestride the room, and pitilessly squeeze the children.' Small scale weaving sporadically continued in small terraces, such as those of the Coventry ribbon weavers in the 1850s. In these cottage factories, 'topshops' or weaving rooms were built along the top of two-storey terraced houses; the weaver could let himself up through a trap door to his loom above his own house. The looms were often connected to a central power system, which was paid for by the weavers.

Rapid expansion of industry in the midlands and the north resulted in a rural labour force flocking into towns. Towns such as Manchester, Liverpool and Leeds were almost doubling their populations within decades: Manchester grew by 40 per cent between 1821 and 1831. All these people needed to be housed as close as possible to the factories and mines, and hundreds of thousands of terrace houses provided the solution. There were different regional configurations but the basic provision was usually two rooms upstairs and two rooms down, with washing facilities and a privy in a yard behind. The houses were primitive and cramped but each family had its own privacy, front door and enclosed yard to hang out washing. Yards usually opened on to back lanes from where the rubbish and privies could be cleared. To pack the greatest density of housing in the smallest space, they were often grouped round small courts that had only one access point to the thoroughfare.

There was one variation that rightly attracted real opprobrium. This was the back-to-back house – cheapest on land and cheapest on building materials. Two individual

houses were built literally back to back, so that each dwelling looked out in only one direction. They opened straight on to the street, so there was neither through ventilation nor yard. In some houses the privies were in the cellar; others were in communal yards which opened out at intervals – not necessarily very close.

Although this housing fulfilled an essential need, conditions within were frequently grim. The importance of good drainage and fresh air were understood, but nonetheless these commodities were generally non-existent. Engels described back-to-backs on the banks of the 'coal-black, stagnant stinking' river Medlock in Manchester: 'Some four thousand people, mostly Irish, inhabit this slum . . . Heaps of refuse, offal and sickening filth are everywhere interspersed with pools of stagnant liquid. The atmosphere is polluted by the stench and is darkened by the thick smoke of a dozen factory chimneys. A horde of ragged women and children swarm about the streets and they are just as dirty as the pigs which wallow happily on the heaps of garbage and in the pools of filth.' Edwin Chadwick, when investigating the state of the 'Labouring Poor' in 1842, cited a report from Stockport of back-to-back houses. In Shepherd's Buildings in Back Water Street, two rows of houses were divided by a lane 21 feet wide, with a central gutter overflowing with putrefying matter. With privies only at the centre of the row, each house had two rooms, one up and one

Dense late nineteenth-century terrace housing in Manchester, photographed in 1930 as due for slum clearance.

down, each room about 9 x 12 feet. A family of nine, with a 'mother on the eve of confinement', lived in one. Four to a bed was usual.

Cities gradually outlawed back-to-backs, Nottingham as early as 1845. However, in Halifax, Bradford and Leeds about 65 per cent of all houses being built in the 1880s were still back-to-back. In Leeds they were built as late as 1909. According to an editorial in the *Builders' Journal,* the extinction of back-to-back houses was 'causing much heart-burning in Leeds. We earnestly plead with the good folk of Leeds to abandon their prejudices, forsake their bad traditions.' Only three years earlier, when writing about housing in the city, F.M. Lupton had aired the view that the lack of a back yard in which to deposit filth was a positive advantage in the poorer parts of town.

'If you're looking for a job and give an address in the Lane, no master'll take you,' was what one man told Gwendolen Freeman. She saw life in back-to-back houses during her weekly visits as a Provident Bank collector in Summer Lane, a particularly poor area of Birmingham, in the 1930s and published her observations after the war in *The Houses Behind.* Her views were those of someone with a 'lawn-tennis voice' – as one of her customers had dubbed it: 'At first I was shocked by the conditions and saw people in a romantic haze of suffering. Now I am so used to the conditions that I hardly notice them.' She described how 'each house may either bake in the sun or never get any . . . The doors open straight into the kitchen, where water may or may not be laid on. Winding steep stairs, almost always without a rail, lead from the kitchen to the bedroom above to what is invariably called "the attic". From the kitchen too, dark steps go down to the coal-cellar, and there cats are taught to relieve themselves as there is nowhere for them in the yard . . . The dwellings are joined together and the bugs run from one to another, so that even a clean woman is visited. Indeed the neighbours frown on too-thorough cleaners, saying that cleaning stirs the bugs up and sends them along the row . . . Gas is the general means of lighting – a penny in the slot – and the poorest go to bed at seven or eight in winter to avoid using more coal and the extra penny . . . Old fashioned ranges, blacked by the house-proud, rusty and filthy by the slothful . . . Pianos, only occasionally played, are in evidence . . . They were once, I think, a sign of gentility, and now they are used for storing things. Old letters and rent-books are slipped under the lids. Every house has a wireless set, and the wireless is always put on over-loudly, so that one may chase one Oxford accent blaring forth from open doors all along the street . . . Sometimes the Lane reminds me of a village. Everybody knows everybody's business in a very small area.' Gwendolen

Freeman admitted that for her such living conditions would be a nightmare. 'But many of the Lane-dwellers – especially the old ones – are attached to the district and dread leaving it.' She recognized its communality and its vitality. 'Life in the courts seems to me far less dull than life in a suburban villa.'

REFORM

VICTORIAN CONCERN ABOUT HOUSING CONDITIONS usually centred on the word 'sanitary' – elements conducive to good health. These were in the main conspicuously absent from workers' terrace housing; cholera, malaria and tuberculosis were rife, life expectation low.

There were a few exceptional employers who took control of housing their labour force rather than leaving matters to speculative builders. Henry Ashworth, a Bolton cotton manufacturer, appalled by an outbreak of fever among his workers, began in the 1820s a programme of house improvement and building. Each of his worker's houses had a living room and a back kitchen, three bedrooms and an individual back yard with a privy. The kitchens had sinks, boilers and ovens and, by 1835, piped water.

Edward Akroyd and Titus Salt, both wealthy wool manufacturers, followed suit in the mid-nineteenth century in building model housing for their workers. They both started from scratch and built new mills in the countryside removed from polluted overcrowding in Halifax and Bradford respectively. At Copley, Akroyd's houses were, for economy's sake, back-to-back but they were flanked by allotments, abutted a church and a village school and were in the fresh air, so even *The Builder*, usually highly critical of terrace housing, acknowledged them to be acceptable. At Akroydon he instituted an experiment by which tenants could gradually buy their own houses. In Saltaire the paternalistic Salt created an ordered and healthy community that was in total contrast to life in Bradford (which Engels's friend and compatriot George Weerth described as like lodging 'with the devil incarnate'). There was the wherewithal for improvement and cleanliness – churches, reading rooms, gardens, concert halls, schools and bath houses. Disraeli in *Sybil* (1845) had created one such benevolent mill owner, Mr Trafford: 'Deeply had he pondered on the influence of the employer on the health and content of his workpeople. He knew well that the domestic virtues are dependent on the existence of a home, and one of his first efforts had been to build a village where every family may be lodged.' For the three thousand employees housed by Salt, there was the possibility of a house in Fanny or Amelia Street, one of the neat

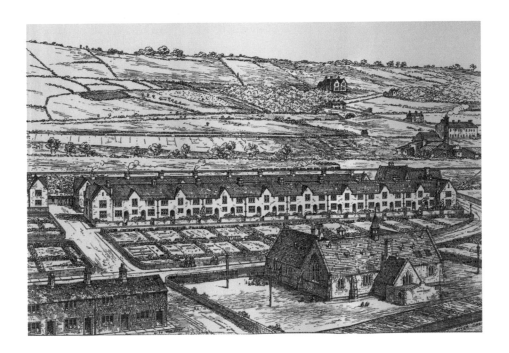

Illustration in J. Hole, *The Homes of the Working Classes*, 1866, showing terraces built in Copley village by Edward Akroyd. This was model housing, with space allowed for green areas and allotment gardens.

terraced streets named for Salt's eleven children, along with proper drains, water and gas, access to the chess room in the Mechanics' Institute and the opportunity to join a brass band. However, you did have to forgo the right to hang your washing outside or visit a pub (there was none).

Public exhibition of washing, inevitable in houses without yards, struck a note of squalor – which is doubtless why Salt banned it. The French historian and critic Hippolyte Taine, on a trip to Liverpool around 1870, left a graphic description: 'It is now six o'clock, and we return through the poorer quarter. What a sight! In the vicinity of Leeds Street there are fifteen or twenty streets across which cords are stretched and covered with rags and linen, hung up to dry. Bands of children swarm on every flight of steps, five or six are clustered on each step, the eldest holding the smallest . . .' There was a mass of evidence relating to the appalling state of housing at this period, but setting it right seemed an insurmountable problem. Yorkshireman James Hole wrote *The Homes of the Working Classes, with suggestions for their improvement* in 1866. He called for central government to compel local authorities to regulate building, supply drainage and water to each house, and to lend money for improved housing, appoint medical and health inspectors in all towns and compulsorily purchase building land where needed. Hole wrote in desperation: 'The fearful condition of great portions of our large towns would not be tolerated were it adequately *understood*. These evils have so long a life because the middle and upper classes have no personal, concrete knowledge of them, but only some dim abstract idea, gathered from newspapers and speeches, that things are not quite as they should be.' Respectable people who made money from letting such houses never came in contact 'with the horrid misery from whose stinted resources that rent is squeezed; [the landlord] never thinks of the anxious daily battle for life, amid filth and fever, from whence his wealth is drawn.'

Rent day marked the week. Reminiscences of a miner from St Helens in Lancashire during the 1920s (collected by Charles Forman for his 1978 book *Industrial Town*) described how a landlord would own a row of ten or twelve houses. 'You never seemed to know your landlord. There was always a rent collector who collected for whoever owned the houses. If the rent collector missed you, he put a notice on the door.' When the rent wasn't paid tenants were evicted, if they hadn't bolted first. 'I've seen doors and windows taken out, or sacks put over the chimneys to smoke him out – all sorts of actions taken.' For some, employer and landlord were one and the same, as railway and dock companies built housing to retain a work force. This was particularly the case in remote areas. The Northern Lighthouse Board, when they commissioned Skerryvore Lighthouse in 1837 from Alan Stephenson, included a short terrace of granite housing for the lighthouse keepers ten miles away on Tiree. Brunel's design for housing at Swindon (then uninhabited countryside) for the Great Western Railway was intended to look good from the train. There was a contrasting stone façade, but each house had only two rooms and they were without kitchens. An early employee, Edward Snell, described them as primitive: 'not a knocker or scraper in the whole. Most of the houses very damp . . . Not a cupboard or shelf . . . and the unfortunate inhabitants obliged to keep the grub in the bedrooms.'

By the mid-1870s the government did draw up a series of regulations or by-laws for local authorities, as housing reformers had hoped. They specified standards of drainage, minimum room sizes, number of windows and width of streets. But the courts and back alleys of earlier housing stock still existed. Some authorities ignored the by-laws, some complained that they raised the cost of housing, but they did result in numerous uniform grids of identical houses built between 1880 and 1914. The minimum size for a living room in so-called by-law housing was 12 feet square. The size of the Woodruff family's front room in Blackburn was 9 x 9 feet. William Woodruff's memoir *The Road to Nab End* describes his cotton-working family's life during the early 1920s in a two-up two-down terrace. The kitchen was the heart of the house: 'There was ever a din going on there at night . . . As the kitchen was three paces one way and two-and-a-half the other, children didn't sit at table, we stood for meals . . . Under the window was a stone sink and a slopstone, or draining board. Above the sink was the only tap in the house. Next to the fireplace was a deep, large metal basin called a setpot or copper. It was heated with free orange-box wood, and had a chimney connected to the fireplace . . . My mother and sisters washed clothes there. Washing was soaked, boiled, rotated with a wooden dolly, rinsed and starched in this small corner. The steaming wet washing was run through a wringer that stood in the yard, and weather permitting, hung out to dry on the clothesline. How forsaken the washing looked through the window when it was left in the rain. Brought inside, it was flung over a clothes rack, fixed to the ceiling in front of the range. Damp clothing usually hung from the ceiling for half the week. The grown-ups got their heads caught in it.'

Being the youngest and put to bed first, he fell asleep to the drone of voices from the kitchen below. 'The cracks in the bedroom floor were so wide that, except when the adults took an unfair advantage by whispering, I could hear all that was going on. When the whispering had gone on too long, I leapt out of bed, and pressed my ear to a crack to listen to the scandal. In our street everybody knew everybody's business: who was sick, who was well; who was richer, who was poorer; who had "got on", and who had "gone wrong".'

Everybody knowing everybody's business was the obvious result of such closely packed living, and this could equally work well or badly. One of the St Helens' residents stated: 'Don't let them fool you with all this stuff about what a great community it was. You'd have eight or ten families in a street, and they'd all be related somehow, but there may be another family just as big. There'd be a lot of feuding going on. You'd have friendly neighbours so long as you were in with the family; otherwise things could be pretty rough.' But another reported that as no one had any money they were all in the same boat, which made people more friendly and neighbourly: 'In sickness, they'd all gather round. They'd lend you sheets or material if you were stuck for something.' When Michael Young and Peter Willmott talked to the inhabitants of Bethnal Green in the mid-1950s for their book *Family and Kinship in East London*, they unearthed the networks of mutual support that had developed in the terraced streets. Such intense interrelations with neighbours were followed by the nation in the television soap *Coronation Street*, first aired in December 1960 and set in a fictional row of by-law terrace housing built in 1902 (and named for King Edward VII's coronation) in the Greater Manchester area. By the end of the decade the programme was criticized as presenting a nostalgic view of the

BELOW Community spirit: the inhabitants of Gladstone Terrace, Northampton, photographed on Coronation Day, 2 June 1953, when they won a prize for the best decorated street.
RIGHT A photograph taken in 1966 of children playing on the site of demolished terraces; a rim of surviving houses stands in front of the high-rise future.

urban working class and not reflecting reality. It was nostalgia for a disappearing world: the city of Manchester announced in 1959 that it had 68,000 'grossly unfit' houses, and demolished 90,000 between 1954 and 1976. Life in an overspill estate, new town or a high-rise block did not foster the same community spirit.

DIVERGING FROM UNIFORMITY

HOWEVER, set against the new green suburbs the old terraces appeared drear indeed. J.B. Priestley, born in a respectable suburb of Bradford, would have known industrial streets well, but coming up from the south to write his *English Journey* in 1933 he wrote of Jarrow in the Depression as 'a mean little conglomeration of narrow monotonous streets of stunted and ugly houses, a barracks cynically put together so that shipbuilding workers could get some food and sleep between shifts. One little street may be rather more wretched than another, but to the outsider they all look alike . . . The whole town looked as if it had entered a perpetual *penniless bleak Sabbath*.'

Distaste for the monotonous similarity of terraces was not new, or confined to those housing the poor. Victorians thought flat-fronted Georgian brick houses were the epitome of dullness. Disraeli, Thackeray and Dickens all implied that living in these houses bred an outlook to match. In *Tancred* (1847) Disraeli described Harley Street as a flat, dull, spiritless street that, with Baker Street and Wimpole Street, were like 'a large family of plain children, with Portland Place and Portman Square for their respectable parents'. Thackeray in *The Newcomes* (1855) described how in every house, 'They had the same entrées, plated ware, men to wait etc.' In the same year Dickens described the Merdles' household in *Little Dorrit*: 'Like unexceptional society, the opposing rows of houses in Harley Street were very grim with one another. Indeed the mansion and

their inhabitants were so much alike in that respect, that people were often to be found drawn up on the opposite sides of dinner-tables, in the shade of their own loftiness, staring at the other side of the way with the dullness of the house.'

Old-fashioned, boring grey brick and pale stucco were thus rejected. Aspirational middle-class terrace houses from the 1860s tended to be red brick or chunky stone. The linear roofscape disappeared as front gables emphasized each individual house, so blurring the differences between detached, semi-detached and terrace houses. Rail transport widened the choice of building material and opened a catalogue of decorative possibilities with which a builder could differentiate one row from another, if only slightly. Multicoloured bricks, pierced ridge tiles, cast ironwork, encaustic tiles, terracotta panels, ceramics, fretted wood and fancy stonework were all options. Sash windows, which Dickens had described as 'expressionless', were dropped in favour of various sizes and shapes of casement glittering with leaded panes and coloured glass. Doors and porches morphed in multiple directions, some featuring house names to further stand out from their neighbours.

SUBURBAN TERRACES

Suburban terrace houses, calibrated in size, continued to provide the habitat for the growing workforce that serviced the expanding Victorian towns and cities, from bankers and stockbrokers to clerks and shop girls. As the journey time from home to work was speeded up, so housing could spread outwards further from the centre. Walking and horse travel – horse buses, hackneys and private carriages – were gradually replaced by railways, the underground, trams and motor buses. The Cheap Trains Act of 1883 forced all railway companies to offer cheap workmen's tickets at less than one penny a mile, enabling working families to move out of cramped conditions in the centre of cities and transforming some areas. The manager of the Great Eastern Company reported: 'Take, for instance, the neighbourhood of Stamford Hill, Tottenham and Edmonton. That used to be a very nice district indeed, occupied by good families, with houses from £150 to £250 a year, with coach-houses and stables, and gardens and a few acres of land. But very soon after this obligation was put upon the Great Eastern Company . . . of issuing workmen's tickets, speculative builders went down into the neighbourhood, and, as a

Revolt against the flat front: red brick terrace houses with bays, turrets and wooden fretwork, *c*.1910, as seen in a promotional postcard for houses in Dudding Hill, Neasden.

consequence, each good house was one after another pulled down, and the district is given up entirely I may say now to the working man.'

The German architect Hermann Muthesius recognized how well the small terrace house fulfilled its purpose: giving a 'measure of independence and quiet, they are nearer to the soil and in a home that is easily reached from the street, they cultivate their gardens and, best of all, know that they are masters in their own houses. The basic form of these houses is immutably fixed, as a mass-produced article, and in every respect they are built so cheaply that, in return for a low rent, the lessee or owner lives in a relatively comfortable and sound house which would not be available to him in any other way.' But he also saw them as dreary and quotes Dante's entrance to hell: 'All hope abandon, ye who enter here. Streets laid out with dull-witted indifference . . . no bends, squares, variety.' That such unexceptional houses could breed a desire to escape them is the theme of Frank Swinnerton's novel *Nocturne* (1917). Jenny Blanchard, a milliner, gets off the tram on her way home from work and turns 'into the side streets among rows and rows of the small houses of Kennington Park . . . The houses were all in darkness, because evening meals were laid in the kitchens: the front rooms were all kept for Sunday use, excepting when Emeralds and Edwins and Geralds and Dorises were practicing upon their mother's pianos . . . Jenny turned in at her own gate. In a moment she was inside her house, sniffing at the warm, odour-laden air within doors. Her mouth drew down at the corners. Stew tonight! . . . O lor'! What a life!'

For those at the other end of the social scale exceptionally large terrace houses were being built, 'mansions' six or seven storeys high. In London houses even larger than those in Belgravia sprang up on the site of Tyburn gallows and became Tyburnia: 'places which were heretofore insufferable nuisances, and the haunts of the thief and vagrant, are now crowded with the luxurious habitations of wealth and high rank', as *Tallis's Illustrated London* put it in 1851. However, the people for whom these houses were intended were by the 1890s moving into less cumbersome housing, leaving many of the large and unwieldy houses to be converted into flats or offices. As early as 1871 Banister Fletcher published plans for converting four-storey houses 'formerly occupied by single families of a rather higher social grade' into four self-contained flats, each with a living room, bedroom, scullery, lavatory, coal box and meat safe. Twenty houses in Kemp's lofty Sussex Square in Brighton were converted into flats in 1903 by Lord Rendel. What had seemed viable half a century earlier was so no longer.

So, in Virginia Woolf's *Night and Day* (1919) Mrs Hilbery remembers the 'old days in Russell Square! I can see the chandeliers, and the green silk of the piano, and Mama sitting in her cashmere shawl by the window.' But then it was let out 'in slices to a number of societies which displayed assorted initials on doors of ground glass, and kept, each of them, a typewriter which clicked busily all day long'. In the attic was the suffrage office.

Builders and developers were always in competition to secure middle-class families as tenants, thus creating pockets of unimpeachable respectability such as Edinburgh's Morningside, Newcastle's Jesmond, Cardiff's Roach Park or Dublin's Rathgar. A church and a row of shops nearby were a lure, whereas being near a lunatic asylum or gas works or on the site of an old fever hospital site was not. As most people rented moving house was easy and areas could quickly rise or fall. Many houses went straight into lodgings. *The Architect* in 1871 pointed to whole streets in places such as Dalston and Clapham full of houses let off from ground floor to attic in single rooms. In the central parts of London, where many of the original leases were falling in, little attempt was made at upkeep and there were 'houses with rich panelling, decorated plaster ceilings, wood dados, inlaid mantelpieces, ornamental staircases etc.' occupied by a poor class of lodging keeper.

LODGINGS AND BEDSITS

Lodgers inhabiting a single room had always been fixtures in the history of the terrace. In 1730 John Wood had Miss Braddock as a lodger in 9 Queen Square, Bath. She was an heiress with a gambling habit fallen on hard times. Taking lodgers was a way to make a house pay for itself or reduce living expenses if financial insecurity struck. An advertisement in *The Times* for 22 January 1813 could have been published at any time during the nineteenth or early twentieth centuries: 'Board and lodging in the house of a Widow Lady of the greatest respectability, in the most eligible part of Brompton, where there are no Inmates or Children. She wishes to receive two Ladies (sisters) who will occupy the same sleeping room, or one single Lady of respectable and genteel habits – as accommodation offered is, in every respect, truly eligible, and possesses advantages too numerous to specify in advertisement, it is trusted none but persons of respectability will apply.'

'Subside into lodgings in Pentonville, or Kensington, or Brompton,' Thackeray suggested in *The Newcomes*, 'and you find yourself very tolerably comfortable.' In this novel Lady Ann Newcome takes lodgings in Steyne Gardens in Brighton with Miss Honeyman, 'who had money losses, took a house and let the upper floors', where every room was 'fiercely swept'. This was not the experience down the road, where, Miss Honeyman's maid reports, 'the family who had taken Mrs. Bugsby's had left as usual after the very first night, the poor little infant blistered all over with bites on its dear little face; . . . [and] Mrs. Cribb *still* went cuttin' pounds and pounds of meat off the lodgers' jints, emptying their tea-caddies, actially reading their letters.' Thackeray opined that most lodgings were kept by retired servants and tradespeople.

Mrs Haweis's advice for newly-weds in her 1887 book *A Bridal Garland, the Art of Housekeeping* was clear: 'Perhaps the wisest thing a young couple can do is to begin life in lodgings. A very few rooms are needed, and a whole house is such a responsibility, especially to an inexperienced housekeeper, that anything is better than hurrying into a house for the purpose of presently hurrying out. In lodgings domestic cares are reduced to a minimum, because the landlady, if kindly and nice, will advise and help her young tenants, and if grasping and dishonest, the victim can leave at a week's notice.' She advised extreme caution in choosing a terrace house, however, listing defects that veer between reality and prejudice. 'The thin walls of houses run up in rows in a fortnight's space, cannot keep out winter frost and wind. Houses which are mainly supported by each other, cannot stand hurricanes or much wet weather. The chimney pots blow down, the windows blow in, the balconies and slates blow off, and the drains, if scamped in the work, as they must be in cheap houses, are none the safer, because the leaky pipes run to the roadway instead of to a cesspool under the kitchen or cellar. In fact between you and me, the old cesspool, *if properly emptied and deodorised*, is preferable to ill-made modern drains which connect every house with every other, and make escape from infectious maladies a clear matter of accident, whilst we are laid on by a pipe to every disease in the town.' She was referring to the novelty of a comprehensive sewerage system begun by the London Metropolitan Board of Works in 1875.

Lodgings such as those envisaged by Thackeray and Mrs Haweis were termed 'genteel'. Plenty were not. *Child of the Jago* by Arthur Morrison was published in 1896. The Jago was based on the Old Nichol, an area between Bethnal Green and Shoreditch which the LCC surveyed in 1890, discovering in its twenty streets a population of 5,566 people occupying 2,545 rooms; 107 rooms had five or more inhabitants. The streets were demolished, and in their place were built the Boundary Estate Flats (see page 156). The Prince of Wales at the opening ceremony referred to the tragic tale of the novel's central character, young Dicky Perrot, bought up in this 'forcing-house of crime'. The density of the housing, the courts, narrow streets and ever-open doors provide an unfailing sanctuary for those on the run or escaping violence. He lives in the 'first floor back' – 'a fair one, ten feet square' with his parents and sisters Looey and Little Em ('unwashed, tangled and weeping'). The Perrots' weekly rent is 3s. 6d., collected in advance. This, Morrison points out, 'made the rent of the crazy den of Old Jago Street about equal, space for space, to those of a house in Onslow Square.'

Charles Booth's *Life and Labour of the People of London* (1889–91) had a social map of London colour-grading streets from yellow for Wealthy down to black for Semi-Criminal, by way of Well-to-Do, Comfortable, Poor & Comfortable, Poor, and Very Poor. Booth's researchers gave a precise analysis of the character of tenement houses, as they were called. In some Paddington streets, 'Many of the houses are let out in furnished rooms from day to day, and among the residents thieves and prostitutes abound. According to the clergy, the rooms are even sometimes tenanted by the day and night, Box and Cox fashion. This district is an example of one that has gone wrong. The houses were built for the well-to-do class, and it is even now difficult to say why they have fallen so low. Probably it has been mainly due to their being too tightly packed upon the ground.' Around Earl's Court they find a contrast between streets where relatively prosperous people live – 'whose houses are homes; they employ few servants, but live in great comfort; with them the pinch of poverty is unknown' – and others where 'great sacrifices are made to maintain appearances . . . Houses are now occupied, now empty; tenants come and go. The house, a home no longer, is made a source of income. There are guests who pay, or the drawing-room floor is let, or boarders are taken, or at length the fatal word "Apartments" appears in the fanlight over the door. Those who can afford to do so leave the stricken district, and those who come or those who do not go are alike in seeking to grasp an elusive advantage, desiring to trade on that vanishing quantity – the fashionable character of the neighbourhood.'

The Irish writer Shan Bullock used his experience as a government clerk in his 1907 novel *Robert Thorne*. Thorne is one of London's thousands of clerks and the story follows his rise up the rented property ladder. On arriving from Devon to look for work, Thorne lodges in Kennington with an Irish widow, who lived 'down with the blackbeetles' in the basement with two children and a servant. 'Up the house were lodgers, dwindling in value and importance, floor by floor, till you came to the attics and the nonentities there. I had an attic, from whose two-paned window I caught a glimpse of squalid yards, dreary backs, chimney pots innumerable; and through whose little skylight came sometimes an appearance of sunshine.' Once he has a job he moves down the stairs to a room with 'a wicker chair in which to lounge' and a view of the street. On marriage he moves to two rooms in Dulwich, with a view from the kitchen windows over back gardens to a railway embankment with trains thundering past. 'Next door on the one side, lived seven people, four above and three below; on the other side lived nine, distributed we never knew how; and so, more or less, it was from end to end . . . We liked to hear neighbours talking over the fences, to watch them tending the flowers, to see men resting after the day's work, women reading the evening paper, lovers sitting in the moonlight. Next door was a man who sang plantation melodies to his own accompaniment on the banjo. Higher up a boy played the flute very well. At a kindly distance was an adventurer on the cornet. We had pianos too and lady vocalists in our street.' They explore Dulwich, gauging the social status of different patches, 'from the humble little roads of our particular zone, each with its two rows of grey-brick houses, all precisely alike, all narrow, crowded, ugly, yet every one of them a home . . . In them lived artisans, small tradesmen, travellers, shop assistants, clerks of all kinds, lodgers innumerable . . . Always struggling, hoping, toiling, always making the best of fate and keeping a bold face to the world.' Then they find themselves in 'brighter zones where the houses had brass knockers and letter boxes and flower beds in front, and small gardens behind, and attics in the roof where the servants slept, [where] two or three hundred a year and a lodger could, with care, make both ends meet.'

For single people there were few alternatives to the rented room. Arthur Ransome arrived in London as a young man in the early 1900s, intending to write. He took a room, with a water supply two floors below, in Chelsea, 'where at least half the ugly, lovable little houses keep a notice "Apartments to Let" permanently in the windows, an apt emblem of the continual flitting that is characteristic of life.' He furnished it with three shillings' worth of packing cases from the grocer that he arranged into table, chair, bed and cupboard. After a scratch supper on his first evening he 'placed a packing case chair by the open window, and dipped through a volume of poetry, an anthology of English ballads, that had been marked at ninepence on an open bookstall in the Charing Cross Road . . . for the first time in my life I was alone in a room of my own, free to live for poetry, for philosophy, for all the things that seemed then to matter

A view from a window in Warren Street, painted by F. Gregory Brown, 1922. Bloomsbury, Fitzrovia and Chelsea were all unfashionable areas with cheap flats and studios to rent and were popular with artists and writers.

more than life itself.' Ransome was young and hopeful, in contrast to a typist whose testimony was published in a 1936 pamphlet published by the Over Thirty Association on the housing problems of low-paid single women workers in London. Box and cox still existed. 'I pay 12/6 for my room, 12 x 12 unfurnished. There is a lobby outside with a sink, but no bath. For the past five years I have been doing temporary work at 30/- to 35/- a week and am about half the time unemployed. I let my room to a night worker who pays me 7/6, but against that I have to go out all day and get my meals out. I go to public libraries or the club or walk about.'

In 1911 40 per cent of Londoners lived in shared houses. Relationships with fellow lodgers must have been as varied as the lodgings, but in no other situation did strangers live in such close proximity. In literature, as no doubt in life, experiences ranged from the grim to the positive. In George Orwell's *Keep the Aspidistra Flying* (1936) Gordon Comstock moves into lodgings of 'mingy lower-middle-class decency', a house 'where you cannot even go to the w.c. in peace because of the feeling that someone is listening to you.' One of his fellow inmates is Lorenheim, a vacuum-cleaner salesman: 'devoured by a lust for company. His loneliness was so deadly that if you so much as slowed your pace outside his door he was liable to pounce out upon you and half drag, half wheedle you in to listen to interminable paranoiac tales of girls he had seduced and employers he had scored off.' However, Noel Streatfeild's children's book *Ballet Shoes*, published the same year, united a group of disparate characters into a cheerful household in a large six-storey house in South Kensington, where the family of Great-Uncle Matthew stave off financial disaster by taking in 'boarders'. A retired ballet dancer spots talent in one of the children, a couple just back from a rubber plantation in Malaya encourage another's interest in engineering, and a pair of learned women take the children's education in hand.

There is an Orwellian description in Lynne Reid Banks's 1960 novel *The L-Shaped Room* of the house where the pregnant unmarried Jane takes a room when turned out of home – 'five flights up in one of those gone-to-seed houses in Fulham, all dark brown wallpaper inside and peeling paint outside. On every second landing was a chipped sink with one tap and an old ink-written notice which said "Don't leave the tap driping". The landing lights were the sort that go out before you can reach the next one. There were a couple of prostitutes in the basement; the landlady was quite open about them. She pointed out there was even an advantage to having them there, namely that no one asked questions about anybody.' Here excessively close-knit living engenders friendship, love and kindness, despite the grim surroundings.

'The planning of new economies': a Ronald Searle illustration for Winifred Ellis's book *London – So Help Me*, published in 1952, charting the struggle of a single girl moving to London and, inevitably, a bedsit.

The popularity of the bedsitter in the 1950s dealt a blow to the old-fashioned boarding house where the landlady's meals were eaten in what Orwell had described as 'a tomb-dark dining-room with a phalanx of clotted sauce bottles'. The bedsit experience was common to thousands, who would easily recognize the world described by Katharine Whitehorn in *Kitchen in the Corner* (1961), later *Cooking in a Bedsitter*. 'Cooking a decent meal in a bedsitter is not just a matter of finding something that can be cooked over a single gas ring. It is the problem of finding somewhere to put down the fork while you take the lid off the saucepan, and then finding somewhere else to put the lid. It is finding a place to keep the butter where it will not get mixed up with your razor or your hairpins. It is having your hands covered with flour, and a pot boiling over on to your landlady's carpet, and no water to mop up any of it nearer than the bathroom at the other end of the landing. It is cooking at floor level, in a hurry, with nowhere to put the salad but the washing-up bowl, which in any case is full of socks.' To the horrors of cooking on a gas ring Diana Athill added in her memoir, 'keeping half one's clothes in a suitcase under the divan or on top of the wardrobe, moving books and writing things from a table to a divan or chair before setting out a meal, and turning a divan from a couch into a bed every night before going to sleep in the froust of one's cigarette smoke.'

In 1915 the government, at a time of housing shortage, had introduced rent control. An unfortunate side effect was that in many cases 'fair rents' meant the landlord did not have the money to maintain their property, let alone keep it up to date. The seedy state many of the Victorian terraces had reached by the post Second World War period is recounted in *The Lonely Londoners* (1956). Trinidadian Samuel Selvon revealed the experience of the Windrush generation, confined by racial prejudice and exploitation to some of the worst housing in London. Of life off the Harrow Road he wrote: 'This is the real world, where men know what it is to hustle a pound to pay the rent when Friday comes. The houses around here old and grey and weatherbeaten, the walls cracking like the last days in Pompeii, it ain't have no hot water, and in the whole street that Tolroy and them living in, none of the houses have bath. You had was to buy one of them big galvanise basin and boil the water and full it up, or else go to the public bath. Some of the houses still had gas light, which is to tell you how old they was. All the houses in

One of Roger Mayne's photographs of Southam Street, Notting Hill Gate, taken in the late 1950s. Built in 1860, the houses in this street were condemned in 1963 as unfit to live in, and demolished by 1969.

a row in the street, on both sides, they build like one long house with walls separating them in parts, so your house jam-up between two neighbours; is so most of the houses is in London. It have people living in London who don't know what happening in the room next to them, far more the street, or how other people are living. It divide up into little worlds, an you stay in the world you belong to an you don't know anything about what happening in the other ones except what you read in the papers.' Some of what was happening was Rachmanism, named for a property developer, Peter Rachman, who by various foul means drove out rent-controlled tenants, enabling him to sell or re-let – in many cases to recent immigrants who struggled to find accommodation – at inflated rents.

GENTRIFICATION

THE OLD WORLD OF LODGERS began to disappear after 1957, when the system of controlled rents was replaced by one based on the rateable value of the house. Inevitably, this increased rent on more valuable houses and many tenants were priced out of their lodgings. Agreements made prior to that date were upheld and tenants staying put with their fixed rent were dubbed 'sitting tenants'. They were a problem to be circumvented – given money to leave or just lived around until they died – by the new breed of terrace house owners. Gentrification had begun – a word first used in inverted commas by sociologist Ruth Glass in a 1965 report of London's housing needs. She was citing the way the middle classes were moving into previously working-class Islington (and thus returning it to its early nineteenth-century middle-class roots). For young families in the 1960s the terrace house had lost the stigma felt by earlier generations and as city air became cleaner the suburbs were losing their appeal.

Home improvement grants were available to install bathrooms, basins and sinks into pre-1961 houses and there was no shortage of potential, as advertised by Roy Brooks, a sixties estate agent with a taste for anarchic copy. 'Fashionable Chelsea. Untouched by the swinging world of fashion an early VIC lower middle class family dwelling, which has sunk to a working class tenement (2 lousy kits. and 3 sinks). The decaying décor lit by 'High Speed Gas.' 6 main rms. And revolting appurtenances which could be turned into bathrm. and kit. A few doors away houses sell for over £18,000 and tarted up twin house to this one makes almost double the modest £8,500 asked for this dump.' Tarting up almost certainly involved the insertion of RSJs supporting ceilings as old divisions between hall and front and back parlours were demolished.

In 1969 *House & Garden* advised using dark colours on brick and stucco with white for woodwork – 'inky blues, spinach greens and deep ochres' to give a street diversity-within-unity – and, incidentally, mark out newcomers. A 1977 report in the *Observer* contrasted the habits of the old working-class population and the new gentrifiers: how the first criticized the second for under-using their housing space, and were rebutted with: 'You couldn't even get a decent camembert when I first came here, now there are delicatessens all over.'

The downside of booming metropolitan house prices and skips lining the street as the improvers and converters got busy was that cheap living space dried up. As a result, in 1968, the squatting movement was born. People moved into empty properties awaiting demolition or refurbishment and set up home without permission or rent book. Although office blocks and luxury flats were also squatted it was principally urban terraces – as usual fitting easily into multi-occupancy – that were occupied all over the country. They sheltered the vulnerable and out of work as well as those politically motivated to fight the status quo, who in many cases formed co-operative communities and saved the houses. Nash's Cornwall Terrace in Regent's Park was occupied in 1975 and

RIGHT An advertisement published in October 1965 for a Leisure Vogue Room Heater, clearly aimed at the new generation of terrace house owners, who at that date had scant regard for original architectural features such as chimneypieces.
OPPOSITE A cartoon by Andy Millman, who squatted in Euston Street, London, in the 1960s, drawn for *Squatting, the Real Story* by Nick Wates.

The two <u>big</u> days in your life

the Divine Light Mission took over some houses for their followers. A squatter called Katherine posted this memory on a squatting history website: 'Before I moved in I walked house to house looking for a room. I remember the Eastern Meditation house I believe number 3, it was really weird, anyway I secured a massive room in number 10. I remember Derek (the Irish guy) was doing a lot of home brewing in the basement kitchens. I made friends with the boys upstairs from me and the highlight of my stay was a massive 3 day/night party we put on. I painted a big mural in the ballroom. It was a glorious summer, the place was magnificent.' Eviction came in October. The same year saw Queen's Terrace in Hebden Bridge, Yorkshire, squatted. Here closure of the mills and unemployment had rendered the houses virtually worthless and the council planned to demolish them, until they were stopped by the arrival of young outsiders desperate for somewhere to live. Plans to turn the hillside terrace into a co-operative community with organic garden, workshops, wind generator, community space and crèche were turned down, but the houses remained, and so did many of the squatters, changing the character of the town.

NEW LIFE FOR THE TERRACE

A REAPPRAISAL OF TERRACE HOUSING had been taking place; in the *Counter Attack against Subtopia* (1957) Ian Nairn and others had compared the higher density of people per acre in a terrace, and better use of land, to an estate of individual houses. Span was a speculative developer led by the architect Eric Lyons, who between 1948 and 1984 specialized in the form, building thirty estates of terrace housing. The houses were two-storey but had picture windows, monopitch roofs, weatherboard cladding and other features that were fashionably fifties and sixties. Although they had back gardens, 'private places for individual foibles, where people can pursue outdoor creative skills, can keep their toddlers in safety and hang out the washing', they were set within landscaped communal ground. The Span T8 type house was advertised as 'positive, modern, elegant and practical. A Town house, conceding nothing to Subtopia. It is quiet, warm, spacious and adult. Built for people who like children and music and laughter, who like entertaining, good talk, Sundays that dawdle between the *Observer* and the *Sunday Times*, and better than average food.' The neighbourliness of terrace housing was revived. The historian Juliet Gardiner, who moved to a Span house in Blackheath in 1964, describes the sense of community – communal spaces for the children to play and mums to have picnic teas, summer parties, babysitting circles with baby alarms trailing from house to house, and an active residents' association. While a Span house, furnished at Habitat and with a Mini in the car parking area, was only for the few, an amended version of terrace housing became popular with developers and planners of the period and plainer, cheaper terraces were similarly laid

Parkend in Blackheath, a Span development advertised in *House & Garden* in 1967, offering 'living and dining area in one spacious 25ft room from which the staircase rose as an elegant design feature'.

among the high-rise and low-rise flats of post-war housing schemes and New Towns. An inhabitant of the Story Hall Estate in Harlow New Town or Eaglestone in Milton Keynes might not have had the colour supplement life envisaged by Span, but their houses were built among green space and trees denied their predecessors.

The desirability, and price, of terrace housing in the south steadily rose: maximized with back extensions, loft conversions and dug-out basements, many were bursting out of their original skin. By contrast, in the north the terraces languished as the old industries declined. Apparently not even considering the idea that many of these too could be renewed and revivified, the government in 2002 pledged several billion to rebuild nine deprived areas under a scheme named Pathfinder. Once more terrace houses were demonized as obsolete, whole neighbourhoods declared surplus and unsustainable and marked for compulsory purchase and demolition. These areas were rebranded as Zones of Opportunity – part of Merseyside was named 'New Heartlands' – the plan was to replace the old terraced streets with developer-built housing at suburban densities. The scheme was, in the main, a failure. When it was wound up in 2010, research by SAVE Britain's Heritage calculated that 16,000 homes had been demolished and only 3,000 built.

The economy of building in terraces hasn't changed, nor has the fact that terraced streets are conducive to neighbourly communities, so when Kevin McCloud started a property company, Hab, to adopt the best practices of sustainable building, his first project, The Triangle in Swindon, was terraces of two-, three- or four-bedroom houses. If Brunel's railway navvies had been catapulted from their Victorian Swindon terraces into these twenty-first-century ones, the hempcrete exterior, rainwater harvesting, eco-cooling system, car pool and Shimmy home information system in each house would have astonished, but the form would have seemed strangely familiar.

FLATS

WHILE MOST NATIONS had flats forced upon them and learnt to live in and love them, the English were resistant, or at least late adopters. Existing horizontally, sandwiched between others, lacked appeal when compared to living in a house with its own front door standing on its own patch of ground.

The Scots had no such problem. They had used the word flat or 'flett' since the fifteenth century to describe accommodation within a house. By the eighteenth century it referred to a floor or storey and by the nineteenth century was generally accepted as the term for living space on one floor. The citizens of Edinburgh had from an early stage been forced to build high, in order to remain on the limited land that was under the protection of the castle. Dwellings of six or seven storeys became usual, and exceptionally even rose to thirteen. As David Buchanan, a well-travelled Edinburgh citizen, wrote in the mid-seventeenth century, 'I am not sure that you will find

anywhere so many dwellings and such a multitude of people in so small space as in this city of ours.' A feature of Scottish law encouraged this: the seller of land could demand an annual fee (feu duty) from the purchaser, who was therefore the more inclined to build the maximum number of dwellings in order to get the maximum return on his land; and the only way was up. In a reversal of what was to become the norm, the most desirable flats were those at the top, farthest away from the street. Nathaniel Hawthorne mused in 1857: 'There is a strange fascination in these old streets . . . This system of living on flats, up to I know not what story, must be most unfavourable to cleanliness, since they fetch their water all that distance towards heaven, and how they get rid of their rubbish is best known to themselves.'

LEFT Mansion flats, St James's, London, designed by Frank Verity, 1905. Verity wrote that blocks were most effective if designed on classical lines, but that the windows could be enriched with suitable balconies.
BELOW Edinburgh: a nineteenth-century photograph of tenement blocks at the head of West Bow in the medieval Old Town.

Even when the Old Town of Edinburgh had finally burst its seams and was extended with rows of Georgian terraces, many of the houses were divided horizontally rather than vertically. Unlike the English, the Scots had no problem with a common staircase and lack of a street door. In Scotland the word 'tenement' was used to describe respectable middle-class flats, while in England it came to describe specifically working-class ones.

CHAMBERS: HOMES FOR THE SINGLE

CHAMBERS WERE, in a sense, proto flats. From the sixteenth century, chambers – one room for sleeping and one for business – were provided within the Inns of Court so that lawyers could be immediately on hand. Food was to be had in a common dining hall, and servants were forbidden. From the same date, the Inns of Chancery, such as Thavies Inn and Furnival's Inn, provided chambers with a similar purpose, housing barristers and law students. A similar pattern of trouble-free living was established in Oxford and Cambridge colleges within very similar quadrangles. This manner of living an easy and undomesticated life was enthusiastically adopted by single professional men. An early and grand example was Albany in Piccadilly. Originally Melbourne House, it was built in the 1770s by William Chambers for Viscount Melbourne but by 1802 belonged to a builder called Alexander Copland. Copland commissioned the architect Henry Holland to divide up the house and build over its long back garden, thereby creating sixty-nine sets of chambers. Here was an early example of converting houses into flats. Byron moved into his set of rooms in Albany on 28 March 1814. 'This night got into my new apartment, rented of Lord Althorp, on a lease of seven years – spacious, and room for my books and sabres,' he wrote in his journal. It must have seemed delightfully manageable and trouble-free, as his move coincided with the foundering of negotiations to sell his ancestral home, Newstead Abbey, by which scheme he planned to escape from debt. Lord Macaulay too was optimistic about living in Albany. He wrote in a letter to a Mr Ellis in 1841: 'I have taken a very comfortable suite of chambers in the Albany; and I hope to lead, during some years, a sort of life suited to my taste, – a college life in the west end of London. I have an entrance hall, two sitting rooms, a bedroom, kitchen, cellars and two rooms for servants, all for 90 guineas a year; and this in a situation which no younger son of a duke need be ashamed to put on his card.' Freed from the responsibilities of a house, he could make a good start on his *History of England*.

An estate agent called Alfred Cox explained in his 1853 *The Landlord's and Tenant's Guide* that many buildings in the Inns, Fleet Street and Strand were entirely occupied with sets of chambers and offices used by merchants, solicitors and private gentlemen. 'By "chambers" is now understood either a barrister's rooms or a few apartments held by a gentleman-bachelor . . . Young bachelors not yet wishing to be troubled with housekeeping, and old bachelors who have renounced all thought of it, find chamber life agreeable, from the independence they can exercise.' As a contemporary advertisement in *The Times* for Jermyn Street chambers put it, 'suit gentleman dining out'. Life could be lived in a club. After the Inns of Chancery became moribund, chambers were available as lodgings. Charles Dickens lived very happily for a short while in Furnival's Inn when just married – although in his essay *The Uncommercial Traveller* he described chambers as places with a 'true kind of loneliness' when compared to rooms in a dwelling-house, 'where there have been family festivals, children have grown up in them, girls have bloomed into women in them, courtships and marriages have taken place in them. True chambers were never young, childish, maidenly; never had dolls in them, or rocking horses, or christenings, or betrothals, or little coffins.'

The advantages of a London life in chambers were eventually offered to independent women, when the Ladies' Residential Chambers Company erected two sets of buildings for 'educated working women'. Molly Hughes, a lecturer at Bedford College, heard of the one in York Street, in the West End, shortly after it opened in 1892. She met 'a dignified Lady Superintendent, who informed us that every applicant must have references and must agree to certain regulations, of which the chief seemed to be that no nail must be driven into the walls.' Either a single room or a pair of rooms could be rented and a single bathroom, charged extra, served two floors. Molly Hughes noted: 'Meals gave us no trouble, for a good dinner was served in the common dining room, lunch was either a picnic affair at home or else taken at a tea-shop, and our gas-ring was enough for breakfast requirements. We met a variety of interesting women – artists, authors, political workers, and so on.' However, other tenants found the constrictions impossibly irksome. A survey by the Women's Industrial Council in 1900 on women's accommodation quoted one: 'I am leaving because of the irritating rules. They should avoid treating tenants as a cross between a pauper lunatic and a rebellious schoolgirl.'

MODEL DWELLINGS FOR THE INDUSTRIOUS

URBAN POPULATIONS IN INDUSTRIAL CITIES exploded in the nineteenth century, exacerbating the problem of housing the workforce, who needed to live close to their employment. Overcrowded housing, without sewerage or water supplies, descended into disease-ridden slums, visible for all to see or read about. In *Oliver Twist* (1838) Charles Dickens described Oliver's impression of Clerkenwell: 'A dirtier or more wretched place he had never seen. The street was very narrow and muddy, and the air was impregnated with filthy odours. There were a good many small shops, but the only stock in trade appeared to be heaps of children, who even at that time of night, were crawling in and out at the doors, or screaming from the inside . . . Covered ways and yards, which here and there diverged from the main street, disclosed little knots of houses, where drunken men and women were positively wallowing in filth.' Edwin Chadwick's Poor Law Board Report of 1842 'on the Sanitary Conditions of the Labouring Population and the Means of its Improvement' spelled out exactly how horrendous the situation was. A section of society had its conscience pricked, and the idea of 'model dwellings' evolved. The earliest were probably the four-storey blocks of flats built for dockers in Birkenhead in 1847. An incredulous report in the *Labourer's Friend* that year stated: 'These workmen's dwellings then: what are they? One hardly knows at first glance what to think of them. They are so totally unlike anything to which we are accustomed . . . they appear more like houses for the upper class of society; and we feel puzzled how to associate them with the limited wants of a working population.'

In this climate of concern the first two organizations were formed to provide solutions: the Metropolitan Association for Improving the Dwelling of the Industrious Classes was founded in 1841 and the Society for the Improvement of the Conditions of

RIGHT Corporation Dwellings, Liverpool: five storeys of flats above a row of shops. OPPOSITE Contented inhabitants of 'model dwellings', as depicted in *Punch* in 1850 (alongside the cellar dwellers shown on page 120). The well-fed workman returns to his family, where he is confident to find food on the table, a kettle boiling on the range and a tap with running water.

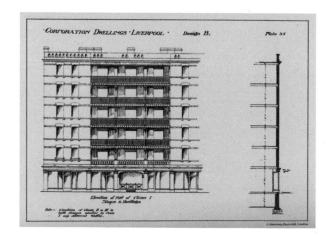

the Labouring Classes in 1844; both organizations constructed 'model' self-contained flats. Model Houses for Families in Streatham Street, Bloomsbury, was an 1850 venture where, as the architect Henry Roberts wrote, 'domestic privacy could be preserved and independence of each distinct family; in addition separate living quarters, and galleries leading off open stairways would prevent the spread of contagious disease.' These buildings were intended to turn a modest profit in order for the scheme to be self-perpetuating and this proved a limitation. Five per cent was generally acceptable but Prince Albert was reported to have said to the architect: 'Mr. Roberts, unless we can get seven to eight per cent, we shall not succeed in inducing builders to invest their capital in such houses.'

One of the most effective of the number of housing organizations established between the 1850s and 1870s was set up in 1862 by George Peabody, a rich and exceptionally philanthropic American merchant banker living in London. The purpose of his Peabody Donation Fund was to provide good-quality housing for artisans, the industrious poor – not seasonal or piece workers. Less than two years later, in 1864, the first Peabody building opened in Commercial Street, Spitalfields, and in moved

RIGHT Corporation Buildings, Farringdon Road, London: a large block erected in 1865, designed by Alfred Allen and Horace Jones. Each tenement had its own scullery and fireplaces. Clothes could be hung out to dry on the roof.
OPPOSITE Banister Fletcher's 1871 design for flats in two-storey houses, each floor having two flats consisting of two rooms. The scullery, larder, sink and WC – and place for rubbish – led off the living room.

(among others) a charwoman, a monthly nurse, a basket-maker, a butcher, a carpenter, a fireman, a shoemaker, a porter, a tailor and a waiter. Slums had to be cleared and suitable sites acquired: a map produced for the Peabody Trustees in 1879 pinpoints eleven estates which between them provided 2,377 tenements for 9,905 people and shows the sites of a further seven. The inhabitants had strict rules, were to pay the rent, lead sober honest lives, be clean and thrifty; they were not the indigent or outcast. Peabody's architect, Henry Darbishire, set a pattern for blocks of flats, preferably around a square which provided a safe place for children to play. The sinks and water closets were on the landings outside the flats; this allowed for regular inspections to be made for cleanliness. An advanced system of chutes took rubbish from each floor down to ground level. Peabody flats were workmanlike, identical, unornamented.

'Barracks' was the word continuously associated with model flats, and their height was, for the period, overwhelming. Streatham Street was described as 'a plain, but handsome and massive building of very considerable size . . .' George Gissing set his novel *The Nether World* (1889) in Clerkenwell, where the Hewett family move from a slum to a tenement flat on the fifth storey of a huge block, Farringdon Road Buildings. This had been built in 1874 by the Metropolitan Association for Improving Dwellings of the Industrious Classes to house 265 families. Gissing places John Hewett and his three daughters here, living in two rooms. The author was alive to the problems of poverty but still regarded the buildings as 'terrible barracks . . . Vast, sheer walls, unbroken by even an attempt at ornament; row above row of windows in the mud-coloured surface . . . An inner courtyard, asphalted, swept clean – looking up to the sky as from a prison . . . millions of tons of brute brick and mortar, crushing the spirit as you gaze. Barracks, in truth; housing for the army of industrialism.' Newly built Farringdon Road also had along it Corporation Buildings, built in 1865 by the City of London to house 168 families on six storeys, and an 1884 Peabody estate of eleven blocks. Size and regimentation were also criticized by James Hole, a housing reformer who worked mainly in Leeds. He thought it unlikely that the independent artisan would be reconciled to living in such blocks in any town or city apart from London, where the price of land was so enormous. He worried (in his book on *Working Class Homes and Suggestions for their Improvement*, 1871) too that the system of building in flats, unless properly watched, increased the evils of overcrowding, and cited some Glasgow blocks where the inhabitants of one building could almost touch the washing hanging out from the opposite block and gossip across the divide. The buildings superintendents' 'continued interference makes the inhabitants feel rather too much like the inmates of a public establishment, and prefer any miserable tenement where their actions are comparatively uncontrolled.' They could seem slightly too similar to the workhouse for comfort.

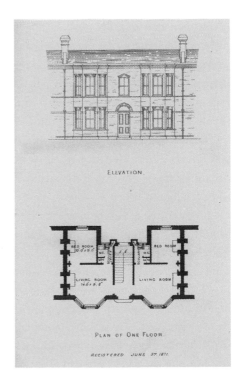

ELEVATION.

PLAN OF ONE FLOOR.

REGISTERED JUNE 5TH 1871.

In 1871 the architect Banister Fletcher proposed disguising flats as terraces of two-storey cottages. Such buildings would, he considered, avoid the odium of living in model blocks, since it would appear 'that the house is the residence of some respectable member of the "lower middle" class of society.' It would give tenants a sense of comfort and 'to coin an expressive word "homishness"', infinitely preferable to 'huge hives containing such large numbers that privacy was next to impossible'.

This was in fact a pattern widely used in Tyneside – Newcastle, Gateshead, Sunderland – where the terraces were divided horizontally rather than on the back-to-back system of other northern industrial towns. Probably the earliest Tyneside flats were on the Shipcote Estate in Gateshead, built by William Affleck in 1866. Here each had its own front and back entrance and its own yard space. This pattern was later used in suburban areas, and self-contained half-house flats were described by a writer in 1907 as being particularly suitable for the aged and 'persons of very slender means'.

Henry Darbishire was convinced that the Peabody model was a good one. In 1884 he told an audience at the Parkes Museum of Hygiene that the system of model dwellings could be extended to the entire working-class population – rather than being limited to artisans earning over 23 shillings per week – but first tenants would have to be divided according to wage and occupation. Sweeps and costermongers, for example, should be put together due to 'their absence of cleanliness'. (The housing reformer Octavia Hill pointed out that the problem with costermongers was that they owned donkeys.) There was a general distrust of block inhabitants. S.F. Murphy in *Our Homes and How to Make them Healthy* feared in 1883 that deterioration might occur 'when the tenements have been constantly occupied for such a length of time that the walls, floors, ceilings etc shall have become saturated with the continual exhalations of their inhabitants.' Henry Spalding, an architect who designed a block for Manchester, blithely asserted in a 1900 RIBA journal that the working classes had not adapted themselves to baths in flats: 'I do not wish to under-rate the importance of hygiene, but hygiene is not valued by the working man and so for its advantages he does not care to pay . . . some years ago it was the custom to provide baths in many of the dwellings; now it is seldom done, and considering that public baths are accessible in most neighbourhoods . . . Also it is no great hardship for people of this class to share a scullery with another family.' Sydney Perks, writing in *Residential Flats of All Classes* (1905), also thought baths unnecessary, citing hot water as a too 'heavy expense' for working-class flats. He also advised that (tenants of this class tending to be destructive) walls should be cement rather than wood – and that knobs placed on stair rails would prevent children from sliding down them. Charles Booth in the 1902 conclusion to his volumes on the state of Londoners decided that block dwellings were 'better than slums – that is all'. He prefigured complaints about tower blocks when he wrote that 'the worst of them have dark stairs without gates, of which sleeping places are made. The condition of such stairs at night is often a scandal.' However, he felt that, on the whole, 'the restrictions make people decent.' Councillor Parkins of Birmingham reported in 1901 that having inspected the 'the flat system' in Manchester he had decided that the Corporation should not build any: they were expensive and inconvenient. He had also noted that some successful candidates in recent elections were men who had placarded the walls with 'No More Barracks'.

The Peabody blocks remain as plain and unornamented landmarks, having frequently housed several generations of the same family, many happy to be identified as Peabody families. Reg Blackwell, who lived in Bedfordbury from 1925 to 1948, described it as 'like living in a village. Everybody knew each other and were friends, not just neighbours. It probably arose from the fact that Peabody set standards which we had to live up to and with rules which we dare not disobey.' Being a family of thirteen children the Blackwells had one of the largest flats, with four rooms. The buildings changed little until after the Second World War and certain features, such as the stone steps, must have seared themselves into the memories of thousands of inhabitants over the years. Alan Kingshott was born in the Peabody Buildings in Hammersmith in 1947 and left when he married in 1967. This estate had been built in 1926 and was the last with separate bathhouses. '66 steps led up to our flat and they have been etched on my mind, carved on my soul and ingrained in my being for evermore. Our rented home was on the top floor of a 5 storey block.' The steps were kept scrupulously clean and had to be washed once a week by the tenants. The coal bunker was in the kitchen alongside the kitchen sink. Deliveries were made randomly, even during supper, at which point the family would be covered in a burst of coal dust as the sacks were emptied. The tin bathtub was stored in the kitchen and laboriously filled once a week, in preference to facing the 'Bath place' with its lack of privacy. Not until the mid-1950s could the regulation green distemper finally be covered by a wallpaper of choice. Alan Kingshott remembers the entire family living in the kitchen, warmed by the heat from the open gas oven, until the purchase of a television in 1953 finally drew them into the living room.

It took the LCC, which became responsible for housing at its inception in 1889, to build something more interesting than rectangular blocks. The Boundary Estate in Bethnal Green was so large that a new road plan was created. At the centre was Arnold Circus, an open space crowned with a bandstand, built on top of the rubble from the Old Nichol slum. Flats were larger and nearly all had a private water closet and their own scullery. With pitched roofs, gables and dormer windows, they could no longer be

Arnold Circus on the Boundary Estate, 1897: photographs of (left) the newly completed flats looking out on to green space and trees, and (right) the interior of the Club Room laid out for lectures.

mistaken for a workhouse. However, like the Peabody schemes, they were intended for the respectable working class, in the belief that such people would learn by example from good housing and move 'upwards'. Only eleven of the tenants came from the cleared slums from which 5,719 people were reputedly moved.

OVERCOMING RESISTANCE TO FLATS

SCOTLAND APART, the urban middle and upper classes did not take naturally to living in flats, unlike their equivalents in, for example, Paris or New York. When he rearranged Paris in the 1850s Baron Haussmann created wide, straight boulevards flanked by palatial stone buildings housing apartments. Façades and floors were of regulation height and uniform balconies formed straight lines at selected storeys. Parisians lodged their servants in the roof, perambulated along the wide pavements and flocked to cafés for a social life. What the French also did – something that was incomprehensible to the Victorian British – was to live in blocks that housed people of differing social classes, a fact noted in *The Architect*: 'It would be difficult to quote any custom of the French which English people might less readily fall in with than that which assigns the tenancy of the half dozen successive storeys of the same house to just as many utterly dissociated and indeed discordant people, ranging from a jaunty viscount on the *premier étage*, not merely to a very small *rentier* on the *troisième*, but to a nest of the humblest work-people on the *cinquième*, all meeting on the common stair.'

New Yorkers too had begun to live in flats; the city's population had burgeoned after the Civil War and land on Manhattan Island was limited. The middle class had therefore to abandon vertical living in single houses for something higher and horizontal. This they did with some trepidation, as multiple dwellings were associated, as in England, with deprivation and with tenements – notorious for catching fire. However, in 1869 Richard Morris Hunt, an architect trained in Paris, built the first apartment block in New York, the Stuyvesant Apartments – often referred to as the French Flats. The term 'French flat' stuck throughout the 1870s and 1880s, despite a nervousness about things French in conservative quarters – a sentiment caught by Edith Wharton in her novel *The Age of Innocence*, set in 1870s New York. Mrs Manson Mingott, too old to climb the stairs of her house, lives solely on the ground floor: 'Her visitors were startled and fascinated by the foreignness of this arrangement, which recalled scenes in French fiction, and architectural incentives to immorality such as the simple American had never dreamed of. This was how women with lovers lived in wicked old societies, in apartments with all the rooms on one floor, and all the indecent propinquities that their novels described.' In fact the Americans soon embraced the convenience of apartments. The exertion of climbing stairs was eliminated by the invention of a lift system by Elisha Otis, who demonstrated his safety elevator in New York as early as 1854. Richard Morris Hunt's apartment block, the Florence, built in the late 1870s, reached seven storeys high. The *New York Times* declared at the end of that decade that there had been a 'revolution in living', with flats appearing in the best quarters of town and occupied by the well-to-do.

In London too it became necessary to demonstrate that the middle-class flat could be quite a different proposition from the working-class block dwellings that were becoming familiar. *The Builder* magazine announced in December 1853 that a Mr Mackenzie had erected a fine set of buildings, at a height of 82 feet from the basement to the roof, 'to supply what has long been a desideratum in London, namely complete residences on flats, as in Edinburgh and Paris . . .' These were in Victoria Street. It was explained that inhabitants would not be abandoned in some giant barracks, but that human contact was nearby. 'A porter resides on the premises, who performs all the duties usually performed by a hall-porter in a private residence, and the hall and staircase are lighted at night at the expense of the proprietor, and kept in a proper manner.'

An account of an early flat visit is given by Nathaniel Hawthorne in his journal entry for 9 July 1856: 'We were invited yesterday evening to Mrs. S.C. Hall's, where Jenny Lind was to sing; so we left Blackheath at about eight o'clock in a brougham, and reached Ashley Place, as the dusk was gathering, after nine. The Halls reside in a handsome suite of apartments, arranged on the new system of flats, each story constituting a separate tenement, and various families having an entrance-hall in common. The plan is borrowed from the Continent, and seems rather alien to the traditionary habits of the English.' The Halls were a literary and slightly unconventional couple: Mrs Hall was an Irish playwright and author of children's books, and her husband, Samuel Carter Hall, was the 'volubly sanctimonious' editor of the *Art Journal*.

As *Building News* noted in 1868, the perception of flats was changing. They were 'no longer built exclusively for the lower classes. They are being adopted by the other extreme of society, and the success of those in Victoria-street have led to the building of others in the aristocratic Grosvenor Mansions at Pimlico. Having thus been partially adopted by both extremes of English Society, we hope before long to see them adopted by the middle strata, when they shall have had experience of their comforts, privacy and convenience.' But it was the lower middle class, sensitive to their position, who were least likely to embrace flat-living.

Amidst all the writing on different sorts of housing, lodgings – rented rooms in private houses – always appeared as the worst option. No one, it seems, ever enjoyed living in them; the idea that the middle classes could be rescued from this terrible fate and put into flats was obvious and attractive. But it met with fierce opposition. The subject was discussed at the Royal Institute of British Architects (RIBA) at a meeting in December 1877, when a Mr White gave a paper on 'Middle Class Housing in London and Paris'. He argued that rather than penetrating ever deeper into the outer suburbs architects should be 'called upon to erect in the central parts of London houses in flats rather than ordinary self-contained dwelling houses. The higgledy-piggledy confusion of lodging houses allowed for no privacy of family life.' Flats were highly acceptable to London's large number of bachelors and people with no families. Discussion on this was heated. The President, Sir Charles Barry, wound up the proceedings with the remark 'that it would be difficult for the generality of Englishmen to imagine anything more miserable or more uncomfortable. Mr. White wanted not only to revolutionise our houses, but our instincts, and habits and modes of life.'

Naming blocks of flats 'mansions' was a step in the right direction, as was using the word in association with a name that conveyed establishment and longevity, such as Addison, Carlyle, Prince's, Mortimer, York Gate, Oxford & Cambridge, Cornwall,

Priory, or Museum. Albert Hall Mansions, looking over Hyde Park, was one of the earliest. This was a scheme conceived by a developer called Thomas Hussey in 1876. After several false starts he employed leading architect Richard Norman Shaw, who designed the block in three stages, so the project could be abandoned if it looked like failing. It was built between 1880 and 1886, rose to six storeys and included wine cellars, bathrooms and a hydraulic lift. With Dutch gables, oriel windows, recessed balconies and generous windows, it was an imposing building that clearly proclaimed it was in no way related to working-class block dwellings. This was a lesson quickly absorbed and fancy architectural detail was rarely missing from the blocks of mansion flats built with dizzying speed over the next twenty years. A sales description of flats in Cadogan Gardens notes the impressive and expensive architectural detail in full: 'There is nothing wanting in the main entrance halls, which are spacious and lofty, being approached through handsome mahogany and plate glass doors, ornamented on each side by massive white marble and stone columns, with floors laid in mosaic.' In addition the building was supplied with Waygood's passenger lifts, day and night porters, tradesmen's lifts and constant hot water. During this period many new thoroughfares were being built and the tall mansion blocks fitted naturally and easily into them. Victoria Street, completed in the 1880s, was particularly popular and included Queen Anne's Mansions, which had risen to an unprecedented fourteen storeys and irritated Queen Victoria as it blocked her view of Westminster from Buckingham Palace. The 'lofty mansions' along Prince of Wales Drive of the 1890s successfully screened the less salubrious parts of Battersea from those enjoying the park.

The existence of a lift, preferably ornamented with veneer and brass, was essential for flats of any pretension, and considered crucial for anything over four storeys. Early mansion blocks, such as Albert Hall Mansions, had hydraulic lifts using power supplied by the London Hydraulic Power Company and transmitted through a vast underground network of pressurized water. Here there was also a 'speaking tube' for communicating with the hall porter. A company called R. Waygood led the field in making the lift cages until the American firm of Otis opened a London office in 1902 and launched their electrical gearless traction lift. Discussion in the *Builder's Journal* in 1905 concluded that electric lifts were superior: hydraulic lifts worked with hand rope control by a lift operator – 'there is a certain amount of labour in stopping and starting and considerable judgement required in accurately reaching the landing level'; whereas with electric lifts it was possible 'to use an automatic push-button control, which can

be operated by a lady or child without the slightest exertion'. The success of electric lifts also boosted the case for electric, rather than gas, lighting. Not only did lift interiors need to be illuminated, but so did the long dark corridors that inevitably occurred in the design of large blocks. One of the early objections to flats was that infectious diseases would spread rapidly: a correspondent in *The Spectator* reported in the early 1890s that in a block where there was a smallpox patient, crisis was averted by banning the doctor from using the lift and by replacing the stair carpet.

An enterprising firm of estate agents, Robins, Snell and Gore (later Terry), launched *Flats, an Illustrated Paper for Owners and Occupiers and all Interested in Flats and Maisonettes* in August 1889. They described themselves as specialists in the letting of flats, chambers and upper parts, and in each early edition relentlessly reprinted the reasons why living in a flat was so desirable.

Fire proof floors
Safety from neighbouring fires
No stairs
Only one servant necessary, two at the most
Drainage perfect, buildings of flats being of modern erection
Burglaries never heard of
No Rates or taxes
No beggars or tramps
No dust to clear away
No caretaker necessary when away for a holiday

In later issues they also listed the advantage of 'No snow to clear away in winter' and added 'or canvassers' to the nuisance of beggars and tramps.

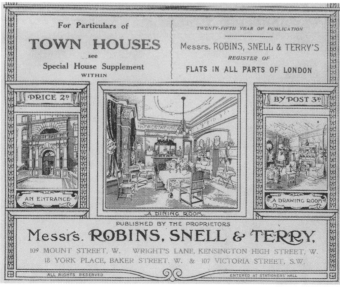

OPPOSITE A lift cage for a mansion block, 1910: carved wood, stained glass, carpet and plush-covered seat.

ABOVE The magazine *Flats*, a promotional tool of the estate agents Robins, Snell and Terry.

The author Mrs Haweis gave her opinion of flats in *The Art of Housekeeping* (1889): they were worth considering since they were often in convenient neighbourhoods. Furthermore, 'To the inexperienced, immunity from the affronts of tax-collectors, and from troubles with repairs, drains, roofs, servants and stairs, shines like a veritable land of promise, and therefore for single persons or couples, flats are often convenient . . . Among its brilliant attractions, one is that a flat can be forsaken and returned to, without any responsibility.' On the 'grave' disadvantages: 'There is a sort of chronic reverberation right up the hollow stairway which is peculiar to flat-life, and particularly disagreeable to some people. There is not much peace if a brother-lodger is musical, or let us say convivial. There is but little real privacy. It is a bore going up and down with the same people in the same lift, and one ends by going as seldom as possible. Without a lift the stairs tire out the robustest friendship. The scandal-mongering is as bad as in any hotel; sometimes the servants belonging to the lower floors are said to levy toll on the goods of the upper storeys – especially confectionery . . . Coals, wine and stores can be laid in only in the most moderate quantities, for want of space . . . In case of a sudden illness at night, a good many people besides one's own servant would have to be disturbed before the doctor can be fetched, for the lights are extinguished at a certain hour, and there is by no means always a night-porter on the premises. For extra trouble tips are expected . . .'

FLAT-DWELLERS

MRS HAWEIS'S INTENDED READERSHIP of late Victorian brides might have preferred to start married life in a suburban house. The flat versus suburb debate was alive at the turn of the century. Estate agent Leonard Snell vociferously promoted the flat not only via the magazine *Flats* but also in the architectural press. If a rose-covered cottage in the suburbs seemed preferable to 'herding in a hotel-flat amid the din and hurry of a great city', then a couple of months commuting on the South-Eastern and Chatham Railway was 'calculated to knock romance on the head'. Snell had first-hand knowledge of flat life, since in the early 1900s he became the manager of Marlborough Mansions at 83–91 Victoria Street. He persuaded the building's owners that they should give him this position with no salary and instead he should take commission on new rentals, and have a bedroom in the building and free meals in the restaurant. His manager's notebook lists his plans: carpet the stairs, halls and lifts; put electric fan in larder; paint water pipes; cease to supply soap; all complaints to manageress; quarterly prizes for best-kept hall and lifts; decide what to do with empty bottles; no shouting down the speaking tube (tradesmen would be banned if they disregarded this). He makes notes on the hall porter's job: they should work from seven to seven; look after the lift boys and report deviation of duty; they must be clean, properly booted and smart; keep servants out of the hall; receive letters and parcels and attend to the telephone. There should be a page in attendance on the hall porter and the lift boys should give 'the necessary salutes and show at all times deference to tenants coming and going'.

As manager he proposed spending £100–£200 on advertisements in all the principal evening papers three days a week, the *Morning Post* every day, also *Country Life*, *The Field*, the *Sporting Times* and *The Observer*. This was a competitive market, as building flats had been considered a good investment in the 1890s. With the enthusiasm of a zealot, Snell came up with the idea that the area covered by London could be reduced by one-third if its entire population lived in flats.

By 1911 there was a glut of flats, and the *Architects' and Builders' Journal* asked the question in its editorial, 'Is The Flat Still Fashionable?', stating 'that period has passed when people took to dwelling in them because it seemed a novel and daring thing to do . . . a desire to flout the common complaint of commonplace people that flats were unhomelike, and thus acquire a sort of spurious reputation for independence of thought by defying public opinion.' Hermann Muthesius was almost certainly expressing the views held by the majority when he stated, in 1904, that for the English 'flat-dwelling can only be regarded as an emergency substitute for living in a private house' and that it was not possible for 'the present-day urban flat to replace all the moral and ethical values that are inherent in the private house'.

Flat-dwellers themselves could be suspect: a shifting, even shiftless population. In his novel *The Whirlpool* (1897) George Gissing depicts two households which could have been perceived as typical: one, that of a woman living on her own in reduced circumstances, the other a rootless couple where the wife is distinctly averse to domestic life. In *The Odd Women*, which Gissing wrote four years earlier, Monica Madden, uneducated but aspiring to a better life, is compromised by young Mr Bevis, who lures her into his flat in Bayswater, pretending that his sisters will also be there. Monica enters and is surprised to find it empty. 'She looked round and saw Bevis's countenance gleaming with satisfaction . . . So perfectly natural was his manner, that Monica, after the first moment of consternation, tried to forget that there was anything irregular in her presence here under these circumstances. As regards social propriety, a flat differs in many respects from a house. In an ordinary drawing room, it could scarcely have mattered if Bevis had entertained her for a short space until his sisters' arrival; but in this little set of rooms it was doubtfully permissible for her to sit *tête à tête* with a young man under any excuse. And the fact of his opening the front door himself seemed to suggest that there was not a servant in the flat. A tremor grew upon her as she talked.' This is clearly a case of Edith Wharton's indecent propinquity. Monica's situation is worsened by another architectural feature: she is seen going into the common entrance of the Bayswater flats by her insanely jealous husband, who assumes she is going to spend time alone with the altogether more alluring Everard Barfoot, who in fact lived on a different floor.

Flats in Earl's Court, designed by R.A. Briggs, 1905. Listed among 'Flats for Moderate Incomes'. An illustration from *Flats, Urban Houses and Cottage Homes*, ed. W. Shaw Sparrow, 1906.

In this novel Gissing also places Mrs Luke Widdowson, a widow living a life of 'feverish aspiration' in a flat in Victoria Street. Here, dressed in mourning garb in the extreme of the prevailing fashion, she holds court among costly and beautiful things, with perfume soothing the air and 'opportunities of freedom'. Her flat attracts 'a heterogeneous cluster of pleasure-seekers and fortune hunters, among them one or two vagrant members of the younger aristocracy. She lived at the utmost pace compatible with technical virtue.' George Bernard Shaw too saw the atmosphere of a Victoria Street flat as louche. In the opening scene of *The Philanderer*, also written in the 1890s, it is past ten at night in the flat in Ashley Gardens of another young widow, Grace Tanfield, whose morals are hinted at by the presence of a yellow-backed French novel. 'She is just now given up to the emotion of the moment.' Her suitor is theatre critic Leonard Charteris, a gentleman a few years older, 'unconventionally but smartly dressed in a velvet jacket and cashmere trousers. His collar, dyed Wotan blue, is part of his shirt, and turns over a garnet coloured scarf of Indian silk, secured by a turquoise ring. He wears blue socks and leather sandals.' In fact, of course, Victoria Street flats proved highly convenient for MPs, government officials and colonial officers.

THE PROBLEM OF SPACE

ATTEMPTS TO PUT A POSITIVE SLANT on the limited space meant that the word 'cosy' made frequent appearances in magazine articles on the subject. In 1897 a feature in *The Lady* worried about the limited area available in modern 'mansions' – 'living in a flat is a liberal education in the art of tidiness.' More importantly, lack of space created its own servant problem. Discussion of how to deal with servants in flats and to what extent they could be dispensed with was perennial. As early as 1870 *Building News* ran an article which pointed out that life in a flat could mean fewer servants: the calculation was made that if a five-storey house required three servants, a flat could be managed with two or even one.

Rarely did flats attempt to recreate all the facilities of a town house, but the 'Flats-de-luxe' in Gloucester House, Piccadilly, built on the site of a Georgian mansion that had been inhabited by a couple of royal dukes, were described in 1907 as being only for millionaires. The architects Collcutt and Hamp created the largest flats in London, complete with servants' hall, housekeeper's room and butler's pantry, plus enough servants' bedrooms for a task force sufficient to look after an entrance hall of 35 x 50

LEFT Photograph used in a feature on the interior design of flats, 1905: 'This illustration suggests a means by which the sitting-room in a flat may be connected with the hall . . . arching of carved wood in the manner of the Morris school.'
RIGHT Design by the architect C.R. Ashbee for Shrewsbury Court in Chelsea, published in *The Studio*, 1905.

feet, a drawing room and boudoir that could be combined to make a 70-foot-long ballroom, numerous bedrooms and three bathrooms. All this within a steel structure faced with Carrara ware 'the colour of old ivory'.

More typical was the flat created by Ada Leverson in *The Little Ottleys* (1908). 'She was seated opposite her husband at breakfast in a very new, very small, very white flat in Knightsbridge – exactly like thousand of other new, small, white flats.' Edith Ottley's husband, Bruce, bemoans the fact that they have no valet: 'But it would be more awful if we had,' said Edith. 'Where on earth could we put him – except in the bathroom?'

Fitting servants into regular-sized flats was a problem. In a house boundaries were easily made: servants could be kept out of sight in the basement or sound-proofed in the servants' quarters beyond the baize door. In a flat a live-in servant generally had to be lodged beyond the kitchen, but there was then the worry of her carrying her slops through the kitchen – and how to find the space to keep the servant's water closet well apart from the larder? While servants complained that flat kitchens were too small, their employers worried that servants walking down the passage to the entrance door would overhear conversations in the principal rooms.

There was an ambiguity to living in flats – on the one hand they were described as places where women could be freed from the tyranny of servants and housekeeping and the 'uncontrollable back door', but on the other it was considered that by living in flats women were shirking their home-making responsibilities. To avoid the necessity

of providing a servants' staircase, service lifts were often installed to manage bulky deliveries such as coal and tradesmen's orders. Increasingly, daily charwomen were favoured over live-in maids, who in any case were being tempted out to far more interesting and social occupations in shops and factories. Part of the attraction of mansion flats, such as Leonard Snell's Marlborough Mansions, was that as they offered 'Cleansing and Arrangement of Rooms' and a Private Dining Room, so it was possible to manage entirely without employing servants. The words 'plus attendance' appear frequently in advertisements for flats: this usually refers to cleaning and laundry. On the other hand, old habits died hard and in Evelyn Waugh's novel *Handful of Dust* (1934), when Brenda Last escapes from her husband and large country establishment to a house just off Belgrave Square subdivided into six flats, each with one room and a bath – 'somewhere to dress and telephone' – she brings her maid, Grimshawe, to London with her. However, 'It's a bore and an expense boarding her out in London', so she thinks she might do without her. The cleaning is done by a woman with a mop and bucket three times a week.

The idea of the service flat, where everything was done by the management, evolved during the 1920s. It was described in *How to Live in a Flat* (1936) by the comic writer K.R.G. Browne as 'guaranteed to do everything for its occupants except pay the rent and blow their noses. Indeed when the tenants of the high class service flat have brushed their teeth, eaten their meals and gone bankrupt they have done all they are allowed to do with their own fair hands.'

Hall porters, managers and superintendents were vital figures in setting the tone of the block – and, incidentally, in acting as the eyes and ears of the management company. Sydney Perks in *Residential Flats of all Classes* made an observation that the easiest flats to manage were those where the tenants had little chance to meet and socialize. A communal ornamental garden, for example, was a very doubtful blessing since in summer the tenants flocked to it, and this engendered 'numerous complaints, petty jealousies and 1001 annoyances, so much better that tenants should remain strangers'. Hall porters, like those in hotels, were put into uniform. An advertisement in *The Times* personal column in 1934 for a small flat ('10 secs. from Portland Place') emphasized the new building, lifts, artistic decoration, central heating and 'liveried porters'. The intention was perhaps to combine the obsequiousness of a liveried servant in an aristocratic establishment with the order and security of the military. The central figure of Charles Lorne's novel *Flat to Let* (1938) is the hall porter, who has a uniform with a peaked cap and sees himself as 'a sort of sergeant-major . . . a man to keep an eye on things and see that people behave themselves and don't go setting the place on fire'.

FLATS AND FEMALE EMANCIPATION

It became clear that the growth of flats was a particular boon to women; they could live respectably either singly or in groups. The Ladies' Residential Chambers had been a small beginning. A flat relieved women of external chores that tended to be a male preserve. At the end of the nineteenth century there were half a million or so women for whom it was said 'there is no making a pair'. This generation struggled to acquire an education, qualifications and skills to lead worthwhile independent lives and earn a living wage. An interview with Fanny Wilkinson, the first woman to be a professional landscape gardener, was written up in the *Women's Penny Paper* in 1890. The journalist enthused about her 'charming flat in Bloomsbury', which was on the newly built Shaftesbury Avenue. 'Her rooms have a pleasant country air about them, and it would be difficult to imagine that one was in the heart of the big city in her pretty drawing room. It is the home of a lady, and instinctively one feels its owner must be a woman of refined taste.'

A novel published in 1896, *Three Girls in a Flat* by Ethel F. Heddle, has the theme of women trying to make it on their own in London. The setting is Wilkie Mansions, Chelsea; three Scottish girls, Lil, Janet and Mabel, in straitened circumstances, are lent the flat by a Miss Madge Fairlie – 'she's the lady who goes in for improving poor people's houses and that sort of thing.' Since they have not been educated up to the standard required for a governess, they scrabble for work. Mabel is offered the post of Lady Mainwaring's secretary for a few hours a day, Janet cooks and decorates the flat with furniture bargains from the Seven Sisters Road painted white, art muslin at three ha'pence a yard and pink shaded lights, while Lil writes novelettes 'for the great middle class, the bourgeois middle class of shop-girls and school-girls and the people who live in the suburbs of London – in little red-brick houses with a balcony and a conservatory'. An impoverished old woman living in one room sublet from the flat below points to a bleak future. As Lil says to an elderly relation who worries what the girls' mother would have thought of the 'three Bohemians': 'It isn't only men who "must work"; Women must, too, nowadays. Don't you know that there are ninety thousand more women than men in England? And, after all, work is a fine thing – the "glorious privilege of being independent".'

Mabel's job with Lady Mainwaring is in an Albert Hall Mansions flat, a great contrast to the Wilkie Mansions walk-up: 'a marvel of comfort and beauty' with 'a luxurious little drawing-room whose balcony faced the large red disc of the Albert Hall . . . in the season this balcony is covered with an awning, and they go right round it to the dining-room, and girls sit here on lounges, and flirt and talk.' Sir Algernon Mainwaring does not quite grasp the girls' poverty, with their suppers of bread and jam and constant worries about coal. '"Awfully plucky and jolly, setting up for yourselves like that! I hope you like it?" The Baronet touched an electric button, and then warmed his hands at the logs in their shiny andirons. "Jolly convenient things, these bells, aren't they?" he hazarded at last, finding the blue eyes rather alarming in their cool survey. "Got them in your flat?"'

Edith Heddle's three Scottish girls would have found life far more congenial in Waterlow Court in Hampstead Garden Suburb. This was a project funded by the Improved Industrial Dwelling Company established by Sir Sidney Waterlow and instigated by Henrietta Barnett. Built in 1909, it provided flats for working women and was designed by the Arts and Crafts architect M.H. Baillie Scott. He took a square plan with a central courtyard, closer in style to an Oxford college than a Peabody building: an arcaded cloister linked all four sides of the quadrangle and made a covered approach to the communal dining room. Each flat had a small kitchen in case the inhabitant preferred home cooking, and a bicycle shed was provided in the grounds. The forty-seven original inhabitants, Ediths, Winifreds, Gladyses and Dorises, presented Henrietta Barnett with a photograph album depicting life at Waterlow Court which shows games of tennis, amateur theatricals, women reading in peaceful interiors with chintz pelmets, fireplaces, art pottery, bamboo tables, bookshelves, prints and thick-leaved pot plants in copper bowls, and sunny afternoons entertaining mothers and children from the Canning Town Settlement for tea on the lawn.

Like the poor, single women were definitely a cause. The Lady Workers' Homes Co. Ltd had established flats in St John's Wood, from where one of the residents wrote to the company in 1911, praising her flat, for 'other flats I have seen seem to be designed by architects who have no idea of the needs of the educated woman of small means,

only recognising the artisan's wife . . . who does all her own washing and cooking.' The company also built mansion blocks in half-timbered Tudor style on Holly Lodge Estate in Highgate, on the site of the philanthropist Baroness Burdett-Coutts's old home (and a stone's throw away from the enclosed Gothic Revival 'hamlet' that she had built sixty years earlier for her old retainers). Both these schemes had communal facilities in the shape of an entertainment room and a dining hall, and the Holly Lodge flats even had a small theatre. It was only at the end of the twentieth century that Camden Council abandoned the women-only policy for these flats.

'Evening brings all home' was the caption beside an illustration of a 'cosy flatlet' with a comfortable armchair beside a glowing fireside. This was put out by Women's Pioneer Housing Ltd, a co-operative founded in 1921 to address the difficulties that 'self-dependent' women had finding homes. Appropriately, they employed Gertrude Leverkus, who the year before had been the only woman among five hundred men to take her architecture finals at University College, to convert large properties into small flats where a woman 'can express her individuality, for the completeness of a woman's life depends on the comfort and beauty of her home.' Some were outside 'the noise of London', in Sussex Square in Brighton.

The 1911 census listed flats for the first time: 3.4 per cent of the population lived in them. After the upheaval of the First World War and the social changes in its aftermath, flats became one solution to the housing shortage. The division of unwieldy Georgian and Victorian terrace houses into flats was a process that occurred in cities all over Britain, accelerating as the twentieth century progressed. Dorothy L. Sayers in *Unnatural Death* (1927) succinctly described 'one of those tall awkward mansions, which originally designed for a Victorian family with fatigue-proof servants, have lately been dissected into a dozen inconvenient band boxes and let off in flats.' Such conversions did not have the convenience of purpose-built flats, but provided cheap alternatives. Winifred Holtby and Vera Brittain were exceptionally focused on their lives after graduating from Oxford in the early 1920s. Needing to be near the British Museum Reading Room, they lived first in a ground-floor studio and then in a top-floor flat in tall late eighteenth-century houses in Doughty Street, WC1. Winifred Holtby wrote to her friend, Rosalind: 'December 3, 1921, Yesterday morning I started off at ten-thirty to look for a flat, rooms, anything at all, where Vera and I could live and move and have our being when neither teaching nor reading ... I went to an agent, who seemed unaware of the existence of anything less than an eight-guinea "mansion".'

On New Year's Day 1922 she wrote again, from The Studio, 52 Doughty Street, 'Vera and I let ourselves in and out of the front door with our latch keys and walk straight along the passage to our own little front door that has a green curtain hanging across it. Inside, it all really looks charming now. We have a hall mantelpiece with some blue Spode plates which mother gave me, and an old brass candlestick, and my polished shell-case, and four blue pots from Malta . . . Does all this bore you? You've had a little flat too, and probably feel very blasé over the delights of our first housekeeping. You know quite well the triumph of entering the ironware department of Shoolbred's and ordering an enamel basin for the kitchen sink, with the air of a housewife of fifty . . .'

They basked in their freedom, their 'independent enthralling London existence' as Vera Brittain put it, with 'few comforts and no luxuries except a tortoise called Adolphus who died prematurely' and the 'pleasant trivialities of daily routine with mop and duster, egg and cheese suppers cooked on a gas ring, adornment by coloured bowls of bluebells and wallflowers picked up cheap from a pavement flower-seller . . . Neither of us had ever known any pleasure quite equal to the joy of coming home at the end of the day after a series of separate varied experiences, and each recounting these incidents to the other over late tea and biscuits, Winifred sitting on the floor in front of a tiny gas fire.' After two years they moved to Wymering Mansions in Maida

Vale. As Vera Brittain wrote in *The Testament of Friendship*, 'our sole object in moving to the unfashionable end of the Edgware Road was to acquire space for a housekeeper who would shoulder all domestic obligations.'

Flats were excellent for providing a temporary solution to life, as novels of the period frequently testify. The novelist John Galsworthy twice dispatches women of uncertain reputations to mansion flats in Chelsea. In *The Country House* (1907), Helen Bellew, estranged from her husband, is described at home, her chin resting on her hand, her gaze fixed on nothing, in a room 'with a sulky canary in a small gilt cage, an upright piano with an open operatic score, a sofa with piled-up cushions'. Fleur Forsyte, after she has abandoned Soames on the death of her lover Bosinney, in *In Chancery* (1920), lives in a mansion block and helps fallen women. Lady Carstairs in *Lipstick* (1925), by socialite writer Lady Kitty Vincent, is 'a little tired of living in the country all the year round', and being, characteristically for the period, no longer able to afford a house in town for the Season, rents a flat in the Brompton Road for four guineas a week, 'an exquisite flat. All panelled in green and gold, with the most beautiful furniture, although perhaps a little flamboyant.' Disaster strikes when it emerges that the owner, Miss Vesey, has failed to inform her two lovers, both of whom have latch keys, that she has rented it out. E.M. Delafield in *The Provincial Lady Goes Further* (1932) takes her heroine, flush with success and a small income from her first book, from her home in rural Devon to enjoy London literary life, again in a Doughty Street flat. 'September 25th – Doughty Street. – Quite incredibly, find myself more or less established, and startlingly independent. Flat – once I have bought electric fire, and had it installed by talkative young man with red hair – very comfortable; except for absence of really restful arm-chair, and unfamiliarity of geyser-bath, of which I am terrified. Bathroom is situated on stairs, which are in continual use, and am therefore unable to take bath with door wide open, as I should like to do.' The explosive pop of the Ascot gas water heater as the hot tap was turned on became a defining feature of converted flats. In 1947 the Ascot Gas Water Heater Ltd even sponsored the informative *Houses into Flats, Key to Conversion* by F.H. Russell.

To live away from home in a flat was a new idea. As John Gloag put it in the late 1930s, it was 'made possible by the dissolution of the old, binding family loyalty which kept the middle class in acrimonious association until marriage or death parted its members. The business girl prefers to share a flat with some other girl who has a job.' Particularly from the fifties onwards, flat-sharing became a rite of passage for most

Cover for the brochure of Northwood Hall, 1935: Art Deco curves in Highgate. Views and sunlight had become desirable features, and by building wings outwards the dark central wells which were the curse of earlier blocks were eliminated.

of the young and unmarried. Diana Athill described in her memoir *Instead of a Letter* (1963) the moment when she earned sufficient money to move into a flat shared with another girl, 'a commonplace event which must be remembered by millions of working women as the turning-point in their lives . . . when I first experienced the delicious freedom of a flat, I was astonished by the violence with which I cast off single-room living . . . In a flat we could give parties.' The Personal Column of *The Times* was pitted with those searching: 'Girl, 24, just back from working in New York, seeks flat or share of flat in Chelsea'; 'Bachelor, 28, seeks congenial flat, preferably with one other, Hampstead, Kensington, Chelsea or thereabouts'; 'Bachelor flat, Little Venice. Young actor has room to let in luxury flat. Full use k. & b. Private Garden. £10 per week'; '2 Funny Girl type girls required for bachelor flat, SW3. Ideally air hostesses.' £4.10s. each.'

MODERNISM

THE INTERWAR PERIOD, from the late twenties through the thirties, saw a boom in flat building, many of the developments on a very large scale. Once again developers made a good return on their money. The modern block had become a different beast, no longer a 'mansion', but a 'court'. It was to Wallis Simpson's 'little flat in Bryanston Court' that Sir Henry (Chips) Channon went on 14 May 1934: 'There I found Emerald, David Margesson, the Prince of Wales and one or two others. The Prince was charm itself . . . He wore a short, black coat and soft collar, checked socks and a tie . . . He shook and passed the cocktails very much the "jeune homme de la maison".' The informality implied by the soft collar and checked socks suggests the relaxed – maybe too relaxed – standards resulting from living in a flat.

The idea that flats were 'foreign' persisted. The fact that a flat, unlike a house, could not be owned outright was seen by the conservative faction as un-British. The analysis of H.I. Ashworth in his supposedly helpful book *Flats, Design and Equipment* (1936) was that 'lack of personal ownership' was 'questionable from a national point of view', since 'a degree of acquisitiveness on the part of an individual tends to produce a communal stability.' In addition, many large blocks of the late 1920s and 1930s were uncompromisingly devoid of ornament and Modernism never sat very comfortably in the British landscape. The famous quote on functional living, 'the house is a machine for living in', made by the arch-modernist Frenchman Le Corbusier in 1923, was applied to blocks of rather foreign-looking flats inspired by Europe and America. John Gloag explained that point of view: 'To those who have mastered the art of comfort, the flat can never be more than an expedient, something of an impermanent convenience . . . those people often have possessions, books, furniture and prejudices that would clash rather badly with the mechanistic functionality of the "machine to live in" flat; and they believe that the deliberate abandonment of all discoveries that were made in comfort before the present fashion in barbaric utility set in is to relinquish the whole idea of living in a home.' Gloag considered the mechanistic clarity of modern blocks of flats and residential towers 'suggest to the English mind the thin end of the wedge of regimentation' – some hateful Brave New World, a stab at the beloved British quality of individualism. Modernism was also easy to mock, as Heath Robinson and K.R.G. Browne showed in *How to Live in a Flat* (1936): 'In the last few years blocks of flats resembling Utopian prisons or Armenian glue factories have sprung up all over the place, to the delight of some and the annoyance of many.'

Heath Robinson illustration for *How to Live in a Flat*, 1936. 'In the old days the average balcony was a flimsy, open-work affair of hopelessly overwrought iron, capable only of sustaining those little old aunts and potted fuchsias . . . The modern balcony is quite another matter, being fashioned usually of the best concrete and strong enough to support three Aldermen or a county cricket XI.'

SPORT AND SOCIAL AMENITIES

HOLIDAY JOYS IN MODERN FLATS

Lawn Road Flats, built in 1934 by Jack Pritchard (the founder of Isokon furniture), and designed by Wells Coates, went as close as possible to being a machine for living. With thirty-four 'minimal' flats aimed at young professionals, the pale concrete modernist block looked shockingly different amidst Victorian red-brick Hampstead terraces. Much of the furniture, including a tiny kitchen and bed recess, was built-in, and provided by Isokon. Food was originally prepared in the communal kitchen and then sent up to individual flats by a dumb waiter system, but shortly turned into the Isobar Restaurant. Heating (electric fire supplied), hot water, cleaning, bed-making, shoe-shining and refuse collection were all available. The early tenants were as cosmopolitan as the architecture. The Pritchard family lived in the penthouse flats, Molly and Jack in one, their two sons and nanny separately in another. Other flats were inhabited by the architects Walter Gropius and Marcel Breuer and the artist and photographer Laszlo Moholy-Nagy – all émigrés from Nazi Germany for whom living in flats was the norm; the painter Adrian Stokes; the Soviet spy Dr Arnold Deutsch; and Agatha Christie, who described it as 'a giant liner'. The liner comparison was apt, since the exceptionally small dimensions led to comparisons with ship's cabins.

'Floor after floor' was, however, the way of the future. One building that pointed the way was Highpoint 1 in Highgate in 1935. This was the first example in Britain of high-rise communal living. The architect was Berthold Lubetkin of Tecton, a Russian who had trained in Berlin, Warsaw and Paris. The engineer was Ove Arup. The seven-storey reinforced concrete building, adhering perfectly to the principles of Le Corbusier, was originally intended as social housing for the employees of Gestetner, but in the end it was progressive and relatively wealthy middle-class north Londoners who lived in the sixty-four flats and enjoyed their central heating and built-in refrigerators.

Despite prejudice there were sufficient people embracing – and paying for – the luxurious modernity of flats for them to appear at seaside resorts and in the suburbs. Embassy Court on the Brighton seafront, also by Wells Coates, was finished in 1935 and advertised as 'the very Shape of Things to come – and what good things they are!' it was 'Luxury Living in the Sun, 60 minutes from London by Electric Train'. Its features included 'Vita glass sun parlours, sun decks, service and meals if required'. Sundecks and balconies suited adherents of the new fashion for acquiring a tan and the general belief in the efficacy of sunshine, 'Oceans of Ozone', as the copywriter put it. A flat here cost £500 a year to rent, at a time when £500 would buy you a freehold bungalow on one of the new estates on the edge of town. A 1937 block in suburban south London could advertise itself as 'Mayfair in Streatham' – an 'irresistible attraction to many distinguished people, planned on suntrap lines, constant softened hot water'.

With little space to deal with, the decoration could be daringly experimental and up to date. Lady Kitty Vincent described a flapper in 1926 as the human equivalent of the furniture you found in furnished flats, 'painted shiny black with vermilion and orange flowers'. Photographs of a Flat in Town in a 1933 copy of *The Lady* show a sitting room with walls of sycamore veneer and all the furniture fitted apart from a sofa with upholstery of 'dull champagne satin'. The dining room, equally minuscule and seating four, had fitted cupboards topped with sand-blasted glass floodlit from below, and the table top was brushed copper. As K.R.G. Browne expressed it in *How to Live in a Flat*, the small size could make the tenant feel 'as might a fly which, having been born and raised in the Albert Hall, was abruptly transferred in the evening of its days to a medium-sized dog-kennel'. Dinner might be produced in the kitchenette – a term recently imported from America. The Vicomte de Mauduit sprang to the rescue with *The Vicomte in the Kitchenette* (1934); his introduction declared that as a member of the very modern generation of 'tin opener cooks' he wanted to help bachelor flat-dwellers (men and girls), and folk who loved good food but who were cramped by their means. He assumed the presence of a maid (who should wear black and not pink, green or blue to harmonize with the dining room colour scheme), who would help serve up such dishes as Sausages à la Deepdene, which involved heating a can of spaghetti and arranging on top some crisply fried sausages surrounded with apple slices fried in sausage fat. Haybox, pressure cooker and self-basting pan from Barkers were essential equipment. *Entertaining with Elizabeth Craig*, published in 1933, had a chapter on 'entertaining without a maid', based on her experience when she first started housekeeping in a London flat and was shocked to discover there was no room for help. An electric table stove, electric coffee percolator and electric kettle were solutions.

Dame Court, the newly built block in Charles Lorne's *Flat to Let*, looks like 'a great anchored ship, waiting to set off on a voyage' and is the 'latest in labour-saving homes, with electric this and electric that and metal window-frames and insulated floors and constant hot water'. The hall porter wonders 'what the people who came to live in them

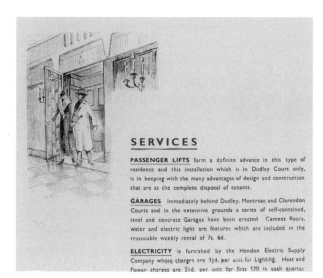

SERVICES

PASSENGER LIFTS form a definite advance in this type of residence and this installation which is in Dudley Court only, is in keeping with the many advantages of design and construction that are at the complete disposal of tenants.

GARAGES Immediately behind Dudley, Montrose and Clarendon Courts and in the extensive grounds a series of self-contained, steel and concrete Garages have been erected. Cement floors, water and electric light are features which are included in the reasonable weekly rental of 7s. 6d.

ELECTRICITY is furnished by the Hendon Electric Supply Company whose charges are 3¼d. per unit for Lighting. Heat and Power charges are 2¼d. per unit for first 120 in each quarter

OPPOSITE Illustration by Mary Shepherd for *The Vicomte in the Kitchenette*, 1934. Space for staff was limited in flats and many flat-dwellers were learning to cook for themselves for the first time.

LEFT A stylish and efficient lift became a selling point, as here at Dudley Court in Hendon.

would ever have to do, beyond listening to the wireless'. In fact they have affairs and cocktail parties, commit suicide and go bankrupt. The demographic of the block covers a range of inhabitants considered typical flat-dwellers. They include a long-distance aviator; Jewish refugees from Germany; a young married couple (the husband disapproves, a flat is only 'fit for a French tart'); a creative pair of Oxford graduates, one a composer and the other a playwright; a politically active couple with a 'sitting room made bleak with a Modigliani portrait'; a businessman and his mistress; an overbearing aunt living with her financially dependent niece and a pair of forbidden dogs; and a couple with a markedly relaxed view of marriage – 'chairs covered in polar bear skin'. There is only one family with children: the adults read Penguin books and the children play in the lift. The message is that the building is modern and the inhabitants are equally so.

MAMMOTH BLOCKS

FOR COUNCILS the national slum clearance scheme inaugurated in 1930 made rehousing urgent, and generally blocks of flats were the best solution. With economy of scale as a motive, two of the largest developments in Britain occurred simultaneously in the second half of the 1930s. Leeds City Council, having cleared the Quarry Hill area of old terraces and industrial buildings, commissioned thirteen blocks in curves and L-shapes to rehouse the previous occupants. Charles Jenkinson, the chairman of Leeds Housing Committee, stated that nothing had been spared to make it the most advanced, magnificent and luxurious estate ever. This was the largest housing scheme in the country, amounting to 938 flats – modern flats, far removed from the tenement. The inspiration was the Karl Marx Hof scheme for workers in Vienna, which was one kilometre in length fronting the Ringstrasse des Proletariats (1,382 flats). Quarry Hill followed the Continental pattern, with lavish communal facilities – a hall with a stage, indoor and outdoor swimming pools, even an estate mortuary. This was the only council estate prior to the Second World War to have lifts transporting residents up to flats with electric light and relayed wireless. The sculleries were fitted with coke bake ovens that connected to the open grate in the living room and were fitted with trivets for cooking pans. There was a revolutionary water-borne rubbish chute system. Each balcony (where the hanging of washing was forbidden) had window boxes carefully designed so they didn't drip on to the balcony below. These and the large troughs placed over the entrances were

LEFT Lupton House, Quarry Hill, Leeds, 1939. An early resident hangs out her washing on the undeveloped garden space.
RIGHT A vignette by H.M. Bateman of how life in Dolphin Square was going to be: a wife need have no worries if her husband forgot to say he was bringing three men home to dinner, for there was a restaurant. This was a feature in many blocks: even Quarry Hill had the Savile Restaurant.

designed to create a flower garden effect flowing over concrete wall slabs. The community spirit fostered during the war survived into the 1950s, with carnivals, weekly dances and whist drives, children's films and even a short-lived community magazine, *The Sentinel*. But the experiment ultimately failed. The jewel in the Leeds social housing programme became a heap of rubble in 1978.

Designed for the professional middle classes, Dolphin Square in Pimlico was similarly vast. The first tenants took possession in 1936. The area, considered unpromising, had been the Thames-side yard for Thomas Cubitt while he was building Belgravia, a tangle of workshops, sawmills and stables, and subsequently a factory making army uniforms. The developers and builders were the Costain brothers, lent money by the bank on the condition that it would be the biggest block of flats in Europe. Nervous that the project might fail, the Costains whetted the appetites of prospective inhabitants by commissioning A.P. Herbert to write a description of the planned 'city of 1250 flats . . . the dwelling of the future' and H.M. Bateman to illustrate it. In a period of financial depression Herbert shrewdly pointed out that in the 'Englishman's Castle' (i.e. an ordinary house), 'roofs leak, food must be bought, entertainment (except the wireless) must be sought outside, exercise ditto, water rates, gas bills, fuses fizzle.' At Dolphin Square there would be flats of all sizes, ranging from one to five bedrooms. The 'Windsor' had two sitting rooms and two bathrooms. There would be a 'sports centre' with swimming pool, gymnasium and squash courts; a children's nursery 'in which babies can be dumped' and, for larger children, 'a play or romping-room surrounded by sliding windows which admit the sun but not bronchitis, and here they may tear each other's hair out, build castles, write plays, debate communism . . .' Most of it happened (though not the river pier for residents' boats). The swimming pool had a wave machine and sunray lamps; the nursery was presided over by the Costains' old nanny; and the gym had an electrical slimming machine and a mechanical horse. The square of plain brick ten-storey blocks, named after famous British admirals, looked on the surface not so very different from a Peabody building, but Dolphin Square had a restaurant and an arcade of eleven shops, a garden in the Spanish style, and a doctor, dentist and vet on site. BBC radio was relayed to each flat.

The concept of such a vast development was so alien to a resident from a Victorian terrace house in adjoining Claverton Street that she wrote to her Aunt Isabel worrying about the flats lowering the tone of the neighbourhood: 'Floor after floor of this hideous red brick edifice to provide dolls house sized pied à terre accommodation for the new secondary schooled semi-professional class of people . . . The rooms are all small. We think the smallest are intended for kitchens, which John says is probably to our advantage. They are not big enough to entertain so we shall be spared the noise of parties. You could not cook much more than a boiled egg there . . . I really cannot make out what sort of dreadful neighbours we are about to have thrust upon us. Let us hope they do not throw things out of their windows, but know how to behave themselves.' They did, and attention to detail was such that during the war the management provided three alternative bomb shelters: for snorers, non-snorers and those with pets.

RISE AND FALL OF THE HIGH RISE

During the war bombs further obliterated much old housing. This presented an opportunity for architects to explore the possibilities of high-rise buildings. High blocks, also known as point blocks, would become a new aesthetic. The architect Frederick Gibberd suggested in the 1950s that they would be 'sculpture in space', giving pleasure to many and offering 'surprise views'. An alternative was the slab block, which stretched out horizontally, most famously at Park Hill in Sheffield, designed by Jack Lynn and Ivor Smith. Here were the 'streets in the sky' – the doors of each flat opening out on to a deck, down which a milk float could theoretically be driven. The term 'urban village' was used: the social reformer Elizabeth Denby had written of a similar scheme how 'on a sunny evening or at the week-end each balcony had its tenants leaning elbows on the rail, smoking, gossiping, happy, like a group of cottagers perched above each other on a steep cliff.' To the converted it seemed blindingly obvious that high-rise blocks would make maximum use of land and prevent urban sprawl, as well as conserving both agricultural land and an unspoilt countryside. The life of city-dwellers would be immeasurably improved as they were lifted out of their squalid old housing and elevated to enjoy a view of bright sky rather than a dingy old brick wall. The modernists were zealous. As Thomas Sharp wrote scathingly in the 1940 Pelican *Town Planning*, 'It is dictatorial, unimaginative and intolerant people who regard themselves as housing reformers who attempt to restrict the range of habitation to the family-house-cum-private-garden type which for some reason or other they regard as the one and only proper Englishman's castle.' Flats suited lots of people, he argued: the unmarried, childless couples, and those whose children had left home. Park Hill,

A War Office public information poster designed by Abram Games, 1942, showing a wartime vision of future housing; bright clean flats replacing old brick terraces.

RIGHT Gee Street, Finsbury, 1954. A woman looks out from the balcony of her eleventh-floor newly built council flat. OPPOSITE An illustration from *Houses and Homes* (Ladybird Book), 1963. 'A modern block of flats . . . steel girders and reinforced concrete, plywood, plastic and aluminium can now be used . . . scores of families can have their homes in a tall block of flats on a ground space which would otherwise house only a few.'

like pre-war Quarry Hill, followed a trajectory from optimism through dilapidation down to notoriety, but was saved from demolition by being listed in 1998, and has been renovated by the developer Urban Splash in partnership with English Heritage. Widened windows and yellow, scarlet and mustard metal cladding send out a message that the flats no longer house council tenants, Sheffield's industrial workers, but rather design-conscious owner-occupiers.

High-rise building had several advantages for town councils. They kept communities intact within the town boundaries, thus fitting in with a green belt, or the idea that there should be one. In addition, their prefabricated building methods meant that they were cheap to erect with relatively unskilled labour, and construction companies were keen to offer authorities package deals. From 1956 to 1967 the government offered local authorities a subsidy for each storey in excess of six. For a decade a tall tower block became a prestige symbol, and blocks reached twenty-three storeys and over in places including Glasgow, Newcastle, Birmingham, even suburban Enfield. Management and maintenance frequently did not live up to the original plan – Martello Court, Edinburgh's tallest block, was referred to as Terror Towers for much of its existence. The sight, on 16 May 1968, of one corner of twenty-two storey Ronan Point falling like a pack of cards on to an East London street after Ivy Hodge on the eighteenth floor struck a match to make herself a cup of tea and caused a gas explosion did nothing for their popularity. The admiration that had been lavished on blocks such as Alton Estate at Roehampton in the late 1950s, standing elegantly on piloti in a simulacrum of eighteenth-century parkland, could not be applied to thirty-storey blocks that 'rise from a sea of concrete and asphalt, inserted on pocket handkerchief sites in areas of semi-industrial squalor', which is how Sir Hugh Wilson, president of the RIBA, described the state of affairs in 1968. The NSPCC issued a report on the bad effect living in a tower block had on families with young children. Lifts, which had made the whole flat system initially possible, had become the fundamental problem. When they were out of order or vandalized tower blocks became impossibly unattractive places to live.

In the early 1970s the twentieth century's highest residential blocks rose more than forty storeys up out of the Barbican in the City of London. The towers were named with reassuringly august historical names, as mansion blocks had been a century earlier: Cromwell, Shakespeare, Wilberforce and Lauderdale, rather than after the chairman of the local housing committee, as Ronan Point had been. By 1974 one in every ten households in England and Wales was living in a flat. Pressure on housing has meant that the subdivision of terraces into flats has continued apace

and redundant building types such as maltings, warehouses, textile mills and lunatic asylums have been reinvented as cool urban flats. The Office for National Statistics recorded that 29 per cent of households in 2012 were single-person households; and it is these, above all, that will trade a garden for a view of clouds, and have a social life that is based around not a family kitchen but a coffee shop in the street below.

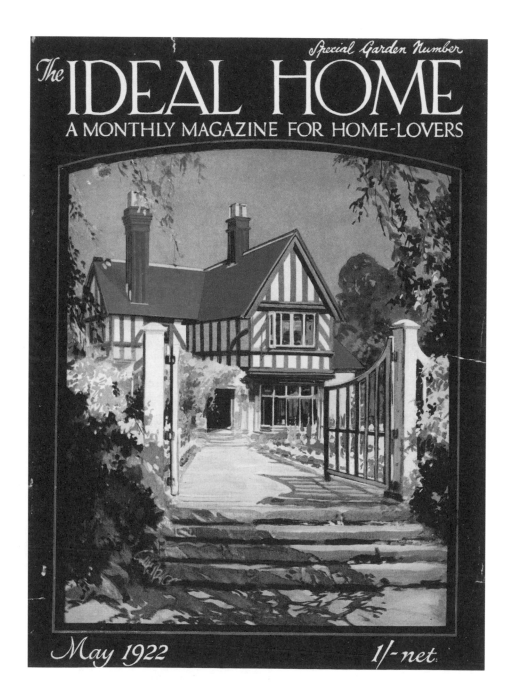

Special Garden Number

The IDEAL HOME

A MONTHLY MAGAZINE FOR HOME-LOVERS

May 1922   *1/-net.*

SUBURBAN VILLAS AND SEMIS

T HE ROMANS BEQUEATHED US THE SUBURBS and a range of words associated with them. The noun *suburbanitas* meant nearness to Rome; *suburbanus* meant a person dwelling close to the city, but was also used as an adjective; *suburbium* meant a suburb. From the Romans too comes 'villa' – an idea with elegant origins which lapsed into banality. A villa is near to town, an easy escape. Pliny the Younger had one in the first century AD near Ostia seventeen miles from Rome: 'so that after getting through all your business, and without loss or curtailment of your working hours you can go and stay there . . . the shore is beautified by a most pleasing variety of villa buildings, some close together, while others have great intervals between them.' It sounds like the original suburban dream – a scattering of houses near town, yet in the fresh air surrounded by gardens. Among its descendants must be counted Chandos Villas in Pinner, semi-detached and newly built, into which the delighted Sam and Isabella Beeton moved in 1856. The builder in his brochure promoted the development as 'Urbs in Rure' – a quotation from the fourth-century Roman poet Ausonius – or, in his own words, 'having the advantages of Healthiness, Situation, Good Society, First Rate Education, Proximity to Town and Seclusion'. By 1928, however, the term villa was stripped of its charming associations; instead, villas were described by the architect Clough Williams-Ellis as springing up 'along the lines of the public services – the roads and sewers, the water, gas and electric light mains – as do rank weeds along an open drain.'

Suburbs have always held great charm for people moving out from the city (as opposed to in from the country) and so the connection to the countryside has often been tenuous and anything smacking of the truly rural – pig-keeping for instance – eliminated from the neighbourhood. In the view of the countryman, suburbs are urban and from that of the townsman, they are dull. The suburban

The magazines *Ideal Home*, *Homes and Gardens* and *Good Housekeeping* were all started in the years after the First World War, catering to a new generation of homeowners.

ideal is to look out on the countryside, but for the route to town to be direct and fast. Their very popularity has been their downfall, since it is their persistent growth that has frequently caused dismay. As towns and cities have expanded so suburban boundaries changed, spreading ever outwards, like 'gravy over a tablecloth', in the words of George Orwell.

GEORGIAN VILLAS

For Georgians a villa was a retreat from town, but, unlike a country house, it came without the responsibilities of land and estate. Successful Georgian professionals, people such as architects and bankers, frequently had a second house within easy reach of the city. Unlike contemporary country houses, these villas were small and compact and usually without a basement. Most were classical in style, recalling the Roman architect Vitruvius and transporting elements of Andrea Palladio's architecture from the Veneto to Middlesex: a conjuring up of Roman perfection. Lord Burlington's Chiswick House, finished in 1729, was among the most famous: 'Some say that with Chiswick-house no villa can compare,' wrote William Pulteney, Earl of Bath, but added:

> But ask the beaux of Middlesex,
> Who know the country well,
> If Strawb'ry Hill, if Strawb'ry Hill
> Don't bear away the bell?

Strawberry Hill, in Twickenham, was built by Horace Walpole. 'I am going to build a little Gothic castle at Strawberry Hill. If you can pick me up any fragments of old painted glass, arms or anything, I shall be excessively obliged,' he wrote to his friend Horace Mann in 1750. The house was loved by its owner, admired by many and criticized by some ('a grotesque house with pie-crust battlements' – Lord Macaulay). Walpole could be held up as an early victim of hostility against suburban fancifulness. 'I did not mean to make my house so Gothic as to exclude conveniences and modern refinements,' he declared.

Earlier, in the seventeenth century, the word suburban had implied licentious habits – life in the badlands outside city limits – but by the late eighteenth century it merely implied inferior manners and narrowness of view. William Cowper included the following lines in a 1782 poem:

Suburban villas, highway-side retreats,

That dread th'encroachment of our growing streets,

Tight boxes, neatly sashed, and in a blaze,

Will all July sun's collected rays,

Delight the citizen, who, gasping there,

Breathes clouds of dust, and calls it country air.

Cowper linked the words villa and suburban and deplored both building over the countryside and the ersatz quality of suburban life. These views – perhaps prejudiced – have stuck, ignoring the fact that for many the suburb has always represented the best of both worlds.

The villa gradually became not just a house for an escape from the city, but, discretely placed on the outskirts of town, a permanent home. A principal attraction of a house in the suburbs has always been the size of garden. In early suburbs this could stretch to several acres, a marked improvement on the narrow strip of land behind an urban terrace. 'Numberless villas in the vicinity of Edinburgh . . . are seen beautiful and distinct, each in the midst of its own plantations,' noted agriculturalist George Robertson in 1795. Many of these villa inhabitants went daily to work in the city, as had the late Thomas Mullet, Esq., of Clapham Rise, whose 'singularly desirable residence' was advertised in *The Times* of 22 June 1815. Its attractions were listed: it was within an easy drive of the Royal Exchange, and had cheerful sitting apartments of excellent dimensions, stabling, a coach house and 'extensive pleasure grounds immediately in

Regency villa, a design by T.D.W. Dearn, 1807. He considered this 'from its size and conveniences . . . well adapted to be a retreat for a merchant and man of business.'

view of the principal apartments, tastefully diversified by plantations of choice shrubs in a state of most luxuriant growth'.

EARLY SEMI-DETACHMENT

INDIVIDUAL VILLAS dotted around the edges of towns and cities and beyond the urban terraces blurred the limits of country and town. The semi-detached house became the house type that linked the two most appropriately. The Eyre family went for this radical

A semi-detached villa, designed by J.B. Papworth in the 1820s. This particular villa was intended to be built in Herne Hill, but it is very similar to the houses pioneered in St John's Wood.

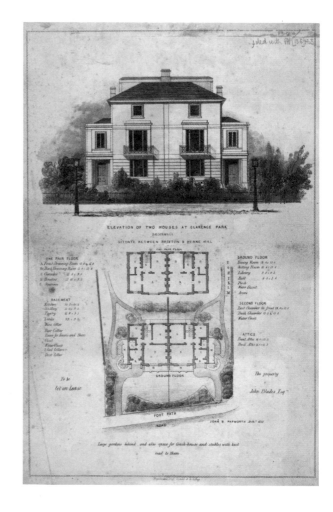

alternative, forgoing both villas and terraces, when they developed their farmland in north London. The 1794 *Plan for the Improvement of the Freehold Estate, called St. John's Wood* showed semi-detached houses with large gardens lining the projected circus, crescent and square and along the sylvan-sounding Lisson Grove and Grove Lane. The estate was advertised as having 'an amplitude of ground' and in 'no instance is one House to be erected opposite another'. The forty-two houses in the circus were to be set amidst shrubberies and a pleasure ground and were advertised in *The Times* as being 'residences of such novel description, as will unite the beauty and pleasure of the Country-House, with the convenience and advantage of a town one'.

The semi-detached house was not in fact completely novel. Landowners had long found that building labourers' cottages in pairs made economic sense. Two houses put together made a more imposing whole than one on its own, a fact which might have appealed equally to a landowner wanting to present his model cottages as substantial and a suburban resident wishing to inhabit a house that at first glance appeared detached.

It took well over a decade for the St John's Wood Estate to materialize, but thereafter Walpole Eyre, the family member who managed the estate, was vigilant that standards of building and behaviour did not slip. Records were kept of concerns and complaints that appear distinctly modern: in 1819 Mr Waters of Alpha Road objected to an unsightly building in front of his drawing room windows and the number of dogs kept by his neighbour. Privacy not expected of a terrace house was maintained in semi-detachment. Eyre instructed that 'a covenant shall be inserted in the Lease that this window shall be a stained Glass Window and that the lower part shall be and remain at all times fastened down so as to prevent the persons in no. 5 overlooking the adjoining prem[is]es'.

EXCLUSIVE PARKS

THE COMBINATION OF SUBURBAN VILLA AND GARDEN within an exclusive space, but close to town, was a winning one. John Nash's plan for Regent's Park in 1811 included fifty-six villas set amidst an undulating leafy landscape. Nash invited the architect Decimus Burton to design eight villas, all that were in the end built. In 1824, at the northern end of Regent's Park, Nash planned Park Village East and Park Village West. This was a collection of small villas, some semi-detached but each one individual, with Italianate, Gothic or Tudor details – no two are alike – setting the pattern for variety that became one of the defining characteristics of suburban

Map of Calverley Park by John Britton, 1832, showing the villas dotted along curving roads. 'In designing and placing these houses the architect has evidently studied variety, but he restrained his fancy to such simple forms and sizes as seemed best adapted to an economical expenditure.'

houses. As the term 'village' suggested, they were small-scale and cosy; the result could be thought of as the suburban ideal. As James Elmes wrote about Regent's Park in his 1826 *Metropolitan Improvements of London*, 'all the elegancies of town, and all the beauties of the country are co-mingled with happy art and blissful union.' This mantra has been endlessly repeated; for example, Laing the builders would describe their Edgware estate in the mid-1930s, 'While modernity is the keynote of the estate, yet a delightfully rustic atmosphere is maintained. It is situated in a beautiful spot close to buses, trains, shops and schools.'

Decimus Burton used his Regent's Park experience at Calverley Park in Tonbridge Wells when he was commissioned in 1829 by the landowner John Ward to 'erect a number of edifices suitable to the reception of genteel families'. Each Italianate villa was to be set on three-quarters of an acre and the boundary fences were to be seven feet back from the road, which allowed for a shrubby green grass verge to provide a bosky screen between house and road. Uniquely for this date, shops, a hotel and pleasure gardens were also in the plan, so that once through the entrance archway the residents need not let the outside world impinge. For himself, Burton built Baston Cottage in full-blown picturesque style, with bargeboards, gables, veranda and fancy chimneys. It was established that a villa could be in any style ranging from Swiss, Anglo-Norman or just 'decorated in the style of Henry VII's times' as delineated in P.F. Robinson's timely pattern book *Designs for Ornamental Villas*, published in 1827 and 1830. 'A Design for a Suburban Villa' in a workaday 1855 pattern book by E.L. Tarbuck, *The Builder's Practical Director*, is captioned: 'this house in planned with studied irregularity, with a view of obtaining the greatest amount of picturesque effect.' Another pattern book by E.L. Blackburne, *Suburban and Rural Architecture* (1869), also illustrated detached and semi-detached villas in the full range of styles: Gothic, German, French Gothic, English Gothic and Italian. The suburban ideal was to get away from the cramped frontage associated with terrace housing, but Blackburne, working on a small plot, managed to squeeze in a pair of semi-detached villas: 'intended for a suburban situation, and suitable for two plots of ground of 21 ft frontage. It has been arranged with the view of meeting the great requirements

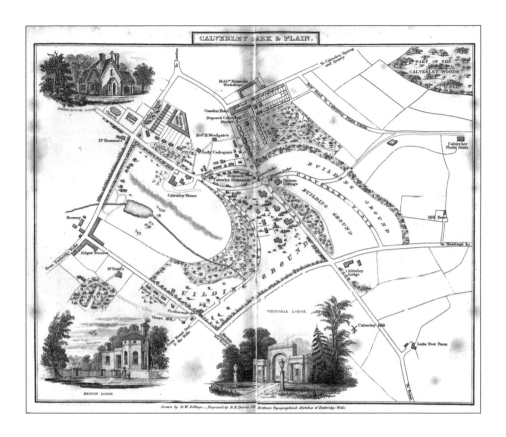

CALVERLEY PARK & PLAIN.

of a suburban residence, viz: as much accommodation as possible at a minimum expense and covering but little ground.' It was always important that suburban layout should marked differ from rectilinear terraces. A handbook of 1885 by one J.H. McGovern, *Suggestions for Artistically and Practically Laying out Building Estates*, advised: 'Everything should be done to give a picturesque and pleasing appearance, with the boulevarde principle, trees planted on footwalks, serpentine curves and nicely grouped semi-detached villas, with well-trimmed lawns and low fence or boundary walls and iron railings.'

Among the prodigious output of John Claudius Loudon was his *Encyclopedia of Cottage, Farm and Villa Architecture*, first published in 1833. He defined villas as being country residences with the land attached designed for recreation rather than profit

A sheet from *Amateur Gardener*, *c.*1890, showing the suburban garden at its most perfect. Space for a garden was always a compelling reason for living in the suburbs.

– what he termed an 'amplification of a cottage of wealth and taste'. He responded speedily to the new trend for suburban living and recycled some of the material as *The Suburban Gardener and Villa Companion* in 1838. He acknowledged the fact that the villa was now most likely on the edge of town. 'We shall prove', he wrote, 'that a suburban residence, with a very small portion of land attached, will contain all that is essential to happiness, [as] in the garden, park and demesne of the most extensive country residence.' All lives would be happier for 'the cheerful aspect of vegetation; the singing of birds in their season; and the enlivening effect of finding ourselves unpent-up by buildings, and in comparatively unlimited space', away from 'close streets of houses' and chimney smoke. Loudon was a great promoter of gardening and recognized that for the master of a suburban villa to enjoy it fully he must have 'knowledge of the resources which a garden, however small, is capable of affording'. This theme was milked in the 1970s television sitcom *The Good Life* in which Tom Good throws in a career as a graphic designer and, with his wife, Barbara, attempts to turn their garden (in, inevitably, The Avenue, Surbiton), into a self-sufficient smallholding.

Loudon saw the suburban house, which could be, as he put it, 'double detached' and on winding roads bordered by trees, as an admirable fit for the middle class. He perceived that the countryside was an unattractive two-class society where 'either you have a display of hospitality, wealth and magnificence or have a life of labour.' It was therefore much better to be where the 'houses and inhabitants were all, or chiefly, of the same description and class'. In these circumstances you would not risk being regarded as the local rich man, or considered unsocial because you had to avoid being 'led to unsuitable expenses by associating with persons of greater fortune'. And, he wrote, 'One immense advantage of a suburban residence over one isolated in the country consists in its proximity to neighbours.'

He grasped that the railway, for travelling back and forth to town, and the suburban house were inextricably linked. He even remarked that in his view a railway could be an attractive visual feature when seen from a moderate distance. He had been 'much struck with the effect of the carriages passing along the line of the Manchester railway, as seen from the beautiful villas, particularly one erected from a design by Mr. Barry, situated on the high bank which overlooks the valley through which that railway is conducted.' The distant sound and sight of the train is a recurring feature of suburban life. In recognizing that the working man's health would also benefit from this semi-rural life, Loudon prefigured Ebenezer Howard and the Garden City movement, and he suggested that with a railway some industries, such as printing, could be moved out of town and the workforce live in nearby cottages with gardens.

The suffix 'Park', as in Regent's and Calverley, was applied to many schemes, the intention presumably being to convey an impression of leafy exclusivity. Rock Park in Birkenhead was laid out in 1837. Dorridge Park in Birmingham was developed mainly by the Muntz family, who shrewdly allowed the Great West Railway through their land in return for a station, which then became a key to their 'park's' success. Cressington Park in Liverpool clustered around Grassendale railway station. Victoria Park, two miles from the centre of Manchester in Rusholme, advertised itself in 1836 as having 'total freedom from manufacturers and their disagreeable effects'. The consortium that developed it consisted of six merchants (who doubtless owed their wealth to the same manufacturers whose effects they were escaping), plus one landowner and the architect Richard Lane, who also included a house for himself.

Lane's first task was the build the boundary walls and the entrance lodges for Victoria Park since it was to be, in current terms, a 'gated community'. It opened with a grand carriage procession to view the first nine elegant 'mansions'. In 1850 Elizabeth Gaskell moved into a Greek Revival villa there. She revelled in both the house ('it certainly *is* a beauty') and the garden for her children: 'Clay soil it *will* be, and there is no help for it, but it will be gay and bright with common flowers; and is quite shut in, – and one may get out without a bonnet, which is a blessing, I always want my head cool . . .' But her conscience pricked her: how it could be 'right to spend so much ourselves on so purely a selfish thing as a house, while so many are wanting – that's the haunting thought to me.' She resolved to make the house as welcoming as possible. She kept a cow, her neighbour Charles Hallé gave music lessons to a daughter, and Charlotte Brontë visited, describing it as 'a large cheerful airy house, quite out of the Manchester smokes'. Victoria Park fought to stay genteel: there was anxiety about putting in gas lighting, public transport was banned and toll gates guarded its entrances until the 1950s. Neville Cardus, writing in 1950, remembered Victoria Park from his childhood as an unattainable 'sequestered purlieu'. 'There were toll-gates at the roads which gave entrance to Victoria Park; no vehicle not possessed by dwellers within these select groves was admitted free of charge. Pedestrians enjoyed right of way, but such was the sense of propriety cultivated by the lower orders of the period, none abused the privilege . . . Inside Victoria Park, the carriages swung by iron gates and pillars, and curved along drives to massive turreted stone houses, at the base of them broad steps leading up to the portals, flanked by lions *couchant*.'

In 1825, while simultaneously erecting terraces in Belgravia, Thomas Cubitt leased 229 acres of Clapham and planned Clapham Park close by the already fashionable Common. Cubitt built himself fourteen-bedroom Clarence Villa, which stood on 22 acres and included stabling, a fruit garden, a vinery and a miniature farm. Some time after Cubitt's death in 1855 the house was sold and renamed Clarence House – a sure marker that the word 'villa' had gone down in the world. In Regent's Park there had been South Villa and St Dunstan's Villa (it incorporated the clock from St Dunstan's Church) and early houses in Victoria Park were named Ivy Villa and Lily Villa, though others – Woodthorpe, Holly Bank, Fairfield, Limes, Hirstwood, High Elms, Firwood, Sunnyside, The Gables, Summerville and Westerfield – simply expressed comforting rurality. Nathaniel Hawthorne chose to live in Rock Park when he was the American Consul in Liverpool in the 1850s, travelling into the city not by steam train, but by steam ferry. His journal paid particular notice to the 'new and neat residences for city people springing up with fine names' that he saw as he walked with his wife on the hills overlooking Birkenhead and Tranmere. He recorded semi-detached villas named

OPPOSITE The salubrious suburb of Victoria Park, Manchester, photographed in 1912. The toll gates kept commercial traffic away.
LEFT House names: in a *Punch* cartoon of 1927, 'Saturday Afternoon in our Suburb', 'The Laurels', talking to 'Mon Repos', comments on the sporting inclinations of 'Clovelly'.

197

Recluse Cottage, Bellvue and Belvoir Villa, with 'little patches of ornamented garden or lawn in front, and heaps of curious rock-work, with which the English are ridiculously fond of adorning their front yards'. Nothing had changed when comic novelist Richard Gordon ruminated on house names in his native suburb of Bromley in 1976: 'We would no more leave our house without a name than our dog.' His observations show how very constant suburban house names have been: the popularity of trees (Two Elms, Three Oaks, The Firs), 'mysterious plurals' (Squirries, Twickets and Cratchetts), and faraway places (Windermere, Adelaide, Lucknow). 'Chez Nous has never been observed in the area,' he noted (it was a bungalow name).

THE COMMUTER'S DREAM

THE DEVELOPMENT OF THE SUBURB and the spread of villas and semi-detached houses were closely linked to transport and easy journeys into town. The early London suburbs, such as Islington and Hackney, were well within walking distance of the city; further out and horses were needed. Wealthy suburbanites owned a carriage or took hackney cabs, but the arrival of the horse omnibus in 1829 made travel relatively cheap and extended the possible distance of a journey to work. Twelve to fifteen passengers were packed in a long coach and later 'knifeboard' models had rooftop seats as well. By the 1840s there was a well-established network of competitive horse bus companies in place which increased the attraction of areas such as St John's Wood for the 'opulent and industrious professional men and tradesmen of London who are for the most part its inhabitants', as estate agent Alfred Cox put it in 1853. Respectable public transport also relieved many suburbanites of the necessity to keep their own horses, with the accompanying smelly stabling. Valuing their peace and seclusion, suburban inhabitants have never been slow to fight for it. A panic-stricken letter sent to St John's College, Oxford, in 1885 regarding one of their houses in north Oxford was an appeal that permission should be withheld for the building of a stable in the house next door, as it would 'render my own occupation of my present house *impossible*. Both my drawing room, the sitting room of my daughter, and my own study – not to speak of two bedrooms, look into the garden, and we have had a balcony built in front of the drawing room, especially to look into the garden, to have tea there, and to occupy it while tennis is being played.'

Figures show that by 1855 around 20,000 people were commuting into London by horse bus, 15,000 by steamboat and 6,000 by rail: the suburban way of life was

Chandos Villas, the semi-detached house on the Woodriding's Estate in Pinner where Isabella and Samuel Beeton set up home in 1856. It was advertised in the brochure as having lobby and entrance hall, dining room, drawing room, five large bedrooms, two water closets and domestic offices, rent £50 per annum.

well established. As the *Morning Herald* had reported in 1848, 'No one who has recently travelled with his eyes open . . . in the environs of this overgrown metropolis, can have failed to observe that houses are springing up in all quarters . . . Money is scarce; the whole nation is in difficulties; but houses spring up everywhere as though capital were abundant – as though one-half of the world were on the look out for investments, and the other half continually in search of eligible family residences, desirable villas, and aristocratic cottages . . .' Sam and Isabella Beeton were typical when in 1856, newly married, they chose to live in the suburbs. They took one half of semi-detached Chandos Villas (rather than Oak, Richmond, Wellington, Cambridge, Cornwall, Lansdowne or Zetland Villas) on a small development in Pinner. It was only

300 yards away from the railway station and a season ticket to London was included in the £50 per annum rent. Furthermore, 'the morning papers are supplied to the regular traveller, who sits at ease in his 1st class carriage and reads The Times, and comes to Business primed with all the news of the previous night.' This in comparison to the poor traveller 'squeezed and jolted' on the Norwood omnibus. 'The country which years ago could only be enjoyed by wealthy bankers and merchants now within reach of even minor clerks' was the boast in the illustrated brochure, attractive no doubt to Sam, a journalist and publisher, who had been living in Milk Street right in the City. Other advantages included post before 8 o'clock, no cholera, good drainage and good water (and therefore no doctor's bills). 'The "paterfamilias", well and happy although he *can* see the house of a neighbour or two, never wishes himself back in Keppel Street, Store Street, or any of the most respectable streets in Bloomsbury.' Living on the estate also entitled you to free education at Harrow, a draw for the aspirational suburban. The Beetons left Chandos Villas after seven years; Sam found his working hours did not fit with catching trains, and although Isabella had abandoned suburban isolation and frequently travelled to Fleet Street too, they moved back to the city to live more economically above their office. Her wish, expressed prior to marriage, that Sam would sometimes say 'I don't think I shall go to town this morning but stay and have a quiet day in the country' had never materialized.

It is impossible to know if the Beetons realized that their house had been named for the area's association with the Duke of Chandos and his extravagant eighteenth-century country house Cannons; that 'minor clerks' could now live in the area demonstrated vividly how it had changed in just over a century. The nineteenth-century demographic persisted: D.C. Houses (Canons) Limited, operating in the same area during the 1930s, offered special loan facilities for a particular 'class of customer. In particular, special attention will be given to the needs of CIVIL SERVANTS, TEACHERS and other persons holding such salaried appointments.'

SEMI-DETACHED PREJUDICE

WHEN THE HON. EMILY EDEN wrote *The Semi-detached House* in 1859 she offered a view of the suburban social scene. Blanche, pregnant wife of promising young diplomat Lord Chester, arrives in the London suburb of Dulham, well out of her normal social milieu. She has rented a semi-detached house, Pleasance, to live in while her husband is abroad on a mission. She is in the suburbs because her doctor wants her to live out of the excitements of London, but close enough to remain under his care. The novel opens with Blanche crying:

'The only fault of the house is that it is semi-detached . . . Oh Aunt Sarah! Surely you
 don't expect me to live in a semi-detached house?'
'Why not, my dear, if it suits you in other respects?'
'Why, because I should hate my semi-detachment, or whatever the occupants of the
 other half of the house may call themselves.'

Blanche assumes (correctly) that her neighbours, the Hopkinsons, family of a sea captain, will be below her class, imagining 'a little boy, who will always be throwing stones at the paling and making me jump; daughters who will always be playing *Partant pour la Syrie*' and their mother, who 'will be immensely fat, wear mittens – thick, heavy mittens – and contrive to know what I have for dinner every day.'

At the other side of the dividing wall, the Hopkinsons, picking up on an item of gossip from a weekly paper, assume that Lord Chester is establishing his mistress in the house. (St John's Wood was, in fact, famous for mistresses.) As the novel progresses their social differences are reconciled and, true to Loudon's remark about suburban neighbours, they become fast friends: 'I could not foresee that I should be housed with such excellent people. What a number of small kindnesses those Hopkinsons have shown me.' The novel illustrates calibrations of suburban status: 'Willis of Columbia House, which boasted of a lodge and an entrance drive, a shrubbery and a paddock, and a two-stalled stable, and every sort of suburban magnificence, married pretty Mary Smith, who merely lived at no. 2 . . .'

A recurring observation is that a suburb is constantly being spoilt as one wave of houses is followed by another, which in turn blocks the view for the next. John Ruskin, raised in a semi-detached house on Herne Hill, was savagely critical of the expanding middle-class suburb of Sydenham. Its houses 'fastened in a Siamese-twin manner together by their sides, and each couple has a Greek or Gothic portico shared between them, with magnificent steps, and highly ornamented capitals . . . The gardens in front are fenced from the road with an immense weight of cast iron, and entered between two square gate-posts, with projecting stucco cornices, bearing the information that the eligible residence within is Mortimer House or Montague Villa.' Having poured vitriol on the houses, he starts on its suburban inhabitants (who, unlike working men

and women, could not cook, sweep, knock in a nail, drive a stake, or spin a thread).
'The men can indeed write, and cast accounts, and go to town every day to get their
living by doing so; the women and children can perhaps read story-books, dance in a
vulgar manner, and play on the piano with dull dexterities for exhibition . . . They know
nothing of painting, sculpture, or architecture; of science, inaccurately . . . of books,
they read "Macmillan's Magazine" on week days, and "Good Words" on Sundays, and
are entirely ignorant of all the standard literature belonging to their own country . . .
The women and girls have no pleasures but in calling on each other in false hair . . . the
men have no faculty, beyond that of cheating in business; no pleasures but in smoking
or eating; and no ideas, nor any capacity of forming ideas, of anything that has yet
been done of great, or seen of good, in this world.'

Ruskin was scathing about how every 'double block' had a drawing room and
a dining room, 'transparent from back to front, so that from the road one sees the
people's heads inside, clear against the light' and the basement kitchen. Space was
now at more of a premium and consequently suburban plots were becoming ever
smaller. A writer in *The Builder* in 1877 even began to question their healthiness: the
commuter 'occupied a small, ill-built, ill-ventilated, and ill-drained box, but which he
called his "suburban villa" . . . In order to pass between his suburban villa and business,
he underwent the toil and anxiety of rushing to a railway station more or less distant
from his house or his office, twice daily and in the course of transit probably shut
himself up in the foul atmosphere of a smoking carriage.'

A NEW SOLUTION FOR THE WORKERS

WELL-FOUNDED CONCERN about urban and rural housing conditions among the poor
led to attempts to improve both. The suburb was not the answer, despite an attempt
of The Artisan's Suburban Cottage Company, which announced in January 1862 that
it had made arrangements with three of the principal railway companies that they
would convey at least a thousand passengers per day from any place within ten miles of
London and back for twopence per day, 'offering a great inducement for the formation
of suburban villages on a large scale'.

At Saltaire, alongside his terraces, Sir Titus Salt began in the late 1860s to put up
detached and semi-detached villas intended for managers and professionals such as
wool-buyers and engineers associated with the company. Similarly, when, in 1879,
George Cadbury moved the cocoa factory four miles out of Birmingham to a new

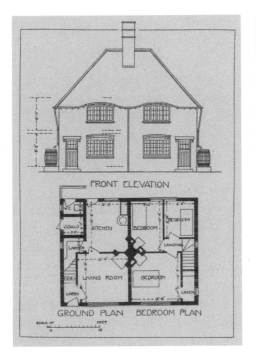
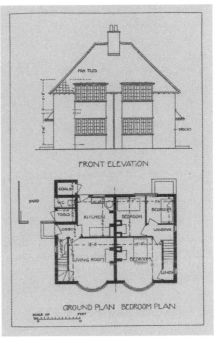

Plans published in 1906 for two variations on the semi-detached cottage built at Bournville. The building cost for each pair was £230 per side.

site conveniently near the canal and a new railway, he began by putting up a few semi-detached houses close to the works for workers who needed to be on the spot. In the 1890s Cadbury expanded the scheme, building a mixture of houses both for his employees and for rent. His ideal was a village community, and roads wound out from the central village green where fêtes and maypole dances were held. The houses, in a variety of sizes, were largely semi-detached in a gentle Arts and Crafts style. Cadbury even transported a fourteenth-century manor house to the site. Nevertheless, Bournville, with its parade of shops, infant and junior schools, an art school, a cricket pitch – and lack of a pub – had more in common with a suburb than a village.

William Lever, equally concerned for his workers' welfare, created Port Sunlight, naming it for his most successful product. He announced at the ceremony in 1888 to

Wherever the Underground was built, housing development followed. A 1912 poster showing the west of London, designed by Charles Sharland for the Underground Electric Railways Company.

cut the first sod: 'It is my and my brother's hope some day to build houses in which our workpeople will be able to live and be comfortable – semi-detached houses with gardens back and front in which they will learn that there is more enjoyment in life that the mere going to and returning from work and looking forward to Saturday night to draw their wages.'

THE MOVE TO THE SUBURBS

THE MASS OF SUBURBAN HOUSING was, however, built for profit. The sheer extent of building in the 1880s was overwhelming. W.S. Clarke offered guidance in *The Suburban Homes of London: A Residential Guide to Favourite London Localities, Their Society, Celebrities, and Associations* in 1881. This listed typical rents and rates alongside snippets of local history for the late Victorian house hunter, 'now that railway and other means of communication have left the choice of situation so free'. He tries to analyse areas, but finds it a problem: Balham is 'like many other suburban neighbourhoods which have grown up since London began to live out of town, it is difficult to say where it begins and where it ends.' But he concludes: 'In the angle formed by the Balham Hill-road and Nightingale-lane are a number of handsome thoroughfares with just that mixture of the practical and the picturesque which appeals at once to the taste of the suburban home-seeker . . . capital choice of homes from 40 l. to 70 l. per annum.' He warns of future development. The situation may currently be delightful and full of the best class of villas, 'but will be less so as time goes on, the estate on the opposite side being now let on building leases.' He notes that the population of Bromley had risen from two thousand to twelve thousand – and soon its Skim Corner, Woodcock Grove and Muzzard's Wood would become the habitation of London citizens. He is impressed with rapidly expanding Ealing and its 'wide choice of buildings for public worship – Presbyterian, Congregational, Baptist, Plymouth Brethren and Methodist'. Clarke also recommends looking in unfashionable Camberwell at old houses 'built about the commencement of the stucco period, and, judged by the aesthetic taste of to-day, must be termed somewhat barbarous'. But he notes their large gardens, and points out that if the peeling stucco can be borne a fine house can be had at a moderate rent.

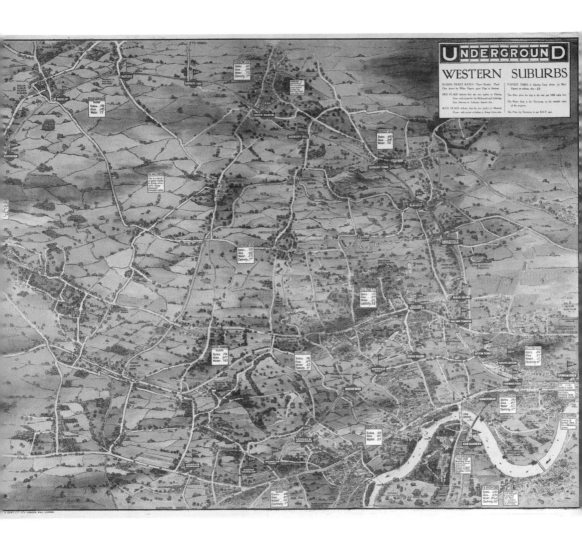

Mrs J.E. Panton – daughter of the artist William Powell Frith and brought up in Park Village West – advised young housekeepers in *From Kitchen to Garret, Hints for Young Housholders* (1888), when 'launching their bark on the troubled seas on domesticity', to live in the suburbs: 'Rents are less, smuts and blacks conspicuous by their absence, and a small garden or a tiny conservatory is not an impossibility.' She thought the expense of a season ticket nothing compared to 'being able to sleep in fresh air, to have

205

a game of tennis in summer, or a friendly evening of music, chess, or games in winter, without expense'. However, she admitted this could be a monotonous existence for wives. 'Of course all the S. or S.W. and S.E. suburbs are the most fashionable and the most sought after; and although to my mind Penge and Dulwich are dreary and damp, they are evidently well supported and much lived in.' Clay was to be avoided. The superiority of living on gravel was a constant in the lists of desirable features in suburban houses.

Her later book, *Suburban Residences and how to Circumvent them* (1896), took a more jaundiced view, based, she said, on four years of living at Shortlands in Bromley. Suburbs 'are not Paradise and can never be made so; yet for people with middle sized incomes and aspirations after fresh air, they are undoubtedly the most necessary evil.' Among the downsides were: the impossibility of coaxing maids away from the entrancements of town; the cold of the average jerry-built suburban villa; letters misdelivered, going to 'Ivy Dene' rather than 'Deneside'; and, confirming Ruskin's view, a low intellectual atmosphere among those 'who love gossip and hate books and art and pictures'.

As suburbs were by their nature supposed to be quiet, individual noises had a particular intrusive clarity. For Jane Panton there was the unacceptable noise of slamming gates, banging dustbin lids and screaming children, and above all the sound of the nearby railway. In Emily Eden's Dulham a screaming macaw induces a headache. By the twentieth century, writers, living in a far noisier world, regard suburbs with nostalgia. The architectural critic J.M. Richards's affectionate portrait of suburbs was written while he was serving in Africa during the war: 'On Sunday the inhabitants remain to worship the suburban gods according to their special ritual, and with all the sight and sounds that accompany it – the sounds especially: the music of lawn mowers, the snip-snip of garden shears, the barking of small dogs straining to be let off the leash at the first turning off the main road, the squeals of a child who is being taught to ride a bicycle down the second quiet turning, the roaring exhaust as a girl friend is whisked off for a day in the sports car and the high-pitched chatter of the group that swings its racquets gaily as it strides in line abreast across the pavement on its way to the tennis club.' In Julian Barnes's 1980 novel *Metroland*, after Sunday morning church bells the afternoon is marked by

Bedford Park, one of a series of lithograph views, 1881. An aesthetically dressed woman sits in the garden, with a view of the church and parsonage.

'the patterned roar of motor mowers, accelerating, braking, turning, accelerating, braking, turning. When they fell silent, you might catch the quiet chomp of shears: and finally – a sound absorbed rather than heard – the gentle squeak of chamois on boot and bonnet.' Richard Gordon, from his work room in the attic of his russet brick, tile-hung Edwardian house in Bromley, hears through shut windows 'the rattle of the electric trains like hastening steel skeletons, the strident wail of police-car and fire-engine, the summer transistor warbling its tuneless note, the competitive snarl of young men's motor bikes, and the lively chatter of schoolchildren, playing their boisterous little sexy games and lighting their fags once out of school.'

ARTS AND CRAFTS

WHEN W.S. CLARKE HAD WRITTEN ABOUT BRIXTON, he stated baldly that it was genteel and 'wouldn't suit the artist'. Bedford Park became the antithesis to Brixton, a magnet for artists and aesthetes. Its developer, Jonathan Carr, acquired land near the new Turnham Green railway station in the mid-1870s and built a suburb in the latest architectural style, Queen Anne Revival, style of choice for adherents of the Aesthetic. Richard Norman Shaw, its leading exponent, was the estate architect. Taking elements from vernacular

building and late seventeenth-century houses, it exuded a friendly and pretty Englishness in harmony with furnishing in the Arts and Crafts style. The houses were red brick, with gables, niches, tile hanging, dormer windows, steep tile roofs and tall chimneys; woodwork and fences were painted a contrasting crisp white. Fine old trees were retained. 'Artistic' folk doubtless also appreciated the healthy lack of basement, excellent plumbing with running hot and cold water and indoor lavatories, and were impressed by an early advertisement proclaiming it the 'healthiest place in the world', with an annual death rate of under six per thousand (and obligatory mention of gravel soil). By 1881 Bedford Park also had its own Tabard Inn, kindergarten, church, co-operative shop, art school and a club which became the hub of the community. An early poll of 168 residents revealed 40 artists, 16 architects and engineers, 9 actors and musicians, as well as lawyers, doctors and army officers. 'The Ballad of Bedford Park', which appeared in *St James's Gazette*, proved its fame (although it didn't prevent Carr getting into financial difficulties and selling up). It included the lines:

With red and blue and sagest green
Were walls and dado dyed
Friezes of Morris there were seen
And oaken wainscot inside.

For floors were stained and polished
And every hearth was tiled
And Philistines abolished
By Culture's gracious child.

As the ballad noted, William Morris's productions, offering as they did a charmed view of the natural world, had an affinity with the newer style of suburban houses. The novelist Mrs Humphry Ward was married to a Oxford tutor and lived in north Oxford on a modest income, 'Yet we all gave dinner-parties and furnished our houses with Morris papers, old chests and cabinets, and blue pots.'

G.K. Chesterton met his wife, Frances, in Bedford Park in the 1890s and set part of his 1908 novel *The Man who was Thursday* there, disguising it as Saffron Park. 'It was defined with some justice as an artistic colony, though it never in any definable way produced any art. But although its pretensions to be an intellectual centre were a little vague, its pretensions to be a pleasant place were quite indisputable . . . A man who stepped into its social atmosphere felt as if he had stepped into a written comedy . . . most of the women were of the kind vaguely called emancipated, and professed some protest against male supremacy. Yet these new women would always pay to a man the extravagant compliment which no ordinary woman ever pays to him, that of listening when he is talking.'

Bedford Park was one small proof that culture and suburb could coexist. However, the view of 'persons of culture', as T.W.H. Crosland put it in *The Suburbans* (1905), had for the last twenty-five years been one of contempt. 'To the superior mind, in fact "suburban" is a sort of label that may properly be applied to pretty well everything on earth that is ill-conditioned, undesirable and unholy. If a man or woman has a fault of taste, of inclination, of temperament, of breeding, or even of manner, the superior mind proceeds, on little wings of haste, to pronounce that fault "suburban".' Helped by the 'ghastly burrow' – the twopenny Tube – estate exploiters had built long, unlovely rows of semi-detached villas for the 'servants and bondslaves of the cits' – 'even in that paradise of all that is suburban, Surbiton'. A view that held good for the entire century ahead.

The name Surbiton derived from the twelfth-century word for southern grange or outlying farm, but alliteration has cast it as archetypal suburb. Keble Howard published in 1906 *The Smiths of Surbiton*, a novel that follows the fortunes of a newly married couple, insurance clerk Ralph and his wife, Enid, and their upward rise through suburbia. Their first house has a garden front and back, a drawing room with little French windows opening on to a tiny balcony, an airy kitchen, five bedrooms and a 'dainty bathroom'. The Smiths dispense with the house number and their notepaper simply bears the address The Pleasance (the same name as that picked by Emily Eden), Eton Road, Surbiton. Before the Smiths have been in residence at The Pleasance one month, they are on nodding terms with fifty people, on visiting terms with twenty, and on 'dropping in' terms with two. Finally, Ralph becomes head clerk and they move up, literally, to a house on a hill, three reception rooms, seven bedrooms, lounge-hall, electric light fittings and a garden large enough for lawn tennis and croquet. 'In short Valley View was just the house to which a man who has worked steadily and industriously for nearly forty years, who has married happily and brought up a family, whose employers have grown to look upon him as a staunch, good friend, whose eldest son is playing his part in the development of the Colonies, and whose eldest daughter is about to take her place as a younger leader of

local society, may fairly consider himself entitled wherein to pass the gentle closing years of his life.' Their society is local, but the money has to come from working in the city. The dogged persistence with which Smith plods through life is in contrast to the path taken by his son George, who rebels against the prudence of the older generation ('You don't make money without working for it'), speculates and loses his money: in much the same way as Lupin Pooter does in *Diary of a Nobody* after he has left home ('I am not going to rot my life away in the suburbs').

When the politician and journalist Charles Masterman wrote *The Condition of England* in 1909 he put the Suburbans between the Conquerors and the Multitude. Identifying them as a product of the second half of the nineteenth century, he saw them as 'detached, self-centred, unostentatious. It is a life of Security; a life of Sedentary occupation; a life of Respectability; and these three qualities give the key to its special characteristics.'

GARDEN SUBURBS

WHILE MASTERMAN WAS DIVIDING THE NATION INTO THREE CLASSES Henrietta Barnett was two years into planning Hampstead Garden Suburb, with the radical aim of reintegrating the classes and proving that suburbs could be lively. The farmland she chose would also be saved from speculative development, since it abutted the newly opened Golders Green Underground station. Henrietta and Samuel Barnett had been social reformers in Whitechapel, and she had first-hand knowledge of slum conditions. She grasped clearly how good housing, a garden and green spaces could vastly improve the lot of the working man.

Both Henrietta Barnett and Ebenezer Howard, the force behind Letchworth, the first garden city in Hertfordshire, chose Barry Parker and Raymond Unwin as architects. Letchworth was different from Hampstead Garden Suburb in that, crucially, places of work were integral to the town plan. 'The town and country must be married, and out of this joyous union will spring a new hope, a new life, a new civilisation.' Both Barnett and Howard fell in with Parker and Unwin's ideas for a new type of house. They proposed that houses should face the sun, 'from whence come light, sweetness and health', and be simpler in design, obliterating dining

Frontispiece, entitled 'Home', to *The Art and Craft of Home-Making*, 1913, by Edward Gregory (of The Nook, Loughton). Watercolour by F.C. Witney. Here all the aspirations of suburban living are epitomized.

A house in Meadway, Hampstead Garden Suburb, by M.H. Baillie Scott, c.1908. Angled to make maximum use of sunlight, this house is, as Baillie Scott described it, 'a dwelling worthy to be ranked with the Englishman's home of the past – modest, serviceable and full of charm withal'.

rooms, libraries and drawing rooms, 'planned largely to meet supposed wants that never occur'. Unwin moved at the earliest opportunity to Letchworth, building a pair of semi-detached houses, Laneside and Crabby Corner, for himself and his friend Howard Pearsall, a board member of the First Garden City Company. He disapproved of the 'common unsatiable desire for detachment'.

At both Hampstead Garden Suburb and Letchworth innovative housing for all classes of inhabitants was planned. There emerged a suburban vernacular with gables, dormer windows, roughcast, catslide roofs and exposed timberwork, inglenooks and craftsman-made furniture. As M.H. Baillie Scott, an architect who worked in both places, had explained in an 1894 edition of *The Studio* magazine, 'An Ideal Suburban House' was simple, sunny, with no money wasted on useless ornament, inspired by the plain bricks and whitewash of a old farmhouse, 'where the marbled wall-papers and oil-cloths which greet us on the threshold of so many modern villas are unknown'. An attic could be used as a study, work-room or studio. Such flexibility was explained to a wider audience in *Modern Suburban Homes* by C.K. Snell (1903). He suggested that a breakfast room could actually be a study, schoolroom or doctor's consulting room, and that billiard rooms, day nurseries, porches, verandas, conservatories, boudoirs and servants' stairs were all pointless. With a bathroom and flush lavatories in place, the days of meeting a maid 'on the stairs with a slop bucket and broom' were finally gone.

This was a style in tune with the pioneering residents of Letchworth, Hampstead Garden Suburb and other co-operative suburbs. In Hampstead a private Act of Parliament waived by-laws that had resulted in dull uniformity in terrace housing and so allowed Unwin the freedom to plan in a density of eight houses to the acre along the Hills, Ways, Chases, Drives, Closes and Walks in a variety of widths that gave a distinctive sense of place. Working people were to be housed in groups of cottages within the twopenny Tube ride to work, the middle classes and professional people further away in squares and culs-de-sac (which make their first appearance here). Henrietta Barnett was restating the long-held goal of a perfect suburban house, that there should be 'consideration for picturesque appearance' and that one should not spoil another's outlook. Hampstead Garden Suburb was to have a choice of churches, an institute and a school, but no pub and, later, no cinema; suburban peace was not be interrupted by church bells, and hedges or trellises, rather than walls, were mandatory. As it turned out, it was expensive for the working classes to get to work and their housing was appropriated by those higher up the pecking order.

The institute was, in Henrietta Barnett's words, intended to be 'an intellectual centre where intellectual people of all standards of cultivation and all classes of society could meet in potential friendship'. To those held within the grip of a rigid Edwardian class structure this was an unattractive idea. But it did appeal to certain strata of society. As reported by the *Architects' and Builders' Journal* in 1911, inhabitants of Hampstead Garden Suburb have 'infinite pity and compassion for those who do not dwell there . . . Everyone knows everyone, like a town in the middle ages, a city walled around from the outside; inside a peaceful haven, everyone meets at the excellent club-house near the village green to play tennis or billiards, or drink tea.' Since it was only twopence a week to join, it was used by 'all types', shoemakers, postmen, architects and doctors up the scale to the prosperous City man. 'To mention idiosyncrasies and not occupations would make a larger list. There are socialists, Fabians, Communists, Suffragists, anti-vivisectionists, and people who are anti everything else. There are a great many serious people in HGS, ladies for instance who wear pince-nez and a severe expression and

who think that the height of dissipation is to dine in Soho with young men who wear loose ties. "Arty" people abound . . . But the "suburb" is by no means a "cranky" place, although artistic temperament is rampant. There is a solid element of business people who know a good place to live in when they see it and who do not bother with the artistic temperament and so keep Utopia steady.'

There was room for experiment and optimism in suburbs, as these were brand-new communities. The idea of escaping the clutches of speculators to create co-operative housing schemes – 'garden villages and garden suburbs' – caught on during the early years of the twentieth century: the principle was that each tenant was a shareholder and the houses were held in common. The first was Ealing Tenants Ltd, formed by six members of Ebenezer Howard's co-operative building firm in 1901 to build nine houses. By 1914 Brentham, as it was called, had about six hundred houses and was well established, with an annual Whit Monday cricket match between Brentham Garden Suburb Club and Hampstead Garden Suburb.

Prior to the First World War, several similar communities were formed, including Burnage Garden Village in Manchester, Rhiwbina Garden Village at the edge of Cardiff, and Wavertree in Liverpool. These were idealistic communities, often teetotal, with a drive for self-improvement and enthusiasm for uncomplicated fun with maypoles, pageants and folk-dancing. Bryce Leicester described life at Wavertree in issue no. 2

of *Garden Suburb and Village Homes* in 1912. Each new family was welcomed with a 'circular letter from the pioneers already established here [that] greeted the new comers and asked them to join the guild of those bent on the quest of a more social life', which centred on the Club House. 'True our vocalist and our instrumentalist may not be so renowned as the artistes at the Philharmonic Hall; our lecturers not so distinguished and so brilliant as those at the University; but there is a charm in seeing and hearing them in our own hall, where we feel at home, at our ease among our neighbours and our friends. Spared the fatigue and expense of a journey to town, the rush and crush of a public assembly hall, the tedious journey back again late at night, we are able to remain by the fireside or in the garden, according to the season of the year, until a few minutes before the hour of commencement . . . Surely under conditions such as these we may look forward to a sturdier race of citizens.'

COUNCIL TENANTS AND HOMEOWNERS

LOCAL AUTHORITIES saw the advantages of building on cheap suburban land and creating something approximating the much-admired garden city communities, but to keep costs down the houses had to be simplified, with rather less gabling and

OPPOSITE In 'Pergola Season in the Garden Suburb', an artistic couple agonize over their pruning. This gently mocking cartoon, originally published in *Punch*, August 1912, was reproduced in *The Town Crier*, the Hampstead Garden Suburb journal.
LEFT The Roehampton Estate, built by the LCC in the 1920s on land previously attached to two large houses, Dover House (demolished) and Putney Park House. The housing was grouped in garden suburb mode.

On the cover of Richard Reiss's *The Home I Want*, 1918, a soldier points to the semi-detached houses under a blue sky.

picturesque irregularity – and built to a higher density. In the early years of the twentieth century the LCC built estates at Old Oak in Hammersmith and White Hart Lane in Tottenham which owed much to Unwin's street plans and to his previously published plans for cheap cottages (see page 42). By the end of the First World War it was clear that a substantial house shortage was brewing and a massive programme of new house-building was needed to appease dangerously disgruntled demobbed soldiery. A report was commissioned from Sir John Tudor Walters to analyse the needs and set the standards. Published in 1918, it promoted low densities, street layouts with culs-de-sac and passageways, houses with a bathroom, three bedrooms if possible; it even recognized that 'wherever possible a parlour should be provided . . . It is a parlour which the majority desire.' This was a source of pain to architects, who believed one large living room at the front of a house a far better solution. A Housing Act of 1919 required local authorities to provide public housing to fulfil Lloyd George's promised 'homes fit for heroes' and supplied subsidies to do it. The cover of *The Home I Want* by Richard Reiss of the Loyal North Lancashire Regiment, published in 1918, is explicit: 'You cannot expect to get an A.1 population out of C.3 homes'. The C.3 home as illustrated is an urban terrace under a grey sky – 'barrack-like rows of dwellings' and 'the repetition of meagre fronts'. The sunny ideal is whitewashed roughcast, gabled, with front garden and picket fence, semi-detached, with a wide frontage doing away with the necessity for gloomy back extensions blocking out light and sun. The living room and the parlour were in the front of the house and the mother at the scullery window could watch her children playing in the back garden. All should have bathrooms. 'Wherever possible, a self-contained house should be our aim,' Reiss wrote.

Nearly three-quarters of a million houses were built by local authorities – suburban 'cottage estates', low-density houses built in small groups and set in gardens around greens or along culs-de-sac. These ranged from a small group on the outskirts of town to the enormous Beacontree estate in Dagenham for twenty-six thousand people. Plain brick, their lack of leaded lights, bay windows, mock timber framing or stained glass proclaimed them 'council houses'. However, when the government abruptly cut off the council subsidies in 1923 it was left to the private builders to fill the shortfall. During the war rents had been fixed, so although that restriction also ended in 1923 the idea of building houses to rent had become less attractive. Instead houses were for sale. Prices and interest rates had fallen, and house-building boomed. Building societies offered increasingly cheap terms on increasingly cheap – and small – houses as the decade progressed; the semi-detached was the smallest and cheapest solution. Tax relief on mortgages was introduced. By the outbreak of the Second World War over four million houses had been built and ownership had risen from a pre-First World War 10 per cent to 30 per cent. By the late 1930s the market was saturated and it was possible to buy a Wates semi in Mitcham for £315 with a weekly payment of 8s.10d.

In *Coming up for Air*, his novel about suburbia, George Orwell's protagonist, insurance salesman George Bowling, living in the inner-outer suburbs, railed against the system. 'A line of semi-detached torture-chambers where the poor little five-to-ten-pound-a-weekers quake and shiver, every one of them with the boss twisting his tail and the wife riding him like a nightmare and the kids sucking his blood like leeches.' It was all 'part of a huge racket called the Hesperides Estate, the property of the Cheerful Credit Building'. With the mortgage, he was 'eaten up with the ghastly fear that something might happen before we've made our last payment'. Speculative builders depended on the building societies for finance and by pooling resources they had succeeded in making the cost of a deposit ever more affordable. Fierce competition among speculative builders led to competing offers of free cars, refrigerators and season tickets and ever more hyperbole: 'Artistry and Utility Combined', 'Estate facing Glorious Woods and Open Heath', 'Each House a Gem'. But there was no increase in rented accommodation for the many unable to save even a small down payment.

The division could be literal. In 1926 a wall topped with broken glass was built cutting off communication between the private owners of houses in Alexandra Crescent, Bromley, and those in the LCC's suburban estate of Downham. The inhabitants of the crescent objected to the estate dwellers using their road to walk into town. This behaviour was repeated in 1934, when Clive Saxton of the Urban Housing Company built a seven-foot spiked wall between the estate that he was building in north Oxford and the council's Cutteslowe estate, claiming dogs and children from there would lower the value of his houses. The wall was demolished by the council in 1938, but the court ordered that it be rebuilt, and it remained until 1959. This self-protective mindset is exemplified by a character in Lettice Cooper's novel *The New*

Cutteslowe, Oxford: a spiked wall blocking off access between the council houses (in view) and the gabled bay-windowed private housing being demolished, for the first time, in 1938.

House, published in 1936. 'Evelyn's view of the housing problem was simple. "Our sort of people" needed, and ought to have, nice houses, because they were accustomed to them. "Working people" ought, she supposed, to have decent houses, but not in any place where they would spoil the view of the neighbourhood for "our sort of people". In any case most "working people" did not want nice houses. If they were given four bedrooms, they all slept together in one. Gladys's young man had told her about a family who did that, and it showed you that it was no use trying to help "that sort of person". Another of Evelyn's articles of faith was that it was a waste of time moving people out of a slum, because they turned any house they lived in into a slum.' The novel's plot concerns a large family house on the edge of an industrial town being demolished and the site developed.

ANTAGONISM TO SPRAWL

FEW PLANNING CONTROLS EXISTED and so houses too big for depressed times and swathes of countryside were rapidly disappearing, and at a speed that caused alarm. The fact that farm values, prices and profits were declining facilitated the ease with which cheap land could be bought for building houses, factories and roads. Architecture was largely abandoned in the free-for-all – and with it architects, who objected to the pick and mix attitude to period style. 'Note the skill with which the houses are disposed, that insures that the largest possible area of the countryside is ruined with the minimum of expense,' wrote Osbert Lancaster angrily. The architects fought back: Clough Williams-Ellis compiled *England and the Octopus* in 1928 and *Britain and the Beast* in 1937, raising consciousness. In the latter, planner Thomas Sharp, while admitting that 'the awful prisoning streets' of cities held no attraction, had little sympathy for those seeking a better life in suburbia. 'Their romantic villas and bungalows with their pebble-dash, their half-timbered gables, their "picturesque" leaded-lighted windows, are certainly in striking contrast to the terrace house of their old congested quarters. But the contrast is merely between one type of barbarism and another.' They were 'selfish and anti-social. Every person who goes to the suburbs pushes the countryside away from someone else – and then he in turn suffers from having it pushed away from him.' The result, Sharp said, was social sterility, aesthetic emptiness and economic wastefulness. Railing against bogus Tudor, the default style of so many suburban houses, was ineffective; Anthony Bertram in the Pelican Special *Design* (1938) described it as both technically and socially dishonest. Tudor, perhaps

conjuring up for its inhabitants some unthreatening golden Elizabethan age, was far more popular than the Modern alternative. Here the minimal lines of Modernism were gussied up with some streamline features, sunburst gates and grass-green pantiles, but with an identical conventional ground plan. Tiled bathrooms, garages and electric kitchens were the desirable features in both. Osbert Lancaster's 1938 diatribe against 'Stockbroker's Tudor', engendered by the sight of numerous Tudor-style cottages complete with central heating and garages, asked the question why 'all over the country the latest and most scientific methods of mass-production are being utilised to turn out a stream of old oak beams, leaded window-panes and small discs of bottle glass, all structural devices which our ancestors lost no time in abandoning as soon as an increase in wealth and knowledge enabled them to do so.'

In 1930 Evelyn Waugh imagined a scene from an aeroplane in *Vile Bodies*: 'Nina looked down and saw inclined at an odd angle a horizon of straggling red suburb; arterial roads dotted with little cars; factories, some of them working, others empty and decaying; a disused canal; some distant hills sown with bungalows; wireless masts, and overhead power cables . . .' J.B. Priestley saw a positive side in his *English Journey* of 1933. 'The northern entrance to London, where the smooth wide road passes between miles of semi-detached bungalows, all with their garages, their wireless sets, their periodicals about film stars, their swimming costumes and tennis rackets and dancing shoes . . . You need money in this England, but you do not need much money. It is a large-scale, mass-production job, with cut prices. Its cheapness is both its weakness and its strength. It is its strength because being cheap it is accessible; it nearly achieves the famous equality of opportunity. In this England, for the first time in history, Jack and Jill are nearly as good as their master and mistress; they may have always been as good in their own way, but now they are nearly as good in the same way. Jack, like his master, is rapidly transported to some place of rather mechanical amusement. Jill beautifies herself exactly as her mistress does. It is an England, at last, without privilege.'

Priestley's journey was, naturally, by car. Increased ownership of motor cars made everywhere accessible and had, as G.M. Trevelyan put it, turned 'every "beauty spot" into an "eligible building site"'. H. G Wells had been too optimistic in *Anticipations* of 1900 when he imagined future car use: 'One will traverse open, breezy, "horsey" suburbs,

A·W·CURTON
PRESENTS HIS HOUSE

1939
EDITION

With compliments
A·W·CURTON LTD.
EDGWARE

OPPOSITE Cover illustration for *Ideal Home*, May 1936, headed 'How, When and Where to Build' and giving a view of unspoilt countryside. LEFT Brochure for north London developer A.W. Curton, 1939. This booklet illustrated ten types of detached and semi-detached houses adjoining Edgware Golf Course. The were designed either in Tudor style – as here – or the less popular modernist.

smart white gates and palings everywhere ... gardening districts all set with gables and roses, holly hedges and emerald lawns; pleasant houses among heathery moorlands and golf-links.' Reality was a landscape of petrol stations, advertising signs, roadside cafés and bypasses lined with ribbons of houses. The fight to stop the rot led to the Town and Country Planning Act of 1932 for the 'protection of rural amenities, preservation of buildings, and other objects of interest or beauty; to facilitate the acquisition of land for garden cities'. Ribbon development was restricted in 1935, although by using a loophole and building a parallel service road to the main road it persisted.

HOME LIFE: DRAWBACKS AND CHARMS

Wherever the Underground emerged, developers clustered. The Metropolitan was London's first underground railway and as it extended out to the north-west through Harrow to Pinner it had been forced to acquire more land than it needed. In 1919 a subsidiary company was set up to develop 'Metro-land', as it was effectively branded. The train door catches were engraved 'Live in Metroland'; an annual magazine, *Metro-land*, detailed developments and highlights of the area, and around 1920 Boyle Lawrence was commissioned to write a popular song. The refrain 'It

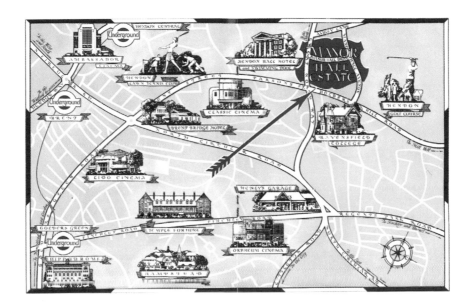

LEFT London Electricity Board leaflet: much of the appeal of a new house in the inter-war period lay in the automatic provision of electricity, which enabled the use of labour-saving equipment.
ABOVE A mid-1930s brochure promoting the Manor Hall Estate in north London mapped suburban high spots: Underground stations, cinemas, garages, shopping parades, hotels, tennis and golf clubs.

is happiness crowned, / It is Paradise found, / Is my little metroland home' came between the morning verse, when the commuter catches the eight fifteen train, and the day's end:

> A smile sweet and rare, and a welcome so gay
> Are waiting me there at the close of the day.
> Each eve'ning at sev'n she is looking for me –
> When I get back by the five fifty three.

The developer's interwar estates, unlike Hampstead Garden Suburb, did not offer a rich mixture of culture and amusement. The house, both inside and out, was for many a canvas for hobbies. Women's magazines, ranging from *Ideal Home*, expensive at a shilling, through the sixpenny *Home Making, Modern Home* or *Women and Home* to the twopenny *Woman's Own*, were packed with information on needlework, homecrafts, fashion, knitting and crochet. 'Household Tools, can you use them properly? Elsie Shand shows you how to be independent.' Miss Ruby M. Ayres, the popular novelist, might warn about 'The Greatest Enemy to Marriage – Boredom! for the women who have no interest outside the task of looking after a home, a husband and children' in *Home Making* (February 1933), but escape could be found a few pages later by reading an instalment of Betty Trask's latest romantic novel, *Camera!*, in which Sue Cooper of Flecker's Grove, a 'nobody', rose to stardom. Sid G. Hedges's 1930s *Universal Book of Hobbies*, aimed at the tidily nuclear family illustrated in the frontispiece, wrote: 'Life can be very drab; mind and spirit can be almost quenched. But hobbies can save them.' He saw no bar to achieving Painting on Wood and Glass, Paper Lampshades, Wood Carving, Mushroom Growing, Stencil Craft, Fretwork, Leatherwork, Model Aeroplanes, Greenhouses, Crochet, even 'Television'. A 1929 collection of essays, *Wonderful London*, had characterized the typical suburban: 'his pipe, his morning and evening newspapers, his tea-shop lunch, his strip of garden, his local tennis, cricket and football clubs. He has his occasional hands of bridge, his gramophone, his wireless set, his infrequent struggles with popular novels or semi-popular non-fiction. He has developed great skill in the manipulation of motor engines and electric lights.'

Writers and planners tended to imagine the lot of the suburban housewife as bleak (most jobs had to be surrendered on marriage). Christopher Isherwood and W.H. Auden in their play *The Ascent of F6*, no doubt to the amusement of their audience, presented a typically patronizing account of a housewife's day in 1936. It began 'I have dusted the six small rooms' and continued:

> The delivery vans have paid their brief impersonal visits.
> I have eaten a scrappy lunch from a plate on my knee.
> I have spoken with acquaintances in the Stores;
> Under our treble gossip heard the menacing throb of our hearts
> As I hear them now, as all of us hear them,
> Standing at our stoves in these villas, expecting our husbands.

The same superiority led Somerset Maugham to proclaim: 'It is unnatural for an artist to live in a semi-detached villa and eat cottage pie cooked by a maid of all work.' Then there was Osbert Lancaster's throwaway remark, also made in 1938, that suburban houses were the slums of the future: 'That is, if a fearful and more sudden fate does not obliterate them prematurely; an eventuality that does much to reconcile one to the prospect of aerial bombardment.' The antipathy is still present in John Betjeman's 1954 poem of regret for the lost Middlesex countryside, replaced by the train disgorging commuters: 'With a thousand Ta's and Pardon's / Daintily alights Elaine.'

In contrast, the novel *Greengates* by R.C. Sherriff (1936) shows rare sympathetic understanding of how thrilling a new suburban house might have been. It is set in 1926. Tom Baldwin, a city clerk, and his wife, Edith, move from 'Grasmere', their basemented Victorian inner suburb house, to a new one in the country in Stanmore. They are astonished by its 'delightful warmth' (central heating, boiler running on kitchen rubbish), the entrance hall, almost a room in itself (Grasmere had nothing but a high-ceilinged, narrow passage, crowded with the coat-stand and umbrella-rack, with doors leading stiffly from it), carpet covering the whole floor, the downstairs cloakroom with wash basin and lavatory (Grasmere involved an ascent upstairs like the conquest of Everest). Then there was the dining room, 'gloriously clean and airy. Its very plainness and simplicity captured the imagination and gave one the feeling of being on a ship bound for some high spirited adventure. One could never feel depressed or old in such a room, with such generous windows and bright cream walls.' The lounge had unexpected little alcoves and recesses and 'an intriguing little oval

An advertisement from the 1933 *Building Societies' Year Book*, which also included news from the Jarrow Permanent, Bishop Auckland Rock, Walsall Mutual Benefit and Sunderland Working Men's Building Society.

window like a ship's porthole high up in the wall . . . the fireplace itself was of small mellowed bricks: it looked like the arched gateway to a miniature Tudor mansion and made one think of crackling logs and moorland peat.' Each bedroom had a basin with hot and cold water night and day and there were built-in cupboards. With its neat gate and electric lights, 'It seemed as if everything in "Greengates" was going to happen in a series of cheerful clicks.' As the Baldwins' neighbour remarks on his new house, 'It's all so clean and fresh – it's nice to know that nobody's ever died in any of the bedrooms.'

By the 1950s the initial freshness of these interwar suburbs had worn off, and the ornamental touches of mock Tudor or Art Deco dated and drab. Towns and cities, on the other hand, were regenerating. Frustration drove Betty Jerman, a journalist feeling trapped by her baby and suburban house, to write a piece for *The Guardian* in February 1960. Under the heading 'Squeezed in like Sardines in Suburbia', she wrote of its incredible dullness and how 'Home and child-minding have a blunting effect on a woman's mind.' Similarly placed, Maureen Nicol, a Wirral housewife, responded and formed the Housebound Housewives' Register to enable liberal-minded women to make contact with each other. As Jerman explained in a 1968 *Good Housekeeping* article, 'How to Survive in Suburbia', rather than hear other young women with families talk about 'colic, measles, pot-training, or give a blow-by-blow account of their confinement', with fellow members of the register you could discuss 'the pill, new parliamentary bills, children's librarians, sterilization and whether or not you should allow someone else to bring up your children.'

In a 1962 feature which caught the mood of the time *House & Garden* praised a more civilized urban life and modern terrace housing as 'the return to sanity'. As usual, suburban dwellers were snobbishly derided, accused of being anti-culture and members of the 'Affluent Society' who only wanted the new: 'They want three bedrooms, a garage, a small garden, a room for the telly and a "nice" neighbourhood, which usually means having neighbours like themselves.' It took *Dunroamin: The Suburban Semi and its Enemies* by Paul Oliver, Ian Davis and Ian Bentley (1981) to put such houses into context, to explain why they were so reviled, but to see them as places also of individuality, where the inhabitants could make of the house and surroundings precisely what they wanted. They summed this up by quoting Cadbury on Bournville: 'I do not call it a waste of land to give a man his own house and garden, where he can feel that it is his own to do with as he wishes, and where at least he can have more than enough fresh air around him.'

A 1963 advertisement from *House & Garden* suggests that with Snowcem the interwar suburban house can be given new life.

THE BEAUTY OF
SNOWCEM
IT COSTS SO LITTLE

You can transform a house like this one for only £8 worth of Snowcem. And because it's a *waterproof cement paint*, Snowcem protects as it beautifies. It's so easy to apply—you just brush it on. But Snowcem is remarkably inexpensive, too. See your Snowcem stockist—find out how much Snowcem can save you. Nine attractive pastel shades and white.

Write for the Colour Chart and Leaflet
SNOWCEM SERVICE, THE CEMENT MARKETING CO. LTD.,
Portland House, Stag Place, London, SW1
Tel: TATe Gallery 3456

American suburbs, viewed in films and imported television shows, did present an alternative suburban vision to post-war Britain. Builders had a brief flirtation with the ranch-style house with feature chimneys, stone and weatherboard panels and picture windows. In some cases the front garden boundaries were even removed to create what a character in Angus Wilson's *Late Call* (1964) termed 'American neighbourliness', but which others probably regarded as scary exposure.

Few towns are now without their housing development on the edge, often encircled and separate, a latter-day suburb. The past is still mined for period features – a half-timbered gable, Edwardian porch or Victorian bay window. The Avenues, Drives and Closes wind and turn into culs-de-sac as they have done for over a century.

On 28 November 2012 Nick Boles, Planning Minister, commenting that more land should be given over to housing, declared that everyone had a moral right 'to a home with a little bit of ground round it to bring up your family in . . . I think everyone has the right to live somewhere that is not just affordable but that is beautiful and has some green space nearby.' The suburban dream.

BUNGALOWS

I N ITS RELATIVELY SHORT LIFE AS A HOUSING TYPE, the bungalow has been subject to enthusiasm and vitriol in almost equal parts. And it has symbolized both unfettered freedom and compressed geriatric living.

By the 1870s the British thought they knew what a bungalow was – a long, low, single-storey house, with a verandah, inhabited by a European in Bombay, Madras, Ootacamond or some such place, perhaps with a copy of *A Guide to Indian Household Management containing hints on Outfits, Packing and Bungalows* (1879) on its bookshelf. Set apart from the local population and generally built of sun-dried bricks and with a thatched or tiled roof, it was designed to be as comfortable as possible in both monsoon and searing heat.

THE HEALTHY LIFE

HOWEVER, THE WORD TOOK ON AN EXTRA DIMENSION when on 15 August 1873 *Building News* ran an article headed 'Mr. Taylor's Bungalows at West Cliff, Birchington-on-Sea' and went on: 'It is very difficult in these days to hit upon a new and successful idea. Mr. John Taylor of 6, Whitehall, has unquestionably done so in his "Bungalow" residences that he has for some time been engaged in erecting in the neighbourhood of Margate.' The accompanying illustration showed a plain single-storey building tucked under a single roof span and faced with a little decoration of whitish bricks and clinker (but no verandah). By naming this fairly ordinary edifice a bungalow, the architect was making it clear that this was something extraordinary.

For a start, the situation of Taylor's bungalows, 'as bracing as our island can supply', was unusual, perched up on the cliffs on the Kent coast, with nothing between them and the sea, and, furthermore, 'nothing but sea between them and the North Pole'. These bungalows offered a superabundant exposure to fresh air together with opportunity for exercise, both increasingly seen as highly beneficial to health. In some quarters there was a growing rebellion over the claustrophobia of Victorian interiors, social ritual and dress. Enthusiasm for the bungalow, with its 'extreme simplicity and adaptability, so generally lost sight of in the over-refinement and finish of the present day', was one outcome, as was the Rational Dress Society

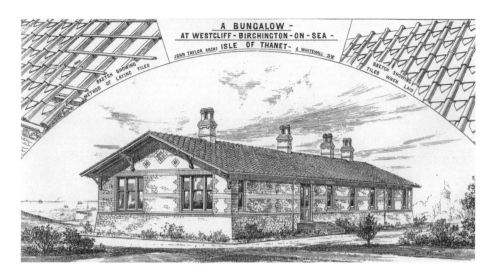

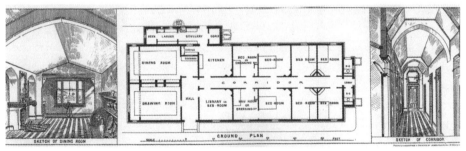

An illustration from *Building News* of 1873, showing one of John Taylor's bungalows at Birchington-on-Sea.

founded by women in 1881 in order to cast off the corsets, high-heeled shoes and heavily weighted skirts that rendered exertion almost impossible. Recommendation of John Taylor's bungalows at Westcliff came from an early buyer, Professor Erasmus Wilson, who praised them as being 'novel, quaint, and pretty, and *perfect as to sanitary qualities. The best sanitary house for a family is a Bungalow.*' Since Wilson was the leading expert on skin diseases and a propagandist for baths and sea-bathing, his views were considered worth heeding.

Their novelty was thought worth publicizing by local resident Athol Mayhew, who published *Birchington on Sea and its Bungalows* in 1881, by which date John Taylor's original bungalows had been augmented by others designed by the architect John Seddon. Mayhew made clear that the 'modified Indian country-houses' were for people who wanted a different (and more modern) seaside experience. There were 'no German bands, nigger minstrels, tea gardens, donkey rides or assembly rooms', but instead 'an uncontaminated playground for large families and secluded sanatorium for invalids'. Here, the most 'jaded professional man in search of ease may pass his well-earned holiday in the most invigorating tranquillity.'

The Kent bungalows quickly gained the reputation of being excellent for invalids. When Dante Gabriel Rossetti, semi-paralysed by a stroke, was recommended a change of air, his brother William suggested a bungalow at Birchington-on-Sea, describing it as 'a new marine health resort'. He arranged for Rossetti, together with his friend and general factotum Thomas Hall Caine and Caine's twelve-year-old sister Lily, to take up residence at Westcliff Bungalow, which had generously been lent free of charge by its owner, a Mr Cobb. The party travelled down by train in early February 1882, Rossetti tetchily prevaricating on the wisdom of the scheme. On arrival at the bungalow he complained to Lily that it looked more like another London, Chatham and Dover Railway station than a house, and that he could see neither beauty nor comfort. Aesthetics were high on the family agenda, and Rossetti's mother, visiting with his sister Christina, also remarked on its lack of beauty. However, she was won over by how convenient the layout was for an invalid – a long corridor flanked by rooms on either side. On Easter Sunday the artist died, his body lying in the bungalow until, at his mother's insistence, the London firm of Brucciani had been down and made a death mask.

The following year Sir Shirley Murphy, editing a collection of 'papers on sanitary subjects' in *Our Homes, and How to make them Healthy*, specifically mentioned the bungalow as 'intended as a summer residence for a family, or as a private sanatorium, the situation being peculiarly favourable for such a purpose from the invigorating quality of the air'. He added that it 'afforded the greatest comfort with the least amount of household labour' – thus latching on to another of what turned out to be one of the bungalow's most appealing features: that it could be run with little or no help.

An early bungalow dweller and perhaps typical in that he fitted into no particular social niche, was Frederick Boyle, barrister and orchid-fancier, who had travelled in Borneo, Sarawak, South Africa, Central and South America, observed the downfall

Frederick Boyle seated among his travel mementoes in his bungalow, photographed for the frontispiece of his book *Legends of my Bungalow*, 1882.

of the Ashanti and been a newspaper correspondent in the Russo-Turkish War. Since colonial Africa had also adopted the bungalow, he may well have become familiar with the form there. The photographic frontispiece of his *Legends of my Bungalow* (1882) shows the author sitting in a long, narrow room stuffed with trophies from his travels, each of which prompted a chapter of his book: the lynx skin on the hearth; the gun rack 'in the glazed porch of my dwelling, nearly hidden at summertime by flowers and climbing plants', and the Ashanti stool at his fireside that 'has a singular attraction for the young of that sex which I admire so warmly and know so little' – the young ladies accompanying their papas on a visit to his 'bachelor abode'. He ends with the observation that on returning to his bungalow in Croydon, after two months away in Eastern Europe, he found it 'quaint and sunny – and damp, as always'.

The Garden Front

Bungalow at Bellagio

One of R.A. Briggs's designs for Bellagio, his East Grinstead estate, named after a village on Lake Como. This home he described as 'a bachelor's summer residence' (cost £800).

The architect R.A. Briggs (or 'Bungalow Briggs', as he came to be known) was another enthusiast who worked hard to widen their appeal. He built an estate of bungalows near East Grinstead, a ten-minute carriage ride from the newly opened railway station, complete with tennis court, fishing lake and recreation ground. Some were illustrated in *Bungalows and Country Residences, recently executed* (1891) a collection of designs with built prices ranging from £250 to £4,500. (His list of subscribers included HRH The Princess Mary, Duchess of Teck.) Briggs was keen to put a positive spin on bungalows: 'A cottage is a little house in the country, but a bungalow is a little country house, a homely, cosy little place, with verandah and balconies, and the plan so arranged as to ensure complete comfort, with a feeling of rusticity and ease.' He quashed any idea that a British bungalow might have any resemblance to a low, squat, rambling, one-storied house under the glaring sun of India or 'some rude settlement in one of the colonies, where houses or huts of wood hewn from the tree with shingle roofs, give us the impression, as it were, of "roughing it". On the contrary, the bungalow was an 'artistic little dwelling, cheaply but soundly built . . . popped down in some pretty little spot with just sufficient accommodation for our particular needs . . . a free and easy dwelling in the country, erected on sites out of the way of the ordinary run of holiday-seekers, or on some river bank or unfrequented shore.' As Briggs shrewdly realized, the bungalow was the perfect cheap retreat for those 'people of moderate means in a city like ours, where the grime and the smoke, the bustle and the hurry, make us long for the country and its freshness'. And, as he pointed out, furnishings should be economic and simple: bentwood and bamboo furniture; floors stained, varnished or covered with matting; woodwork painted white and decorations 'of the airiest description'.

The journal *Building News* continued to monitor the bungalow's progress, identifying the 'extensive verandah' as its essential feature and showing, in 1895, a selection of bungalows built in brick and roofed in tile and slate. This was to refute the idea 'that the bungalow is of necessity a very temporary kind of structure – something like a dismantled railway carriage deprived of its wheels and fitted up as a residence'. That, in fact, was a fair description of many of the ad hoc and temporary buildings that were popping up all over the place, a state of affairs highly unpopular with architects and the building trade. Maybe in an attempt to wrest the initiative from the self-builders and the carriage-shunters, *Building News* ran competitions for bungalow design. The brief for the May 1898 competition was a Hill Side Bungalow. 'Restrictions are few, and chances for artistic originality are unfettered, provided all attempt at a monumental style of building is avoided and the suitability of simplicity is acknowledged.' The imagined client was to be a gentleman, the site well wooded and a few miles from London, and the building intended only for summer occupation. It was to have a belvedere smoking room, hall, living room, drawing room, full-size billiard room, four best bedrooms and two for servants. Responding to its recreational purpose, one of the winners incorporated storage for bicycles and golfing irons.

In *The Whirlpool* (1897), George Gissing created a character who might well have been the client for that competition. A millionaire 'quasi-aristocratic' inhabitant of the demi-monde, Cyrus Redgrave, has persuaded his sister to let him build a bungalow among the trees in her large garden in Wimbledon, with a separate entrance from the road. Redgrave cites its advantages: 'One is free there; a member of the family whenever one likes; domesticated; all that's respectable; and only a few steps away, the bachelor snuggery with all that's – .' Redgrave invites Alma Frothingham, an aspiring violinist, to come down to one of his afternoon gatherings: 'I assure you it is perfectly respectable.' Alma 'had a curiosity about the bungalow. Its exotic name affected her imagination; as did the knowledge that Cyrus Redgrave, who she knew so particularly well, had built it for his retreat, his privacy.' She agrees to go there and 'it was the first time in her life that she had acted with deliberate disregard of grave moral compunction.' A feature that contributes to the bungalow's dubious moral tone is that the bedrooms have French windows: 'The front door may be locked and bolted, but people come and go for all that.' A jealous husband subsequently punches Redgrave, who dies of a broken neck as his head hits the verandah door.

BOHEMIAN SHACKS

THE BATTLE FOR THE ARCHITECT-DESIGNED BUNGALOW was in fact rapidly being lost, as recluses and adventurers, dubbed 'Back-to-the-Landers', hauled railway carriages and what amounted to little more than wooden sheds on to sand dunes, hills and riversides, in search of an instant and very cheap place to set up camp. Shacks could slowly acquire the accoutrements of a bungalow. In *The Thames and its Story*, compiled in 1909, the Surrey bank near Staines is described as giving 'hospitality to a ragged array of those wooden shanties which are dignified by the name of "bungalows", and which with their fluttering flags and enamelled trellises, impart a tawdry flippancy to the banks of the river.' River trades were dying, leaving vacant riverside and islands such as Eel Pie, Tagg's and Pharoah's that were perfect for summer colonization.

Shoreham Beach in Sussex was a site typical of many that clustered on marginal land around the country. The long shingle bank, hitherto inhabited only by fishermen and flint-pickers, began to acquire a scattering of railway carriages, ferried over from Shoreham town by boat, fixed on to concrete rafts and used as dwellings. This motley collection was discovered in 1900 by Marie Loftus, at the height of her fame as the 'Sarah Bernhardt of the Music Halls', while exploring on an afternoon off from performing in nearby Brighton. Enchanted with the set-up, she commissioned a bungalow and named it 'Cecilia' after her daughter Cissie (by then as famous a performer as her mother), but later moved to 'Pavlova'. Shoreham rapidly became a magnet for other music hall and variety stars who congregated there while resting between engagements. Some families spread into chains of bungalows: the comedian Will Evans appropriately named his first one 'Hop o' My Thumb' for the tiny boy in the

Examples of very cheap bungalows from a 1930 catalogue for a company called Bath. Designated 'marine' and 'riverside', they illustrate the carefree holiday life they were intended to provide.

Perrault fairy tale, and followed this by building 'Puss in Boots' and 'Sleeping Beauty', named for two of his most successful shows. These were used by his extended family, which included Jimmy Nervo, the Coster Queen and Fred Evans, who, in the character of 'Pimple', was an early silent film star. They were joined, among others, by the prolific Lupino family and two Australian variety artists, Billy Williams and Albert Le Fre, who built 'Coogee', 'Hoo-Hoo', 'Timaru', 'Kangaroo' and 'Emu'. Vital supplies of fresh water and paraffin for cooking and heating were delivered by the Bungalow Stores.

By 1907 Shoreham Bungalow Town was literally on the map, and featured in the *Homeland Handbook for Shoreham, Southwick and Steyning* (published to encourage

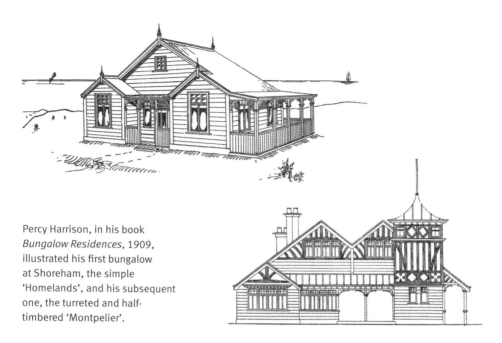

Percy Harrison, in his book *Bungalow Residences*, 1909, illustrated his first bungalow at Shoreham, the simple 'Homelands', and his subsequent one, the turreted and half-timbered 'Montpelier'.

touring holidays in Britain), which noted that it had been transformed from 'a ramshackle colony into one long picturesque village of summer houses with wide verandahs'. Gas, telephone and electricity had been laid on and there was a new railway station. A developer had plans for adjoining Southwick beach that were to include a motor racing track, a motorboat racing canal and new bungalows 'to meet the taste of visitors whose Bohemianism does not despise the comforts of modern life'. The push for racing tracks was presumably influenced by local bungalow resident Malcolm Campbell, journalist and motor racer. Shoreham Bungalow Town was also the site of an early film studio. Will Evans, in partnership with the scenic artist F.L. Lyndhurst (who lived with his wife, Dora, in an imposing bungalow called 'Lyndora'), set up the Sunny South Film Company to film comedy sketches using the bright coastal sunlight. They built a studio on the beach and a twenty-bed bungalow to accommodate artists working on the films.

H.G. Wells, at that time living not far down the coast at Sandgate, depicted a seaside bungalow village in his 1906 futuristic novel *In the Days of the Comet* in which William Leadford searches for his girl Nettie, who has bolted with a rich young man. He finds her in this 'odd settlement of pleasure-squatters' inhabited by 'artistically minded and carelessly living people'. Here are railway carriages turned into habitable little cabins.

'The thing had become a fashion with a certain Bohemian spirited class – gaily painted with broad verandahs and supplementary lean to's . . . Art muslin and banjos, chinese lanterns and frying are the leading "notes".' In the epilogue the four main characters live communally, the future being one where the stifling individual home is obsolete.

Significantly, it was a small magazine called *The Sandgate Budget* that transmogrified to a larger publication called *The Bungalow* in the summer of 1899, when its editor, Max Judge, moved from the resort up to London. The magazine set out to celebrate Bohemianism and its title was chosen to epitomize this ideal. Characteristic statements from its pages were: 'Everyone is on a level in the Bungalow – you are either above or below in the towering city dwelling.' Or: 'Nobody has his liberty, but perhaps the Man in the Bungalow has most. There is no limit to his building. His house can extend on and on. Room after room can be added, and as he wants it, and according to the position of the sun, so he can select his position in the shade of the never-ending verandah.' An article in the first issue on Bohemianism by Guy Wilfred Hayler exclaims: 'what jolly fellows we Bohemians are (although I say it myself), "enjoying life without mummery fummery".' Other articles covered Japanese prints, Aubrey Beardsley, Rossetti, Ruskin, the ethics of picnicking, Cornwall as a health resort, 'A scamper to Egypt' and 'On behalf of Canoeing'. However, evening canoe excursions along the river by the light of Japanese lanterns to the sound of mandolins could only be a temporary respite from everyday life, and 'the enviable dwellers in far-away, cool sounding Bungalows' had, inevitably, to return to 'the hot, tiring pavements of London, on tiresome business instead of being left in peace'.

RESPECTABILITY

As THE TWENTIETH CENTURY PROGRESSED, the bungalow as home to rackety Bohemianism began to lose ground. Two famous examples were built for distinctly un-freewheeling characters, Queen Alexandra and Sir William (later Lord) Lever, the soap magnate. The Royal Bungalow stuck out on the shingle of Snettisham Beach in Norfolk was typical in its position. However, any idea that the 'bungalow' might shelter unorthodox behaviour was knocked on the head by the Latin motto carved out along the roof ridge, 'Nisi Dominus', and the date 1908 in Roman numerals. The complete line 'nisi dominus aedificat vanum laboraverunt qui aedificant eam' opens Psalm 127: 'Unless the Lord build the house, they have laboured in vain.' There was a loggia to one side and photographs show the royal party lunching off white damask. With a

The Royal Bungalow at Snettisham, Norfolk, 1910, a snapshot from Princess Victoria's album. It is probably Princess Victoria who is photographed in the foreground walking her dog.

porch formed by an upturned boat and an interior decorated with shells and pebbles, it seems more like the final fling of the *cottage ornée* than a bungalow.

When Lever bought the Rivington Hall Estate, outside his home town of Blackburn, he turned the house into a museum. For himself he had constructed in 1902 a wooden bungalow high up on Rivington Pike. His architect, Jonathan Simpson, adapted what was originally a simple prefabricated wooden building to make it suitable for displaying Lever's collection of Stuart embroideries, which were to hang in the corridors and inglenook. When the bungalow was torched by the suffragette Edith Rigby in July 1913, its remote position high on the Pennines (just right for a bungalow) made it a fiery beacon that could be seen for miles. Rigby announced: 'I want to ask Sir William Lever whether he thinks his property on Rivington Pike is more valuable as one of his superfluous homes or as a beacon lighted to King and country to see some of the intolerable grievances for women.' Lever rebuilt in concrete.

Providing plans for the increasingly conventional owner, Percy Harrison bought out *Bungalow Residences. A Handbook for all interested in Building* in 1909, with a second edition in 1920. It featured 'Homelands' in Shoreham, his first bungalow, built eight years earlier, which he acknowledged was 'more Bohemian' because the bedrooms opened directly out of the saloon, an economical arrangement 'but never entirely satisfactory'. Most designs such as 'Montpelier', his second bungalow, were more substantial, with upstairs bedrooms and a belvedere smoking room (which, judging from the earlier *Building News* competition, was the latest thing in bungalow design). Harrison and Briggs both insisted that their buildings could have upstairs rooms yet remain bungalows in spirit – conveying a sense of unrestraint and easy comfort. Bungalows should be as rural as possible and command 'views of white cliff and restless sea, of verdure-clad hills or winding river, where for a time a least, the rattle of motor-bus may be forgotten, together with many other obtrusive indications of the triumph of machinery, indispensable as such may be in these days of rush and hurry'. With a hint that the good times might be ending, Harrison mentioned that the government was considering by-laws governing the erection of bungalows.

INSTANT BUILDINGS

THE SIMPLICITY OF BUNGALOWS meant that, unlike most other types of housing, they could be prefabricated and dispatched by rail anywhere in the country and speedily erected on insubstantial foundations. John Taylor had prefabricated timber frames and some furniture for his Westgate bungalows, but corrugated iron proved to be the perfect material. There was already a flourishing trade in instant buildings: barns, billiard rooms, cricket pavilions, mission halls, shepherds' huts, piggeries, game larders and dairies; bungalows were added to the list. A corrugated iron fisherman's cottage had been exhibited in the 1883 International Fisheries Exhibition and by the end of the century companies such as William Cooper of the Old Kent Road and Boulton & Paul of Norwich had copious catalogues of single-storey buildings. Some were exported to the colonies, but there was a substantial British market too. There were two categories: the 'cottage' – a 'cheap and serviceable structure suitable for Gardener, Groom, Gamekeeper and others' with bedroom at 9 x 7 feet, for cash price £72, and the 'bungalow' – a 'picturesque erection, with Verandah, for the Country or Seaside. Built on a raised terrace it is particularly striking.' Cash price £250. Prefabricated bungalows could also be found in the catalogue of the company William Colt, which set out in 1919 to produce high-class wooden poultry sheds. These were much favoured by the ex-soldiers taking advantage of the post First World War smallholding scheme, and the realization that some chicken sheds were being used to live in encouraged the firm to expand its range.

TOP A corrugated iron 'Bungalow' from the William Cooper catalogue, c.1900. At this date the word was sometimes also used to describe two-storey houses, as here, but the implication was that they would be for holiday use in a rural situation.

ABOVE Postcard printed to promote Oetzmann's portable bungalow, exhibited at the Franco-British exhibition in London, 1908.

Prefabricated bungalows were easily portable, and therefore also easy to exhibit. Thomas Oetzmann & Co. of Hampstead Road, London, moved from manufacturing pianos to cheap furniture and by the early 1900s were selling a complete bungalow called the 'Week-end' for £200–£230. For an additional £45 it could be fully furnished, and that included half a dozen napkins, an art printed bedspread and a folding bath for 'baths without bathrooms'. The Oetzmann bungalow was exhibited in 1908 at the Franco-British Exhibition and then two years later at the Japan-British Exhibition, alongside 'a typical Japanese peasant village'. It had a living room with inglenook, entrance hall, porch with two seats, best bedroom, second bedroom and a maid's bedroom 'in dainty pink'. The inclusion of an inglenook spoke more of cosy country cottage than healthy exposure on the verandah.

BUNGALOW MYSTERIES

THREE IN A BUNGALOW, a novel for girls written around 1914 by M.F. Hutchinson, reveals some contemporary opinions of the form. The story begins: 'A quaint little bungalow, with a verandah, stood in the middle of a field; only a rough cart track led up to it. Three gay girls, ankle deep in dust, trudged happily towards it, the spirit of adventure strong within them, their hearts thrilling with the sense of possession. For the sum of twelve shillings a week that bungalow, furnished, with a verandah and a bath-room, had been rented by them for two months.' 'Pine-wood Bungalow', an hour from London, had been built by a 'mad artist', who ran out of money when it cost twice as much as he had planned and he still couldn't get water to it. Hence the bathroom, much to the girls' horror, is illusory, as are the kitchen taps. The water must be brought in pails by an obliging labourer. Although 'the spirit of sheer gaiety' returns 'in full force', when they explore the nearby pinewood, they are unnerved by the bungalow's lack of boundary and gate to shut at night: 'Anybody can get in and steal everything. Because there is no fence our movements here can be seen for all we know by someone in the wood.' The three independent girls – one is on sick leave from Newnham – are taken by the locals to be suffragettes, and therefore potential arsonists. Being middle class, they are upset when no one comes to call on them: 'I have told you before, goosey,' says Betty, 'that people don't call on those who are in furnished houses or rooms. This bungalow is peculiarly cheap.' When Lady Upperton does appear, bumping precariously down the track in her chauffeur-driven car, there is consternation because there is no bell to ring. She enters 'a place she considered hardly fit for human habitation'. 'I can't

'One Tree Bungalow stood facing nearly west in a dip in a wild stretch of rugged coast, close to the edge of a low grey cliff overlooking a small sandy cove and the sea.'

help hoping you will tell me how three such charming girls come to be staying in this dreadful little bungalow.' The local squire has a similarly predictable attitude: 'Terrible place, it should never have been erected . . . Three girls in that bungalow! What extraordinary young people they must be.' At the end of the adventure they muse on their bungalow's future: 'It is too expensive for working people and not nice enough for others.'

The association between the unconventional and the bungalow was often exploited, particularly in popular crime fiction, where shady bungalow dwellers abound. In Annie Haynes's *The Bungalow Mystery* (1923), the body of a middle-aged reclusive artist is found lying in the bungalow in a pool of blood. Frederick M. White's *The Green Bungalow* (1930) is set in Shoreham, where there are no bodies but there is smuggling by 'the most accomplished and daring card-sharper and swindler in Europe'. *The Yellow Bungalow Mystery* (1935), by Leonard Gribble, has an actress 'well known in London, and on films too' stabbed with an Arab dagger in the woods beside her summer retreat. *The Lonely Bungalow* (1931), by Henry Taprell Dorling writing as 'Taffrail', has a murderous Russian prince signalling from the cliff top bungalow to enemy submarines.

ENCROACHMENT OR ESCAPE?

WHAT BEGAN AS local tut-tutting at randomly erected bungalows in wild beauty spots (as Briggs's 'unfrequented shore' or Harrison's 'verdure-clad hills') turned into full-blown fury when they began to engulf famous landscapes. Peacehaven, on the Sussex

Downs, threatened exactly that, and its developer, a consummate publicist called Charles Neville, made sure that everyone knew about it. Neville was motoring in his imported Hupmobile with his wife along the south coast in 1914 when he spotted a perfect cliff top site to the east of Brighton. He was fresh from land speculations in Canada, where he had built estates called Belgravia, Coronation and the Garden Suburb of Mayfair, and well understood housing development. Neville bought up land until he owned five miles of prime flat cliff top, which he then divided into a regimented grid of plots – the very antithesis of the bungalow spirit. In order to kick-start the scheme at such an unpropitious time – in the middle of the war – Neville took out advertisements in all the major newspapers announcing a competition to find a name for the new town. The first prize was a plot of land worth £100, with fifty £50 plots for the runners-up. Neville claimed that 80,000 entered, and the short-lived winning name was New Anzac on Sea – jettisoned in favour of Peacehaven the following year when the Anzac Gallipoli expedition was deemed a tragic failure. In fact Neville pronounced almost 2,500 people 'winners' of the £50 plot prize, but then presented them with a three guinea 'conveyancing fee', which garnered him an instant profit. The *Daily Express* denounced the whole scheme as a fraud and took Neville to court; by the time the claim and counterclaim had reached the House of Lords everyone had heard of Peacehaven.

In September 1921 with a handful of residents *in situ*, Neville started the *Peacehaven Post*, a magazine stuffed with Neville-type homilies such as 'PEACE – thrice blessed word to hearts that seek a HAVEN from the storm and stress of life' and 'A Haven of Frolic, Freshness and Fun. There are no cages in Peacehaven for birds or human beings.' He also came up with the sobriquet 'Lureland':

'Land Ahoy!'
'What land?'
'Why, my land, your land, our land,
Care free and freehold happy land – LURELAND.'

Notes by the 'Peacehaven Pedestrian' (Neville) gave cheery reports of goings-on: 'Mr Sankey, busy about his poultry farm where at present he lives in an army hut whilst his permanent bungalow is being built . . . Towards the top of Roderick Avenue the smart bright bungalow of Mr. Denne (built by Mr. J. Wagstaff) strikes a gay note against the

RIGHT A cartoon published in the 1921 edition of the *Peacehaven Post*, encouraging the belief that people were clamouring for plots.
OPPOSITE The milkman delivers to the Parks's bungalow, Valencia, in Tor Road, Peacehaven.

rising green of the reservoir hill, ready and waiting for the human animation which will soon give life to it . . . On the far side of Valley Road, the 077 white bungalow, with red tiled roof, built by the Company for Mr. Rowntree (Acres 312 and 313) is all ablaze in the sun, and looks a most desirable nest to snuggle in.'

By the end of the decade the population of Peacehaven was over four thousand, and there were four churches, tennis courts, Girl Guides, a Philharmonic and Dramatic Society, and a Literary and Debating Society. The 'histrionic gifts of Miss Flora Robson' had been appreciated at a performance in the Rosemary Tea Gardens. Neville kept up the stream of publicity for Peacehaven. In 1925 and 1926 he ran a lottery for the prize of a free house and land worth £1,125.

It is easy to imagine the emotional appeal of owning a plot of land that could represent a stake in the future. Frank Parks was an early resident who moved to a rented bungalow in 1922 while he built his own – finally leaving it just before his death in 1992. He started with just a bedroom and living room, but like thousands of other bungalow owners extended as he had time and money – adding extra bedrooms, a kitchen and a garage for his motorbike and sidecar. He was a carpenter and worked on many of the bungalows, photographing their progress. The significant change was that the majority of Peacehaven inhabitants were permanent residents rather than holidaymakers.

In an early issue of the *Peacehaven Post* Neville had expressed a mission to help the residents 'look upon all that lies within their Land of Romance with the eyes of understanding, and to realize not only the beauty and charm of that land, but the part that it has played in the making of the history of England, the England guarded still by that inviolate sea which foams and breaks for ever against the high white cliffs of the Great Down Country'. It was, in fact, the 'high white cliffs' that conservationists had hoped would remain inviolate. However, a Housing Act of 1924 had worked in favour of bungalow building as the government granted subsidies for building houses under a certain size. This was intended to increase the stock of small working-class houses, but also naturally included bungalows. In response the Council for the Preservation of Rural England was founded in 1925 by the architect Guy Dawber and the architect-planner Patrick Abercrombie. The loudest salvoes yet in the war against the bungalow were fired in 1927, when William Inge, Dean of St Paul's, writing an article in the

Evening Standard on the demise of the country house, stated dramatically that, within twenty years, 'the whole country will be spotted with bungaloid growths within which childless couples will sleep after racing about the country in little motor cars.' The coining of the word 'bungaloid', so close to fungoid, is attributed to Inge.

The architect Clough Williams-Ellis was another fierce warrior in the anti-bungalow brigade, denouncing 'the anti-social placing of these little buildings with their gratuitously flashy or exotic appearance'. In his 'Devil's Alphabet', a coda to *England and the Octopus* (1928), B was for Bungalow: 'they constitute England's most disfiguring disease . . . Peacehaven may still be cited as the classic example of ravages of this distressing and almost universal complaint.' Attacks followed in *The Observer* ('the distressing sacrifice of rural beauty involved in the uncontrollable erection of bungalows . . .'), *Country Life*, *The Spectator* and the architectural press. In a sense these attacks are unsurprising, for they come from those who upheld the status quo in the countryside, those who felt it should still be ordered by the landowning classes, and largely for their benefit. They felt threatened by incursions on to their land, not only by buildings, but also by those who considered the countryside should be enjoyed by all, a movement which culminated in the Kinder Scout Trespass in 1932 when ramblers claimed the right to walk on the Duke of Devonshire's Peak District estates. The architectural profession, too, was being sidelined by an army of self-builders and speculators. In many ways it was a class war. Sir William Beach Thomas, writing about the Home Counties in *Britain and the Beast* (1937), edited by Williams-Ellis, contributed this thought: 'The trouble is that the week-end visitors and a great number of those who live in the newer "concrete mendacities" or villa-nous excrescences, or bungaloid growths, and caused them to be erected, are by habit and occupation urban in sentiment and alien to the district.'

While *Country Life* magazine campaigned against the bungalow, its book-publishing arm had been churning out, since 1920, successive editions of *The Book of Bungalows*, by the editor of *Homes and Gardens*, R. Randal Phillips. Phillips makes a case that the bungalow could be an appropriate and respectable form of housing for the middle classes – 'that middle class upon whose shoulders every new burden is thrust. The middle class have to shift for themselves in the matter of housing, and many are turning eagerly to the bungalow as a hopeful solution of their difficulties.' It offered cash-strapped middle-class families a selection of bungalows, all designed by architects. Included was work by Clough Williams-Ellis, who had in fact hedged

An architect-designed bungalow, illustrated in *The Studio* magazine in 1927. The architects were F.J. Horth and H. Andrew of Hull.

his bets in his Bungalow diatribe in 'The Devil's Alphabet' with the sentence 'there is nothing intrinsically vile about a one-storied dwelling'; and S.D. Adshead, whose view in 1923 was that: 'Young married people of the middle class flock to bungalow towns. There they can live a sort of aboriginal existence for a time.' Phillips allowed that white-painted weatherboarding redeemed a bungalow from any suggestion of either hut or shanty, and he approved of casement windows which could be thrown open for an abundance of air, 'bungalow life going hand in hand with open-air life'.

There was a yawning chasm between the taste of the bungalow owners and that of the critics. Roof colour was a particularly contentious issue – asbestos tiles of a pinkish colour being singled out as repellent, alongside red and green Ruberoid tiles. *Bungalows, Pavilions and Cottages: How to Build or Adapt* by Sidney Vant (1929), one of 'Warne's Useful Books', aimed at self-builders and priced at sixpence, offered 'the most lucid method of instructing the unskilled handyman in the erection of a bungalow'.

While he warned against bad taste – 'meaningless tricking out with paint and timber' – this was precisely the sort of home-made ornament that made bungalow owning fun for many. Vant 'regretted that the word "bungalow" seems in many areas to have been confounded with the shorter and aptly descriptive word, shed.'

PLOTLANDS

A BUNGALOW IN THE COUNTRY OR BY THE SEA, as the success of Peacehaven had proved, was a dream for many in the years between the two world wars. The custom of going away for holidays or weekends was spreading down the social scale. Acquiring a small plot of land was not difficult during a period when agriculture was in depression: farmers were pleased to sell off parcels of their most unprofitable land for cash. Land at Dunton in Essex was advertised in the *Hackney and Kingsland Gazette* for £5 a plot (20 feet wide and 160 feet deep). Vant warned against cheap plots that might prove to be swamp or on eroding coastline, and the difficulty of building without an approach road; he also gave instructions for digging wells and cess pits, as the usual amenities were inevitably unavailable. Despite the difficulties, thousands of families from the East End of London decamped to plots in Essex such as those in Laindon, Langdon Hills and Dunton, travelling out by train at weekends to live in tents, sheds or old trams while they slowly constructed their bungalows. This pattern was replicated around the country.

A short cut to bungalow ownership, as for the pioneers at Shoreham Beach, remained the conversion of an old railway carriage: Southern Railways rolling stock provided the core of bungalows at, for example, Dungeness and Selsey on the south coast. *The Woodworker* magazine in 1925 gave a plan for adapting a corridor coach into a bungalow, and the Great Western Railway advertised 'camping coaches' that could be rented for holidays in beauty spots. Ex-army huts, also, could be pressed into service as bungalows – or even, as at Sandhills Meadow by the Thames at Shepperton, a single-decker Midlands bus.

Families mostly used their bungalows for weekends and summer holidays, but some eventually moved out of London altogether. Charles and Mary Page lived in Barking and built their three-room weatherboard bungalow, appropriately called 'Peacehaven', in Laindon over five years, moving there permanently in 1938. Their son, Ken Page, who was brought up there, described it: 'The inside of the bungalow was lined with asbestos sheeting and the roof had asbestos tiles. We had a bucket toilet in the usual small shed

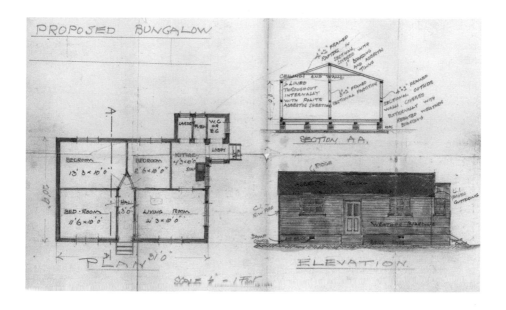

Plan for 'Anthelen', at Dunton, Essex, on a plot belonging to the Anthony family from Whitehorse Lane off the Mile End Road. The annexe, with the lobby, larder and lavatory, was never built. The Anthonys moved permanently to Anthelen after their East End house was blitzed in 1940.

and over time a "scullery" was added and my brother and I had a bedroom in the loft accessed by a ladder. Lighting was by oil lights. Mum cooked on the paraffin oil stove for a number of years until the coming of Calor Gas, when she got a "proper" cooker, plus Dad put in a Rayburn slow combustion stove and plumbed in hot and cold water fed from header tanks in the roof. We dug a "well" in the garden which was fed from the roof run-off, then, using a hand pump, transferred water to the header tanks every few days. Primitive, but it worked very well.' The family had a large vegetable garden, they kept chickens, and his father raised pigs, fattening them on scraps from his factory canteen; the loft was full of bottled pears, plums, apples and blackberries. Such self-sufficiency was typical of bungalow dwellers, and refutes Sir William Beach Thomas's charge that they were irredeemably urban. Families often bought double or treble plots in order to create smallholdings. During the war some families took up permanent residence in their bungalows to escape the Blitz and many of the original self-builders chose to retire to them. But the 1947 Town and Country Planning Act established the fact that ownership no longer included the right to develop land without permission and marked the end of the opportunity for the adventurous to build on a small piece of their own land. In many cases these pre-war 'rights' turned into a post-war 'problem' and Dunton, for example, was demolished in the 1980s by Basildon Development Corporation; other settlements gradually acquired proper roads and services.

POST-WAR PREFABS

IRONICALLY the ending of one form of bungalow coincided with the beginning of another when, in the aftermath of the Second World War, government provision of over 150,000 prefabricated bungalows went some way to alleviating the housing shortage. The Temporary Housing Programme was established in 1944 to provide factory-made bungalows, particularly for families with children, until the construction industry got back on its feet. There were thirteen different types, made from a range of materials – steel, asbestos-cement, timber, concrete and even aluminium – manufactured by an aircraft industry that had only recently built bombers. Ready-made sections were loaded on lorries at factories and transported directly to bomb-hit cities, where they could be rapidly assembled by unskilled labour following standard-issue step-by-step guides. Churchill had announced that as much thought would go into prefabricated housing 'as went into the invasion of Africa', and the interior design did indeed make a radical and meticulous use of space which delighted the new occupants. Kitchen, living room, bathroom and two bedrooms were fitted into a floor area of 635 square feet. Fridges, fitted kitchens, built-in cupboards, proper plumbing and ducted hot air heating were novelties to most inhabitants. As a child in South Wales Neil Kinnock moved into a 'prefab' with his parents in 1947 and described the fridge, the kitchen table that folded into the wall, and the bathroom: 'Family and friends came visiting to view the wonders. It seemed like living in a spaceship.' Although they were scheduled to last fifteen years, roughly ten thousand survived into the twenty-first century, much loved by their inhabitants.

BUNGALOWS FOR ALL

THE DAILY MAIL IDEAL HOME EXHIBITIONS had always pinpointed precisely what middle Britain found most attractive, and regularly featured bungalows. The 1922 exhibition included a 'Bungalow Town' and the newspaper ran a competition for the best labour-saving bungalow. In 1936 the Next-to-Nothing bungalow was exhibited,

Mr L.T. Jackson, photographed in 1948, after Camberwell Council had awarded him first prize for the smartest prefab garden.

including a mattress of plaited inner tubes. The *Daily Mail Book of Bungalow Plans* came out annually from 1958 until the late 1970s. Off-the-peg bungalows were available in their thousands: some system-built and some from licensed plans. 'Get the 1962 edition of the *Planahome Book of House Plans* featuring 160 designs of houses, chalets and bungalows, from £2,200 to £8,250, exclusive of land. The book costs 20/- and a set of plans, comprising six prints on paper and one on linen (coloured to meet Local Authority requirements) and two specifications, costs only 25 guineas.' With ranch-style frontages, 'feature panels' of random masonry, 'feature chimneys', wood cladding and picture windows, many of these bungalows of the fifties and sixties pay homage to America suburbia. Though a 1962 'bungalow for dog lovers', where the

The Ranch III Bungalow, advertised in the 1975 *Daily Mail Book of Bungalow Plans*, supplied by a company called Berg.

picture windows provide a floor-level view into the garden for dogs, has a distinctly British take on the style.

Many were specifically aimed at retirement. Single-storey living was tirelessly promoted as the solution for old age, as it had been for invalids in the 1880s. The building trade met the need with thousands of bungalows, many spilling over the edges of seaside towns and beauty spots. Specifications of post-war bungalows frequently show layouts as being 'primarily designed to meet the requirements of an elderly couple with a modest income': 'Two bedroom bungalow on a frontage of 34 ft compact and pleasing in appearance'. Or, scaled up: 'Here is a design for a medium-sized bungalow which would suit a retired couple. It has a wide frontage facing south. All rooms are spacious enough to accept large items of furniture.' Griff Rhys Jones, in his autobiography *Semi-Detached*, writes of his grandparents' retirement from running a greengrocer's shop in Wales to 'dreary exile' in a bungalow by the sea at

Weston-super-Mare, where, as he put it, they had 'elected to die'. 'The bungalow, although new, was a gloomy mausoleum inside. The net curtains were never drawn. A pallid light illuminated the heavy brown furniture, the piano, the polished mahogany table and the Welsh clock that ticked and whirred heavily in the gloom. It was prison ... Days were often spent just sitting in the gloom, visited by other decrepit old people like Aunty Betty, with her frizz of grey curls and currant eyes, and Uncle Jan, whose idea of amusing children was to let them look at his pocket watch ... the few "holidays" when my parents dumped us at Granny's ... are lodged in a yellow jelly made of furniture polish: the laborious preparation of tea; the clink of cutlery against a plate; the shuffling feet in the corridor; the endless, inert waiting.'

An explosion of bungalows in Ireland, where it remained permissible to build on your own land without planning consent, was put down to *Bungalow Bliss*, a book of 250 plans devised by architect Jack Fitzsimons which sold over 150,000 copies between 1971 and 1989. Selling plans at £10 per set, it enabled thousands of Irish – many returning home to retire – to build. The resulting 'one-off' bungalows scattershot over the hills caused uproar against 'bungalow blight'. In 1990 an unrepentant Fitzsimons published a defence in *Bungalow Bashing*: 'I believe that bungalow bliss – rural housing – is the right policy. It is a policy endorsed by the majority of the population.'

The fight between blight and bliss is almost as old as the bungalow's history. What is evident is that they have historically given thousands the opportunity for a free and easy life, even if only temporarily. Some, in their never-to-be repeated locations, have provided opportunities for tearing down and rebuilding, but any innovative contemporary replacement – say a glass pavilion with a flat sedum roof – will be described as a single-storey house, never as a bungalow. The appeal of the bungalow is now only for those with a taste for the retro.

BIBLIOGRAPHY

COTTAGES

Adams, Maurice, *Modern Cottage Architecture*, London, 1904

Aronson, Hugh, *Our Village Homes, Present Conditions and Suggested Remedies*, London, 1913

Austen, Jane, *Sense and Sensibility*, London, 1811
Pride and Prejudice, London, 1813
Sanditon, London, 1817
Persuasion, London, 1818

Baillie Scott, M.H. , & A.E. Beresford, *Houses and Gardens*, London, 1933

Barley, M.W., *English Farmhouse and Cottage*, London, 1961

Bartell, Edmund, *Hints for Picturesque Improvement in Ornamented Cottages and their scenery including some observations on the Labourer and his cottage*, London, 1804

Batsford, Harry, & Charles Fry, *The English Cottage*, London, 1938

Bermingham, Ann (ed.), *Sensation and Sensibility: Viewing Gainsborough's Cottage Door*, New Haven & London, 2005

Birch, John, *Examples of Labourers' Cottages etc.*, London, 1871

Britton, John, *Specimen of the Autobiography of John Britton*, London, 1850

Burnett, John, *A Social History of Housing 1815–1970*, Newton Abbot, 1978

Campbell, Beatrice (Lady Glenavy), *Today we will only gossip*, London, 1964

Chadwick, Edwin, *Report on the Sanitary Condition of the Labouring Population of Great Britain, 1842*, Edinburgh, 1965

Cobbett, W., *Cottage Economy*, London, 1822
Rural Rides, London, 1853

Crosland, T.W.H., *The Country Life*, London, 1906

Darley, Gillian, *Villages of Vision*, London, 1975, revised 2007

Davies, David, *The Case of Labourers in Husbandry Stated and Considered*, London, 1795

Dearn, T.D.W., *Sketches in Architecture consisting of Original Designs for Cottages and Rural Dwellings*, London, 1807

Dick, Stewart, *The Cottage Homes of England*, London, 1909

Eden, Frederick Morton, *The State of the Poor*, London, 1797

Elsam, Richard, *Hints for Improving the Condition of the Peasantry in all parts of the United Kingdom by promoting comfort in their habitations*, London, 1816

Graves, Robert, *Goodbye to All That*, London, 1929, revised 1956

Gyfford, E., *Designs for Elegant Cottages and Small Villas*, London, 1806

Harling, Robert (ed.), *House and Garden Book of Cottages*, London, 1963,

Horn, Pamela, *Life and Labour in Rural England, 1790–1850*, Basingstoke, 1987

Howitt, William, *The Rural Life in England*, London, 1840

Kent, Nathaniel, *Hints to Gentlemen of Landed Property*, London, 1775

Loudon, J.C., *Encyclopaedia of Agriculture*, London, 1844
(ed.) *Cottage, Farm, and Villa Architecture and Furniture*, London, 1846

Lugar, Robert, *Architectural sketches for Cottages, `Rural Dwellings, and Villas, in the Grecian, gothic and fancy styles*, London, 1823

Malton, James, *An Essay on British Cottage Architecture*, London, 1798

Mayor, Elizabeth, *The Ladies of Llangollen*, London, 1971

Murphy, S., *Our Homes*, London, 1883

Panter-Downes, Mollie, *Good Evening, Mrs Craven: the Wartime Stories of Mollie Panter-Downes*, London, 1999

Parker, Rowland, *The Common Stream*, London, 1976

Plaw, John, *Rural Architecture*, London, 1796
Ferme Ornée, or Rural Improvements, London, 1800

Pocock, W. F. *Architectural Designs for Rustic Cottages, Picturesque Dwellings, Villas, Etc.*, London, 1807

Price, Uvedale, *Essays on the Picturesque*, London, 1810

Ravetz, Alison, *Council Housing and Culture*, London, 2001

Starforth, John, *The Architecture of the Farm. A Series of Designs for Farm-houses and farm-steadings, factor's houses, and labourers' cottages,* Edinburgh, 1853

Stevens, Francis, *Views of Cottages and Farm-houses in England and Wales, etched by FS from the designs of the most celebrated artists,* London, 1815

Tinniswood, Adrian, *Life in the English Country Cottage,* London, 1995

Ward, Colin, *Cotters and Squatters, Housing's Hidden History,* Nottingham, 2002

Wood, John, *A Series of Plans for Cottages or Habitations of the Labourer,* London, 1781

COUNTRY HOUSES

Athill, Diana, *Instead of a Letter,* London, 1963

Bailey, Brian, *English Manor Houses,* London, 1983

Bailey, Catherine, *Black Diamonds, The rise and fall of an English Dynasty,* London, 2007

Baker, C.H.I., *The Life and Circumstances of James Brydges, First Duke of Chandos,* Oxford, 1949

Balsan, Consuelo Vanderbilt, *The Glitter and the Gold,* Maidstone, 1973

Barley, M.W., *The House and Home,* London, 1963

Barstow, Phyllida, *The Country House Party,* Wellingborough, 1989

Bath, Daphne, Marchioness of, *Before the Sunset Fades,* Longleat, 1951

Bedford, John, Duke of, *A Silver-plated Spoon,* London, 1959

Briggs, R.A., *Homes for the Country,* London, 1904

Channon, Sir Henry, *Chips, the Diaries of Sir Henry Channon,* ed. Robert Rhodes James, London, 1967

Creevey, Thomas, *The Creevey Papers,* ed. Herbert Maxwell, London, 1903

Defoe, Daniel, *A Tour Through the Whole Island of Great Britain,* Exeter, 1989

Edgeworth, Maria, *Letters from England, 1813–1844,* ed. Christina Colvin, Oxford, 1971

Fiennes, Celia, *The Journeys of Celia Fiennes,* ed. Christopher Morris, London, 1949

Galsworthy, John, *The Country House,* London, 1907

Gascoigne, George, *The Complete Works,* Cambridge, 1910

Gill, Richard, *Happy Rural Seat: The English Country House and the Literary Imagination,* London, 1972

Girouard, Mark, *Life in the English Country House,* London, 1978

Robert Smythson and the Elizabethan Country House, London, 1983

Hartcup, Adeline, *Below Stairs in the Great Country Houses,* London, 1980

Howitt, William, *Rural Life of England,* London, 1838

James, Henry, *English Hours,* London, 1905

Jenkins, Alan, *Men of Property, Knight Frank & Rutley,* London, 1986

Kerr, Robert, *The Gentleman's House, or how to plan English Residences from Parsonage to the Palace,* London, 1865

La Rochefoucauld, Francois de, *A Frenchman in England, 1784,* Cambridge, 1933

Lees-Milne, James, *Some Country Houses and Their Owners,* London, 1975

Mitford, Nancy, *Christmas Pudding,* London, 1932

Morrell, Ottoline, *Memoirs of Lady Ottoline Morrell,* ed. Robert Gathorne-Hardy, *1915–1918,* London, 1974

Morris, Christopher (ed.), *The Journeys of Celia Fiennes,* London, 1949

Morris Revd F.O., *A Series of Picturesque Views of Seats of the Noblemen and Gentlemen of G.B and Ireland,* London, 1866–80

Mowl, Timothy, *Elizabethan and Jacobean Style,* London, 1993

Muthesius, Hermann, *Das Englische Haus,* 1908, trans. *The English House,* London, 1979

Neale, J.P., *Views of the Seats of Noblemen and Gentlemen in England, Scotland and Ireland,* London, 1818–1823

North, Roger, *Of Building: Roger North's Writing on Architecture,* ed. Howard Colvin & John Newman, Oxford, 1981

Paston Letters and Papers of the Fifteenth Century, ed. Norman Davis, Oxford, 1971–76

Pembroke, Anne, Countess of, *The Diary of Lady Anne Clifford,* ed. V. Sackville-West, London, 1923

Powys, Caroline, *Passages from the Diaries of Mrs. Philip Lybbe Powys of Hardwick House, Oxon.,* ed. Emily Climenson, London, 1899

Pratt, Sir Roger, *The Architecture of Roger Pratt,* ed. R.T. Gunter, Oxford, 1928

Puckler Muskau, Hermann, *Tour in England, Ireland, and France, in the years 1828 & 1829,* trans. Sarah Austin, London, 1832

Sackville-West, Vita, *The Edwardians,* London, 1930

Saltonstall, Wye, *Picturae Loquentes,* Oxford, 1946

Saussure, César de, *A Foreign View of England in the Reigns of George I and George II,* London, 1902

Smollett, Tobias, *The Expedition of Humphry Clinker,* London, 1771,

Strong, Roy (ed.), *Destruction of the Country House, 1875–1975,* London, 1974

Tayler, William, *Diary of William Tayler, footman, 1837,* ed. Dorothy Wise, London, 1962

Torrington, John Byng, 5th Viscount, *The Torrington Diaries,* ed. C. Bruyn Andrews, London, 1954

Trollope, Anthony, *The Duke's Children,* London, 1880

Walpole, Horace, *The Yale Edition of Horace Walpole's Correspondence,* ed. W.S. Lewis, New Haven, 1937–1983

Waugh, Evelyn, *A Handful of Dust,* London, 1934 *Brideshead Revisited,* London, 1945

Wells, H.G., *Tono-Bungay,* London, 1909

Whatman, Susanna, *Her Housekeeping Book,* Cambridge, 1952

Williamson, Tom, & Liz Bellamy, *Property and Landscape,* London, 1987

TERRACES

Austen, Jane, *Jane Austen's Letters to her Sister Cassandra and Others,* ed. R.W.Chapman, Oxford, 1952

Banks, Lynne Reid, *The L-Shaped Room,* London, 1960

Barbon, Nicholas, *An Apology for the Builder,* London, 1685

Booth, Charles, *Life & Labour of the People in London,* London, 1902

Brooks, Roy, *A Brothel in Pimlico,* London, 2001

Bullock, Shan F., *Robert Thorne,* London, 1907

Burman, Peter, & M. Stratton (eds.), *Conserving the Railway Heritage,* London, 1997

Burney, Frances, *The Early Diary of Frances Burney, 1768–1778,* ed. Annie Raine Ellis, London, 1889

Clark, Mrs Godfrey (ed.), *Gleanings from an Old Portfolio,* vol. 3, London, 1898

Cosh, Mary, *Edinburgh: The Golden Age,* Edinburgh, 2003

Cox, Alfred, *The Landlord's and Tenant's Guide: A compendium of information upon the procuring, occupying and disposing of Estates and Houses,* London, 1853

Crawford, E., *Enterprising Women,* London, 2002

Cruickshank, Dan, & Peter Wyld, *The Art of Georgian Building,* London, 1975

Daiches, David, *Edinburgh,* London, 1978

Dale, Anthony, *Fashionable Brighton 1820–1860,* London, 1947

Ellis, Winifred, *London – So Help Me,* London, 1952

Elsam, Richard, *The Practical Builder's Perpetual Price-Book,* London, 1842

Engels, Friedrich, *The Condition of the Working Class in England in 1844,* trans. F.K.Wischenewetsky, London, 1888

Freeman, Gwendolen, *The Houses Behind,* London, 1947

Forman, Charles, *Industrial Town, St Helens in the 1920s,* London, 1978

Forster, Margaret, *Elizabeth Barrett Browning,* London, 1988

Gascoigne, Caroline Leigh, *Belgravia, A Poem,* London, 1851

Gaspey, William, *Tallis's Illustrated London,* London, 1851

Gissing, George, *The Odd Women,* London, 1893

Grant, J.C.,*The Back-to-Backs,* London, 1930

Grosley, Monsieur, *A Tour to London: or, New Observations on England, and its inhabitants,* trans. Thomas Nugent, London, 1772

Grossmith, George & Weedon, *Diary of a Nobody,* London, 1892

Gwynn, John, *London and Westminster Improved,* London, 1766

Haweis, Mrs, *The Art of Housekeeping,* London, 1889

Heape, R.G., *Buxton under the Dukes of Devonshire,* London, 1948

Hobhouse, Hermione, *Thomas Cubitt, Master Builder,* London, 1967

Maitland, F., *Building Estates,* London, 1883

Morrison, Arthur, *Child of the Jago,* London, 1896

Muthesius, Stefan, *The English Terraced House,* New Haven and London, 1982

Neale R.S., *Bath 1680–1850, A Social History or A Valley of Pleasure yet a Sink of Iniquity,* London, 1981

Olsen, Donald J., *The Growth of Victorian London,* London, 1976

Orwell, George, *Keep the Aspidistra Flying,* London, 1936

Priestley, J.B., *English Journey,* London, 1934

Ransome, Arthur, *Bohemia in London,* London, 1907

Saussure, Cesar de, *A Foreign View of England in the Reigns of George I and George II,* trans. Madame Van Muyden, London, 1902

Selvon, Samuel, *Lonely Londoners,* London, 1956

Simm, Barbara (ed.), *Eric Lyons & Span,* London, 2006

Simond, Louis, *Journal of a Tour of Residence of Great Britain during the Years 1810 & 1811,* London, 1817

Southey, Robert, *Letters from England,* ed. Jack Simmons, London, 1951

Stewart, Rachel, *The Town House in Georgian London,* London, 2009

Streatfeild, Noel, *Ballet Shoes,* London, 1936

Strike, James, *The Spirit of Span Housing,* London, 2004

Stuart, James, *Critical Observations on the Buildings and Improvements of London,* London, 1771

Summerson, John, *Georgian London,* London, 1945

Swinnerton, Frank, *Nocturne,* London, 1917

Taine, H., *Notes on England, Letters from Albion to a Friend on the Continent (years 1810–13),* 1814, trans. W.F. Rae, London, 1872

Thackeray, W.M., *The Newcomes,* London, 1854–55

Ware, Isaac, *The Complete Body of Architecture,* London, 1756

Wates, Nick (ed.), *Squatting, the Real Story,* London, 1980

Weightman, Gavin, and Steve Humphries, *The Making of Modern London 1815–1914,* London, 1983

Whitehorn, Katharine, *Cooking in a Bedsitter,* London, 1963

Wood, John, *A Description of Bath,* London, 1765, reprinted Bath, 1969

Woodruff, William, *The Road to Nab End,* London, 2002

Woolf, Virginia, *Night and Day,* London, 1919

Young, Michael, & Peter Willmott, *Family and Kinship in East London,* London, 1957

FLATS

Ashworth, H.I., *Flats, Design and Equipment,* London, 1936

Brittain, Vera, *Testament of Friendship,* London, 1940

Craig, Elizabeth, *Entertaining with Elizabeth Craig,* London, 1933

Crawford, Elisabeth, *Enterprising Women, The Garretts and their Circle,* London, 2002

Cromley, Elizabeth, *Alone Together: a History of New York's Early Apartments,* New York, 1990

Flatland, published monthly by Fred. Hazell, 117 Victoria Street, Auction Land and Estate Offices, March 1894–

Flats, An Illustrated Paper for Owners and Occupiers and all Interested in Flats and Maisonettes, 1889–1921, Robins, Snell & Terry

Fletcher, Banister, *Model Houses for the Industrial Classes,* London, 1871

Gissing, George, *The Whirlpool,* London, 1897
The Private Papers of Henry Ryecroft, London, 1903

Glendinning, M., and S. Muthesius, *Tower Block: Modern Public Housing in England, Scotland, Wales and Northern Ireland,* London, 1994

Hanley, Lynsey, *Estates, An Intimate History,* London, 2007

Heath Robinson, W., and K.R.G. Browne, *How to Live in a Flat,* London, 1936

Heddle, Ethel F., *Three Girls in a Flat,* London, 1896

Herbert, A.P., *Dolphin Square* (a brochure advertising a block of flats), London, 1935

Hole, J., *The Homes of the Working Classes,* London, 1866

Holtby, Winifred, *Letters to a Friend,* ed. Alice Holtby & Jean McWilliam, London, 1937

Lorne, Charles, *Flat to Let,* London, 1938

Mauduit, Vicomte de, *The Vicomte in the Kitchenette,* London, 1934

Perks, Sydney, *Residential Flats of All Classes,* London, 1905

Ravetz, Alison, *Model Estate, Planned Housing at Quarry Hill, Leeds,* London, 1974

Shaw, G.B., *Plays: Pleasant and Unpleasant,* London, 1898

Shaw Sparrow, W. (ed.), *The Modern Home, a book of domestic architecture for moderate incomes,* London, 1904

Sutcliffe Anthony (ed.), *Multi-Storey Living, The British Working Class Experience*, London, 1974

Tarn, John Nelson, *Five Per Cent Philanthropy*, Cambridge, 1973

Verity, F.T., *Flats, Urban Houses and Cottage Homes*, London, 1906

Yorke, F.R.S., and F. Gibberd, *The Modern Flat*, London, 1937, 1948, 1950

SUBURBAN VILLAS AND SEMIS

Arnold, Dana (ed.), *The Georgian Villa*, Stroud, 2006

Auden, W.H., and Christopher Isherwood, *The Ascent of F6*, London, 1936

Barnes, Julian, *Metroland*, London, 1980

Bertram, Anthony, *Design*, Harmondsworth, 1938

Bidlake, W.H. & others, *A Book of British Domestic Architecture for Moderate Incomes*, London, n.d.

Blackburne, E.L., *Suburban and Rural Architecture*, London, 1869

Branson, Noreen & Margot Heinemann, *Britain in the Nineteen Thirties*, London, 1971

Briggs, Asa, *History of Birmingham*, London, 1952

Chesterton, G.K., *The Man who was Thursday*, London, 1908

Clarke, W.S., *The Suburban Homes of London, A Residential Guide to Favourite London Localities, Their Society, Celebrities, and Associations*, London, 1881

Clegg, Gillian, *Clapham Past*, London, 1998

Cooper, Lettice, *The New House*, London, 1936

Crosland T.W.H., *The Suburbans*, London, 1905

Eden, Emily, *The Semi-detached House*, London, 1859

Elmes, James, *Metropolitan Improvements*, London, 1826

Galinou, Mireille, *Cottages and Villas: the Birth of the Garden Suburb*, New Haven & London, 2010

Gaskell, Elizabeth, *The Letters of Mrs Gaskell*, ed. J.A.V. Chapple & Arthur Pollard, Manchester, 1966

Girouard, Mark, *Sweetness and Light, the 'Queen Anne' Movement 1860–1900*, Oxford, 1977

Gissing, George, *In the Year of Jubilee*, London, 1894

Gordon, Richard, *Good Neighbours, Suburbia Observed*, London, 1976

Greeves, T., *Bedford Park, the First Garden Suburb*, London, 1975

Harvey, W.A., *The Model Village and its Cottages: Bournville*, London, 1906

Hawthorne, Nathaniel, *The English Notebooks, 1856–60*, Columbus, Ohio, 1997

Hedges, Sid G.,*Universal Book of Hobbies*, London, n.d.

Hinchcliffe, Tannis, *North Oxford*, London, 1992

Howard, Keble, *The Smiths of Surbiton, A Comedy without a Plot*, London, 1906

Hughes, Kathryn, *The Short Life and Long Times of Mrs Beeton*, London, 2006

Kerr, Robert, *The Gentleman's House*, London, 1865

Loudon, J.C., *Suburban Gardener and Villa Companion*, London, 1838

McGovern, J.H., *Suggestions for Artistically and Practically Laying out Building Estates*, London, 1885

Masterman, C.F.G., *The Condition of England*, London, 1909

Maugham, W. Somerset, *The Summing Up*, London, 1938

Middleton, Charles, *Picturesque and Architectural Views for Cottages, Farm Houses and Country Villas*, London, 1793

Miller, Mervyn, *Letchworth, the First Garden City*, London, 1989

Nairn, Ian & others, *Counter-attack against Subtopia*, London, 1957

Oliver, Paul, Ian Davis and Ian Bentley, *Dunroamin*, London, 1981

Orwell, George, *Coming up for Air*, London, 1939

Panton, Mrs J.E., *From Kitchen to Garret, Hints for Young Householders*, London 1888

Suburban Residences and how to Circumvent Them, London, 1896

Papworth, J. B., *Ornamental Villas*, London, 1827

Parker, Barry & Raymond Unwin, *The Art of Building a Home*, London, 1901

Quiney, Anthony, *House and Home, A History of the Small English House*, London, 1986

Ravetz, Alison, *Council Houses and Culture*, London, 2001

Reiss, Richard, *The Home I Want*, London, 1918

Richards, J.M., *Castles on the Ground, The Anatomy of Suburbia*, London, 1946

Robinson, P.F., *Designs for Ornamental Villas*, London, 1827

Ruskin, John, *Fors clavigera, letters to the workmen and labourers of Great Britain,* Orpington, 1871–1884

Saint, Andrew (introduction), *London Suburbs,* London, 1999

Sharp, Thomas, *Town Planning,* Harmondsworth, 1940

Shaw Sparrow, W. (ed.), *The British Home of To-Day,* London, 1904

Sherriff, R.C., *Greengates,* London, 1936

Snell, C.K., *Modern Suburban Homes,* London, 1903

Spiers, Maurice, *Victoria Park, Manchester,* Chetham Society, 1976

Stevenson, J.J., *House Architecture,* London, 1880

Swenarton, Mark, *Homes Fit for Heroes,* London, 1981

Tarbuck, E.L., *The Builder's Practical Director,* London, 1855

Unwin, Raymond, *The Art of Building a Home,* London, 1902

Ward, Mrs Humphrey, *A Writer's Recollections,* London, 1918

Waugh, Evelyn, *Vile Bodies,* London, 1930

Wells, H.G., *Anticipations,* London, 1900

Williams-Ellis, Clough, *England and the Octopus,* London, 1928

(ed.) *Britain and the Beast,* London, 1937

BUNGALOWS

Boyle, Frederick, *Legends of my Bungalow,* London, 1882

Briggs, R.A., *Bungalows and Country Residences,* London, 1891

The Bungalow, London, 1899–1909

Fitzsimons, Jack, *Bungalow Bliss,* Kells, 1971

Bungalow Bashing, Kells, 1990

Hardy, Denis, *The Plotlands of the Thames Valley,* Middlesex Polytechnic, 1981

Harrison, Percival, *Bungalow Residences. A Handbook for all interested in Building,* London, 1909 (2nd edition 1920)

Hutchinson, M.F., *Three in a Bungalow,* London, n.d., *c.*1912

Jackson, Peter, & and Deanna Walker, *A Portrait of the Basildon Plotlands,* Chichester, 2010

Julian, Francis W., *Bungalow Plans for Everyone,* London, 1956

King, Anthony D., *The Bungalow,* London, 1984

Mornement, Adam, & Simon Holloway, *Corrugated Iron, Building on the Frontier,* London, 2007

Murphy, S., *Our Homes,* London, 1883

Peacehaven, A Brief History, East Sussex County Library, Lewes, 1979

Peacehaven Post, London, 1921–23

Phillips, Randal, *The Book of Bungalows,* London, 1920

Rhys Jones, Griff, *Semi-Detached,* London, 2006

Rossetti, D.G., *His Family Letters with Memoir by William M. Rossetti,* London, 1895

Stevenson, Greg, *Palaces for the People, Prefabs in Post-War Britain,* London, 2003

Vant, Sidney, *Bungalows, Pavilions and Cottages. How to Build or Adapt,* London, 1929

Walter, Felix, *Fifty Modern Bungalows,* London, 1955

Wolters, N.E.B., *Bungalow Town, Theatre and Film Colony,* Marlipins Museum, Shoreham, 1985

Weightman, Gavin & Steve Humphreys, *The Making of Modern London, 1914–1939,* London, 1984

Wells, H.G., *In the Days of the Comet,* London, 1906

INDEX

ACKNOWLEDGMENTS

AUTHOR'S THANKS

Reading a manuscript in progress is a daunting task and I am extremely grateful to Gillian Darley, Juliet Gardiner and Margaret Willes, who all patiently read this and contributed valuable suggestions and improvements. Any mistakes are mine alone.

So many people were generous with ideas, references and in answering questions. I should like to thank in particular Nick and Sheila Carey-Thomas, Nicholas Cooper, Martin and Liz Drury, Bettina Harden, Lisa Heighway of the Royal Photographic Collection, Tim Hart, Jenny Hartley, Elisabeth Ingles, Julia Jones, Patrick Lorimer, William Macnair, Jan Prebble, Amoret Tanner, Christine Wagg of the Peabody Archive, Nick Wates, Lisa White and Lucy Wood.

Pictures frequently convey far more than text, and the works of Mark Boxer, Osbert Lancaster, Andy Millman and Posy Simmonds are each worth at least a thousand words; many thanks to them/ their estates for permission to reproduce. I am also very grateful to Barry Parks for his grandfather, Frank Parks' photographs of Peacehaven and to Michael Anthony for the plan of his family's bungalow at Dunton.

For the finished product I should like to thank my editor Jo Christian for her boundless enthusiasm, Anne Wilson for her sensitive design, Nancy Marten for her meticulous proofreading and Douglas Matthews for the index.

Families are traditionally thanked at the end, but as they can't escape the project from start to finish they should really come first, where they belong: to Miles, Tom, Hannah and Ned Thistlethwaite, the co-inhabitants of variously a flat, a converted church, a terrace house and a mill, my love and gratitude.

Philippa Lewis
January 2014

PICTURE ACKNOWLEDGMENTS

Amoret Tanner Ephemera Collection 108, 130, 194, 240
Bridgeman Art Library 16 (Bristol Museum & Art Gallery), 19 (Belvoir Castle, Leicestershire), 22 (British Library), 39, 54 (Chatsworth House, Derbyshire), 58 (Tichborne House, Hampshire), 61 (Chatsworth House, Derbyshire), 71 (Wimpole Hall, Cambridgeshire, The National Trust), 79, 94, 98, 99 (National Coal Mining Museum, Wakefield), 112 (Cheltenham Art Gallery & Museums), 207
Bristol City Library 25
Christie's Images 14
City of London 156
Fine Art Photographs 26
Getty Images 128
Hatfield House Archive, by courtesy of the Marquess of Salisbury 75
Leeds Library and Information Service 180
Manchester City Archive 122, 196
Mary Evans Picture Library 45, 65, 89, 129, 140, 183
Museum of Domestic Design and Architecture, Middlesex University 174, 179, 221, 223, 235
National Portrait Gallery 88
National Trust 84
Oxfordshire County Council - Oxfordshire History Centre 218
RCAHMS, Scottish National Monuments Record 147
RIBA 63, 104, 190
Royal Photographic Collection, Windsor, by permission of HM The Queen 238
TfL from London Transport Museum 205
Topfoto 184, 251

TEXT ACKNOWLEDGMENTS

Every effort has been made to trace the copyright holders. Any that we have been unable to reach are invited to contact the publishers so that a full acknowledgement may be made in subsequent editions. The author and publishers are grateful to the following for permission to reproduce copyright material.

'Design for Living', from *At the Drop of a Hat* by Flanders and Swann, copyright © 1957. By permission of the estates of Michael Flanders and Donald Swann.
James-Lees-Milne, *Some Country Houses and Their Owners*, Penguin, 1975. By permission of the estate of James Lees-Milne, c/o David Higham Associates.
Nancy Mitford, *Christmas Pudding*, 1932. By permission of the estate of Nancy Mitford, c/o Rogers, Coleridge & White, Ltd.
J.B. Priestley, *English Journey*, published by W. Heinemann, 1934. By permission of United Agents on behalf of the estate of J.B. Priestley.
Griff Rhys Jones, *Semi-Detached*, 2006. By permission of Penguin Books.
William Woodruff, *The Road to Nab End*, first published under the title *Billy Boy* by Ryburn in 1993, republished by Abacus 2002, republished by Eland in 2011, copyright © 2008 by Asperula, LLC. By kind permission of Helga Woodruff.